THE RUMOUR OF CALCUTTA

THE RUMOUR OF
CALCUTTA

Tourism, Charity and the Poverty of Representation

JOHN HUTNYK

ZED BOOKS
London & New Jersey

The Rumour of Calcutta was first published in 1996 by
Zed Books Ltd, 7 Cynthia Street, London N1 9JF, UK, and
165 First Avenue, Atlantic Highlands, New Jersey 07716, USA.

Typeset in Monotype Bembo by Lucy Morton, London SE12
Printed and bound in the United Kingdom
by Biddles Ltd, Guildford and King's Lynn

A catalogue record for this book is available from the British Library
US CIP data is available from the Library of Congress

ISBN 1 85649 407 1 (Hb)
ISBN 1 85649 408 x (Pb)

CONTENTS

Preface   vii

1   Introduction: Calcutta Cipher   1

2   Travels in Calcutta: The View From Modern Lodge   40

3   Writing Calcutta: Travelling with Lévi-Strauss and Günter Grass   86

4   Cartographic Calcutta: Amazement   117

5   Photogenic Calcutta   143

6   Cinematic Calcutta: Camera Angles on the City   176

7   Conclusion: The Gifts of Calcutta   214

Bibliography   224

Index   241

ACKNOWLEDGEMENTS

There are many people, travellers and fellow-travellers, scholars, critics and friends, who have helped me with this project over the years and I thank them all for the advice they provided. Those I would most like to mention, not in any particular order then, and travellers all, include: Biren Das Sharma, Michael Dutton, Eli Wong, Ben Ross, Chris Francis, Peter Phipps, Nick Lenaghan, Ashis Nandy, George Marcus, Klaus Peter Koepping, Gaston Roberge, Kuhu Das, the staff and students of Chitrabani, Cassandra Bennett, Stephanie Bauer, Diana Tresno, Dom Tillen, Anil Chandan, Catherine Yeatman, Angela Jones, Beth Spencer, BJ, Raghu, Rachel Brighton, Nigel D, Françoise the Cheese, Nicole divine, Monia cinemas, Mitch ('which?'), Vicki Kirby, Wei-Ying Ho, Adrienne Timmermaus, Cecelia Hornell, Diana Rees, Far Chiang, Tinzar Lwyn, Kathy Grattan, Mel Hood, Vanessa Chan, Left Alliance, Jellyheads, Toby Borgeest, Tieu Tieu, Lucy Blamey, Marcus Strom, Virinder Kalra, Uma Kothari, Raminder Kaur, Sanjay Sharma, Shirin Housee, Bobby Sayyid, Tim Eadensore, Vishvapriya Iyengar, Ulrike, Fiorinda Koch, Fiona always, Fabian Hutchinson, Emma Grahame, Don Miller, Gary and Greg, Julie Stephens, Jack and Jackie, Jadran Mimica, Jit Uberoi, Kankabati Datta at Kolkata 2000, Kate (in Tassie), Kath Kenny, Katherine Tyler, Kathy Harding, Katie Fisher, Katrina Collet, Catrin Evans, Joseph Chandy, Abdul's 2, Alison 2, AJ 1, Amy Muscoplat, Amanda Perry-Bolt, Angie Mitropoulos, Georgia Flaskas, Danny Sullivan, Gerard Goggin, Glenda Sluga, Hannah Harborrow, Helen Searls, Jo Higginson, Ian Wilson, John Lord, John Wiseman, John Lam Po Tang, the Latrobe Students' Representative Council, the UTS Students' Association, the UWS Students Union, the Department of Political Science, University of Melbourne (and its coin and its crew), the International Centre for Contemporary Cultural Research and the Department of Social Anthropology at Manchester University, Malcolm Crick, Nikos Papastergiadis, Phillipa Rothfield (and travelling cash from Deakin University School of Humanities), Mary Leahy and Amanda Lawrence – the Paper Tigers, Madeleine Fogharty, Peter Donald, Penny Harvey, Marcia the wise, Mary Madness, Margaret Crawley, Max Ryan, Karen crime, Christine, Laura Turney, Liza Hopkins, Lucy Cooper, Mary Louden, Natasha Soares, Robert Candler, Ruth Brittain, Saiffudin, Shirin Hanfi, Zawar Hanfi, Scott McQuire, Rajinnie Verma, Ruchira Ganguly-Scrase, Shiv Vishvanathan, Sarboni Sarkar, the Lokayan group, Sonya and Matt of Manic Ex-Posuer, Sophie Pavlovski, Ruth Catty, Sadie Belling, Safdar Hashmi, Ramona Mitussis, Michael Healy, Stephanie Cauchi, Susan Fry, Suzanna Williams, Sven H. Thesen, Teresa Tjia, Suzie Q, Raju, KWarK, Tammy King, Damien Lawson, Denise C, Debra Dun, Aroup Chatterjee, Antoine B, Annie X, Anna Ferguson, Anna Davis, Andrew Hindle, Andrew Lattas, Anand Patwardhan, Tom T8, my mother Ann, brother Kim, sisters Marie-Ann and Cheryl and the rest of the family (especially the newer members), editorial powerhouse Louise Murray, Lucy Morton and all the fabulous gang at Zed, the Charterhouse Posse, everyone cited, everyone quoted, the Blackboard Hakka Chinese stall, the crew at the Khalsa, the curd shop staff (now 'curd corner'), the denizens of the Lodge, the distribution system, the corporate conspiracy, the transformatory project and, of course, good old Nomadic Action. Red Salute.

Previous sections of this book appeared in the following places: Sections of Chapter 5 in 'Photogenic Calcutta: Instamatic Anthropology', *In-Me-dia*, Calcutta 1992; Sections of Chapter 6 in 'Cinematic Cities: Camera Angles on Calcutta and the Politics of Representation', *Agenda*, 29/30, 1992; and sections of Chapters 2 and 5 in 'Calcutta Cipher: Travellers and the City', *Social Analysis*, 32, 1992. Snippets also appeared in the newspapers *Filmnews*, Sydney, and *The Telegraph*, Calcutta. Thanks to all concerned.

PREFACE

Je haïs les voyages et les explorations. (Claude Lévi-Strauss)

Rumour has it that Calcutta is a city of between ten and fifteen million people. Located on the banks of a tributary of the Ganges, it has known human settlement for something over three hundred years. As a trading post for the British East India Company, and geopolitical centre of British imperialism, the untold wealth of the subcontinent passed through its port. Portrayed as an overcrowded place of poverty and despair, of desperation and decline, the rumour of Calcutta travels all over the world. Yet popular Western notions of this incredible city are scant, wrong, contemptuous, ideological, vicious and shitty. There is little good said about the place, and what is said is so often extreme: Calcutta, crowded and stinking, brutal and dark, black hole and slum: saved only by the vague association with the Missionaries of Charity. Calcutta suffers from a bad press.

It is not my intention to set the record straight. Rumour is a luxury for those with leisure to waste and squander, to give over to its circulation and elaboration in a counterfeit economy. A rumour is also a gift of truth lying under cover of deceit – a surplus representation, a doubled sign. There are no doubt numerous ways to tell the story of Calcutta: the beginnings of the Indian independence struggle could be traced here; it could be given a place in history as the crucible of revolutionary anti-imperialism; it has a heritage which could claim some of India's foremost social reformers, writers, painters, poets and several Nobel prizewinners – it has its Roy, its Tagore, its Bose – and its Mother Teresa... Latter-day fame accrues to the city via filmmakers like Satyajit Ray and industrialists like Birla. Capital of the state of

Bengal, it has been a communist stronghold since...

...I did not want to write a conventional book which settled the conventional accounts, and so this Calcutta story is less epic. Yet not more or less fictional, not more nor less imaginary – as all histories are. This book is a version of Calcutta culled from the ideological production of Western travel and charity work. It is not a Calcutta that will necessarily be recognized by all Calcuttans, or for that matter by all travellers, but it is Calcutta. This is a study of the ways particular Western visitors understand Calcutta; the ways writing, photography and film condition this process; and the ways touristic representations fit into the practices and ideologies of aid work and cultural imperialism. It is an ethnography of budget travel drawing upon Heidegger's work on framing and Marx's work on the circulation of value to open a space for a critique of development narratives maintained by conventional representations of the city – imagery of decay, absolute poverty, teeming millions, squalor and leprosy.

The analysis bears upon the 'technologies' which frame travellers' understandings and experiences at the Modern Lodge Guest House; the first chapter plots a theoretical context; Chapter 2 attends to traveller 'gossip' and travel-guide 'lore' as exchanged in Modern Lodge; Chapter 3 reads more famous Western visitors to the city; Chapter 4 explores maps to link travel to the circulation of meaning in a wider economy; Chapter 5 focuses upon photography and representations of poverty; and Chapter 6 offers a study of a cinematic Calcutta, particularly Roland Joffe's film *City of Joy*, with which a number of Modern Lodge travellers became involved. Cutting across this version of Calcutta I collect images of gifts, coins, red flags, nuns, police chiefs, towers, cameras, *Octopussy*, Louis Malle, Michel Leiris (versus Lévi-Strauss), Günter Grass (versus Frankfurt book fairs), Jorge Luís Borges and Mahasweta Devi, chai stalls and cottage industries, monsoon and flooded drains, Raj relics and five-star dinners, postcards and taxi drivers...

Technologies of representation give focus to the imagery which enframes Western views of Calcutta: decay is not simply there, it is sought out, foregrounded, represented, and becomes a tourist attraction. Yet, for those involved in volunteer charity work with leprosy sufferers and other destitutes on the streets of Calcutta, explanations of their experience fit into a framework which attributes blame locally, and cannot acknowledge complicity in production of the 'rumour' of Calcutta. This is where questions can be raised about charity and what actually is given – the problem of the gift – in exchanges between travellers and locals. The gift-rumour here is more than one of misrepresenting the city, but of doing so in ways that are not innocent of violence, of exploitation and of plunder. The correlation of Calcutta as a 'natural' site for the lending of charitable care, with the division of the world into developed prosperous nations and struggling 'in-need-of-help' places, indicates for me all that is wrong with our current global predicament. Travellers with good intentions only contribute further disorder to this predicament – I will argue that charity is dysfunctional in that it helps to keep the 'Third World' in the state of an impoverished and disenfranchised recipient of limited 'aid', rather than as partners in redistribution and just exchange. This suggests that tourism and charity in the 'Third World' represent the soft edge of an otherwise brutal system of exploitation. It deserves no alibi.

I want to render this problem in a way that also acknowledges my own complicities in writing on this topic, and writing with a view to both challenging the protocols of ethnographic and social science description, and to furthering, in however small a way, an anti-imperialist project that is not just mere writing, and is not naive about representation and presentation. The code-words here are the proper names of culture theory such as Spivak, Nandy, Foucault, Derrida, Trinh, Bhabha, Said, Virilio, Deleuze, Guattari, Jameson, Agamben and others, all sampled like souvenirs alongside the café pronouncements of travellers, friends and chatterboxes.

This morass of travelling voices, however, is not the 'trinketization' of commentary; rather, it is to be seen as the contested forum in which hegemonic understandings of how those mostly middle-class children of privilege who are able to travel – even, or especially, as 'alternative travellers' giving 'aid', as people who 'care' – see their relation to the rest of the world, or at least to the 'Third World'. As played out, embellished and confirmed in Calcutta, representations of the city in even the grottiest little tourist dive can have much wider significance. At this level, I have not attempted to arbitrate strictly between the categories of the tourist, traveller, exile, expatriate or volunteer worker, since all these categories overlap to some extent in the clientele of the Modern Lodge. I am not overly interested either in any psychological or psychoanalytical evaluation of travellers, volunteers, exiles, or charity workers in general. Just as this project does not purport to be a history of Calcutta nor of all visitors' experience of Calcutta, it is also not a detailed survey of all that travellers and tourist-volunteers are doing in the city. I have little to say specifically of those who work for Mother Teresa: 'religious' volunteers are largely ignored in favour of travellers and volunteers from the Calcutta Rescue group associated with Jack

Preger. But from the particularity and peculiarity of the Modern, I attempt to understand the situation of voluntary 'service' within an international context where varied practices and technologies of tourism, representation and experience combine.

The 'context' of budget tourism and charity work is thus a situation where, in the 'developed' parts of the world, a good portion of the workforce are 'free' to pursue leisure activities (so long as these also involve the consumption of goods and services, and so the recovery of surplus-value as profit). Technological and global market integration, especially through transportation and telecommunications, then facilitates a consumerism in which seemingly all could participate (given full implementation). But this promise is not fulfilled, and despite globalized transportation and accessibility to all cultures, all sites, all markets, for the children of the bourgeoisie, this global accessibility relies upon both a view of the world as resource to be developed (production, progress, development aid, for the benefit of some), and upon the systematic occlusion of actual conditions of production in the peripheral capitalist or comprador sites (and exploitation for almost all). No equitable re-distribution of productive resources (otherwise stolen, squandered and hoarded by capitalist elites, and comprador brethren) can be broached in this view, where 'holidays' remain an exclusionary, and exclusive, luxury. Representations in travel guides, notions of exotic adventure (say, trekking in the Himalayas) and the 'good works' ethic of many aid and charity organizations are not of a monolithic or uniform code but offer, rather, a multiplicity of often contradictory scenes which reinforce and cross-reference an ongoing project: the occlusion of inequalities through ideological work in even the most progressive and well-meaning of tourisms. Budget or 'alternative' travel, like the alternative trade promoted by many organized aid groups, can be criticized as an illusion of 'nice' cottage capitalism, soothing ideological anxieties while extending commercialization and the tourism industry. Rather than working towards social transformation, alternative travel and charity work seems often to tinker at the edges of capitalist expansion into new market niches. This book attempts to articulate these connections, starting from the rumour of the Modern.

INTRODUCTION:

CALCUTTA CIPHER

'Everyone thinks that Calcutta is saying something. That it is a message, a sign, and all we need to do is crack the code.' (Suzie)

It bears repeating: the Frommers guide to India declares: 'everything you ever heard about Calcutta is true' (1984: 195)! This astonishing statement proclaims Calcutta as a cipher, an icon that comes to stand for many different, contradictory and even impossible things. Distanced from 'truth' through the extravagance of this touristic claim, the sensations and curiosities of Calcutta take on a surreal shape and are consigned to the categories of myth and mystique. It is possible, for example, for Jean Racine to describe Calcutta in quite different ways; he begins with the words, 'multitude, misery, dilapidation, violence ... Calcutta, an urban monster, a city of hell', but notes that we 'have heard too much about these clichés broadcast by the international media moved by the lame beggars outside five-star hotels', and suggests that Calcutta's street scenes have become the stuff of myth; he queries these myths of the 'greatest urban disaster of our times? Sinking Calcutta? Hopeless Calcutta?' (Racine 1990: 1). These first moves then. But, now it is something of a commonplace among expatriates and long-term visitors to India that an old British Raj slogan, and sign of confusion, is often repeated: 'for everything that is true here, its opposite will also be true'. In Calcutta, Racine does seem to want it both ways:

One cannot understand Calcutta without looking at it from two angles... there is no major event or influence of India that has not found an echo in Calcutta's bubbling cauldron. It is Calcutta where for centuries *sahibs* and *bhadralok, babus* and pavement dwellers, socio-religious reformers and terrorists,

I

authors or activists have mingled. A brilliant symbol of power and wealth, Calcutta was the second city, after London, of the greatest empire in the world. But as the decay set in, Calcutta became a symbol of misery, the problem city par excellence. (Racine 1990: 51)

With a distinguished and contested history, and with a 'difficult' reputation that almost everyone can cite (if asked to offer three words that sum up Calcutta, what would you say?) and yet few can confirm, it is not so strange that Frommers and Racine take a wide view. But such clichés offer no easy opening for a book on Calcutta.

In this context of Calcutta as a site of which 'everything' can be heard, then everything said or written about the city, all the deliberations of academics and politicians at the Calcutta 300 tercentenary seminars commemorating Job Charnok's 1790 visit, the planners' versions of the future of the city, every commentary and documentary, every photograph, travel guide, home movie, memoir, and so on, could appear as an illusion. In this incarnation Calcutta exists as a metaphor, an imaginary space, a restless marker and a code-word for irregular meanings that are located ... where?

This book is concerned with those who visit Calcutta, starting with contemporary Western travellers doing volunteer work in the city, but also taking into account the experience of other visitors, and the representational technologies used to make sense of that experience. The perceptual 'tools' which both structure and are structured (or enframed) by what I will call 'the rumour of Calcutta' are roughly the subjects of separate chapters on the voice, writing, the camera, and so on – although certain continuities and themes, such as the issues of poverty, difference, space, vision and exchange, cross these mechanical demarcations. I am interested in the ways a small section of the tourist market (backpacker or budget traveller) can be used to open up a topic so vast as the urban conglomeration that is Calcutta. This exploration, and my topic, is also broadly that of representation, of travel and of perception or interpretation. I try to limit the slippage of this project – which always seems to threaten to become a study of international capitalism and more – by beginning with what travellers say in the confines of a small (cheap) guesthouse at the bend of a tiny laneway in the city: the 'Modern Lodge' of Chapter 2. Starting with travellers and 'The Modern' provides a vantage point for all that follows.

Corresponding to the separate parts of this study, I take different theoretical motifs as guides: dialogue and 'gossip' to make sense of what travellers say; texts and writing as a script for experience; and camera technology as an organizing frame of perception. These motifs overlap and are sometimes woven together in a way which may appeal to the current fashion for 'hybrid texts', but which is also a consequence of the main thesis of this work: that Western visitors consume Calcutta through machineries of perception carried as baggage in minds, texts, snapshots and backpacks. This consumption serves particularly dubious ends, not much to the benefit of Calcuttans or, for that matter, to anyone much at all.

The 'rumour' of Calcutta refers to that imaginary Calcutta of guide-books and charitable Western sympathies, but also to the experience of Calcutta which sometimes impinges upon those who visit *despite* the guidebook protocols. Needless to say, I am not claiming this Calcutta as any real or 'local' one, since this too is rumoured not to exist... so I heard, or overheard. Ways in which travellers then understand the city can be calibrated alongside the logics of – to sound redundant – the *ways* they understand the city. By *way* of the things that are part and parcel of what visitors bring to Calcutta – travel guides, tourist visas, tourist lore, gossip, cameras, souvenir hunting, good intentions, charitableness, and so on – their perception of the city is inevitably quite different from that of those who live there. While 'locals' may understand in some, many, or sometimes all of these *ways*, in general the conjunctions of tourism and charity ways of understanding the city are not experienced locally. This book is about versions of the city fashioned – with various mediations – in ways probably unrecognizable to non-tourists.

No doubt Calcutta is locally produced by those of privileged classes also. Government propaganda is circulated largely to serve the interests of the middle class (Mallick 1994), etc., and so any reference I make to the 'authenticity' of local versions of Calcutta should be treated as the easy 'Easternization' that it is. A valorization of otherness named as the limit of the West; another project would deconstruct this still further as a symptom of the fascination for India that is also the subject of this study.

A CITY OF INTENSITIES

So kaleidoscopic is the city that a dozen classic essays on each city still could not capture all its meanings. Not all the efforts of Kipling, N.K. Bose, Geoffrey Moorhouse, Günter Grass, Pritish Nandy and Arpana Sen have exhausted the polysemic power of Calcutta, its repeated attempts to mediate between hope and despair, good and evil. The city keeps re-writing itself, constantly producing new variations that need to be grasped. (Vishvanathan and Sethi 1989: 51)

This aside, an article on the Bhopal gas leak eloquently captures many of the first moves I would want to make in an essay on representations of Calcutta. A discussion that occurred in the IUMDA library (Information Unit on Militarization and Demilitarization in Asia, in Delhi) a year before this article appeared gave me these first steps. More than an elaboration of its meanings, a possible extension would be to consider the limits of meaning in Calcutta; more than its polysemic power, rather a critique of this polysemy; more than a mediation between binaries like hope and despair; more (or less) than the city rewriting itself: I wanted to explore my own involvement in an entire industry of description and explanation implicated within an international inscribing apparatus which constituted the many 'meanings' of Calcutta. Vishvanathan and Sethi offered a further aside that was prophetic: 'The city has not only been a site for the drama of modernity but a metaphor for speculating about it' (Vishvanathan and Sethi 1989: 51). For me, the ways an anthropological/biographical project which could mirror the displacement they describe became an obsession, linked with a certain voyeurism and activism, for a number of years, continuing. Kaleidoscopic.

From the beginning the French writer Marguerite Duras also haunted writing on Calcutta for me, since the evocations of *India Song* and *The Vice-Consul* seem so much more alive than those of other Raj literature I had read. Perhaps this is because her fame in literature and film imposes itself, and because Duras was more a traveller than an administrator, and her words are always more poetic. Somebody – I no longer remember who – pointed out a passage that I would like to use as the emblem for my travel to and fro in Calcutta. Duras wrote:

> you can't just talk without starting out from a particular point of knowledge or ignorance, and arrive somewhere at random amid the welter of other words.... And so this book, which I'd have liked to resemble a roadway going all directions at once, will merely be a book that tries to go everywhere but goes to just one place at a time; which turns back and sets out again the same as everyone else, the same as every other book. The only alternative is to say nothing. But that can't be written down. (Duras 1987/1990: 8)

In short, then, this work begins in a specific place, and while it tries to go everywhere and cover everything, it cannot, and so it becomes a sequence of locations, anecdotes and, I hope, insights into what is at stake in the polysemy of Calcutta in so far as it applies to the city's Western visitors. It is 'about' travellers to Calcutta and how they imagine, make sense of, and explain their experience. This is Calcutta from, in a certain way, the inside-outsiders. Those who visit the city, but imagine it from afar, even when they are closest to it – in its centre, from the low-budget accommodation of the Modern Lodge Guest House.

While this purports to be an anthropological study, it is tempting to proclaim it as a fragmentary entity. The multiple and confused meanings that circulate among visitors trying to make sense of the city necessarily tend towards a polyglot text. Demarcation of the limit of Calcutta, or of the subject of this study, is difficult when everything threatens towards undecidability. It is not clear – as Horne, among many others, has pointed out – that the traveller ever even leaves home (Horne 1992; Virilio 1984/1989), carrying their own culture around inside their heads as we do (change of subject intended). The Indian political psychologist and essayist Ashis Nandy says the West is no longer a geographical category but a state of mind (Nandy 1983 – I will come back to this: the 'West' cannot be homogenized). Given a possible indeterminacy of the specification of the 'West' in the current state of international relations, is it so strange to ask if a tourist is in the 'West' or the 'East' when in Calcutta – this great city, administrative centre of the Raj, imperial wonder, Black Hole, place about which, as the Guide puts it: 'everything you ever heard is true'? Obviously it is not simply a matter of boarding a plane and heading east – for to visit Calcutta as a tourist, north-west from Melbourne, Australia (where I come from), south-west as well as east from Manchester, UK (where I live now) is, as much as staying home, an exploration of the perforated sheet of the worldwide West, where the West is everywhere, and possibly no 'place' at all. In another part of India, in Salman Rushdie's *Midnight's Children*, the foreign-returned Dr Aziz examines his future wife for a variety of ailments shown to him, apparently without compromising the woman's modesty, through the facility of a bed sheet with a small hole torn in it. Fervent exploration of a new portion of the body each month under the strict supervision of parents and through the charade of medical consultation entails a voyeurism, which in this scene is evoked intentionally to focus upon the ways in which Western disciplines (of medicine – and literature) came to investigate India in the hands – never quite fully grasping – of an exoticizing yet empowering knowledge. Similarly, perhaps, the disciplines of knowledge, the protocols of perception, and the charity mentality of some Western tourists can be interrogated as voyeurism, and thus seen more clearly for the ways in which they condition what can be known about Calcutta.

When the 'West' is abandoned in favour of psychological or semiotic spaces, it is all too easy to find Calcutta in every place and then conclude that somehow it doesn't exist geographically, as if a tourist need not even visit Calcutta. And then what of the status of the souvenirs (and memories, experiences, images) that might be carried away from Calcutta? Do they remain Calcuttan, or have they been transmuted into the 'West', as artifacts of Western appropriation, as part of the world market? Calcutta turns up in so many places, projected on to living-room walls and pasted into scrapbooks, worn, eaten, displayed, broadcast on television, submitted in PhDs and analysed in books; and yet it should not be confused, as an unthinking postmodernist might do, with a purely imaginary place. A deterritorializing essentialism, as contrived as that which some who are called postmodernist condemn, would operate here to ignore the effects of a geographical Calcutta to the exclusive favour of an imaginary one; and inversely, an allegedly empirical Calcutta is sometimes taken more seriously than its imaginary manifestations. What this amounts to is a spatial bifurcation of 'Calcuttas' – the ones people carry with them in their heads and in their baggage, and another that is there – where? Calcutta.

Calcutta could be described as a 'city of intensities'. In many ways it is overdetermined in the understandings of travellers – for example, in the anthropomorphic attribution of certain qualities to the city. It is the face of a woman for some, one eye crying, the other smiling; this was mentioned by the filmmaker Mrinal Sen at a Calcutta 300 seminar and repeated by several of the traveller-volunteers who had attended.[1] In another similarly anthropomorphic conception, 'the city has a soul, you can feel it' (Alan). This possession of a soul was identified by Alan after just three days in the city, although it is notable that the most popular travellers' guidebook ends its Calcutta section with just the same words: 'Calcutta has a soul' (Wheeler 1982) – guidebooks provide short-term visitors with a language through which the mismatch of expectations and experiences can be resolved.

There is, perhaps, a corresponding visitor's psychology for Nandy's 'intimate enemy' of the 'West' inside the heads of Indians, and that is the way the 'West' is carried to India in the visitor's mind – as something securely owned – and yet also as something in a process of transformation, in varying degrees of abeyance while experiments with something considered 'other' go on. Of course Western travellers retain their cultural anchoring even in their experiments with versions of what they might call 'local culture' (an ideally non-Western construction for tourists or, if not 'purely' other, a hybrid topsy-turvy West of misspellt menu items – cornflex – and the curiosities of Indian English. I promise more of this). A travellers' Westernness crosses the tarmac and travels too – within the intimacy of the backpack. The enemy in all this might be the too-Western lifestyle, the ethnocentrisms and prejudices, the racists, and perhaps the inability to face up to difficulties and differences without contest; a spectrum of positions from renunciation of the West, through incomprehension, to outright rejection of the validity of those who seem different.

What, then, of the various images of the city constructed by these travellers? My response to this complex is to pursue a critical itinerary which requires construction of another city, called Calcutta, from metaphors and comparisons, the whispers of tourists, snippets of news and rumours, chance glances and visions, in order to open up further problems. I take as justification for this Edward Said's formula for his study *Orientalism*, where he suggests that the 'things to look at are style, figures of speech, setting, narrative devices, historical and social circumstances', rather than some naive reaction seeking 'correctness of presentation' or 'fidelity to some great original' (Said 1978: 21).

IDENTITIES

Said pointed out in *Orientalism* that the machineries of understanding employed by Western scholars were inseparable from the political structures within which and for which they wrote. Against this, he often quotes Fanon: 'Europe is literally the creation of the third world' (Fanon 1961/1967: 96), and contends that the politics of knowledge still operates to occlude much of what is important in world history. In a later book, Said has argued that 'most accounts of European cultural history take little notice of the empire', and that 'today's scholar and critic is accustomed to accept [great novels, etc.] without noticing their imperial attitudes and references along with their authoritative centrality' (Said 1993: 289). While extending the focus of his project to an interest in the 'globalised process set in motion by modern imperialism' (Said 1993: xxii–iii), and in 'new alignments that now provoke and challenge the fundamentally static notion of identity that has been the core of cultural thought during the era of imperialism' (Said 1993: xxviii), he still, however, confines his studies largely to past specificities in a way that remains, perhaps, too local. This can be brought forward so that the 'identity' of travellers, as well as the identity of contemporary places, can be questioned under his recognition that all cultures are 'hybrid, heterogeneous, extraordinarily differentiated and unmonolithic' (Said 1993: xxix). This rubric might usefully be carried into a consideration of the ongoing 'orientalisms' of today. What is required, beyond historical commentaries which would rewrite European cultural history (however important this remains; see especially Kabbani 1986; Viswanathan 1989 and Suleri 1992[2]), is an intervention which challenges the identities so described, and can begin to challenge the continued operation of those identities in contemporary cultural relations – the 'identity' of Calcutta included.

Among the most prominent 'positive' images of old Calcutta is that of the city as the site from which the wealth and riches of India were exported to Europe under the Raj. I want to consider this alongside the privilege accorded to images of poverty in contemporary Calcutta; to examine how available literature and the experiences of tourists doing volunteer work in the city fit into an imaginary polysemic zone. And from here, to tell the story of visitors to the city, travellers and volunteers, working alongside the impoverished and reading Lonely Planet's *India: A Travel Survival Kit* in what was the premier city of empire.[3]

Such work requires a degree of enthusiasm for India, and for Calcutta. Geoffrey Moorhouse can call Calcutta a 'definition of obscenity' (Moorhouse 1971: 132), but this ethnocentric denial does not fit my own experience as a visitor to the city. Moorhouse's prejudice deserves to be quoted:

> It is the easiest thing in the world to come close to despair in Calcutta. Every statistic that you tear out of the place reeks of doom. Every half mile can produce something that is guaranteed to turn a newcomer's stomach with fear or disgust or a sense of hopelessness. It must be a generation at least since anyone stayed here for more than a day or two unless he was obliged to, or had a phenomenal sense of vocation, or a pathological degree of curiosity. (Moorhouse 1971: 350)

Sometimes I did feel that writing a book like this had a certain 'pathology', but not for Moorhouse's reasons – he says: 'writers struggle for the words to describe what has happened' (Moorhouse 1971: 356-7). My pathology was that of the tourists I study, a self-analytical unlearning/learning and attempt to negotiate a politics of representation with regard to the city, and to international tourism. Rather than Moorhouse's writing-blocked fleeting newcomers, I began with quite different visitors in mind (though some of these do profess a 'vocation'). An early essay by Richard Lambert describes, in a generalized way, a set of 'signs' of the enthusiast for India which I more easily recognize, and which would form the beginning of what must become a broad, critical, characterization of many of the travellers I have met in Calcutta:

> Aside from items of dress, the mark of the enthusiast is the preference for Indian-style food; attending night-long musical recitals; making the grand and the local tour of temples; a fondness for Indian films; a smattering of language lessons; some social welfare work in a captive village; rummaging for oriental miniatures, brass work, textiles, and other handicrafts; attending weddings and other public ceremonials; and collecting, specimen fashion, acquaintances with as great a number of Indians as possible. (Lambert 1966: 161)

The Western travellers who live in the Modern Lodge do not all, or always, fit this outline, and certainly many of those who visit short-term would recognize only some of these characteristics in their own experience, but – with a number of more Calcutta-specific items – this list does identify characteristics of the main subjects of this work.

Many, if not most, of the backpacking travellers who pass through Calcutta are not unreflective about their situation in travelling. Their reflections reveal the presence of a form of popular alternative critique of travel, a perspective on the ethical problems of otherness, and some recognition that their experience is filtered through the technological aids of perception they carry with them. Their critique of tourism manifests itself in (a) the search for 'authentic' experiences; (b) dismay at the effect of tourism; and (c) condemnation of other tourists and sometimes themselves. The correlates of these three moments are (a) claims to the 'once-in-a-lifetime' experience; (b) nostalgia for the days when such and such a place was not so well known; and (c) 'of course I'm doing it differently' stories.

The confusion which reigns in this kind of tourism derives from a predicament where the consumption of its product – in so far as the product of tourism is more than snapshots and souvenirs – entails no obvious or easily accumulatable tangible possession. 'Good works', experience, and cultural capital are less easy to reinvest. However, all the productions of these travellers – comments, letters, photos, and so on – amount to an overwhelming ethnographic archive that would repay investigation as the script of the ongoing dynamics of capitalist appropriations and ongoing constructions of cultural difference. More than this, low-budget backpacker tourism plays a significant role in the world order of the capitalist cultural economy, and not only through the enormity of representations it helps produce. The ability to move to conveniently inexpensive market and service centres through the facility of international travel yields a relatively high buying power with attendant ideological, habitual and attitudinal consequences — back-packers who can live like Rajas in Indian towns at low financial cost. An expanding economy revolves around middle-class youth travellers, and engraves the principles of consumption upon even the most ethe-real aspects of their lives. The hypocrisy with which some travellers are condemned for renouncing materialism while looking for the cheapest guesthouse room or dorm for their ashram stay is relevant here. It would be an error to think that the global low-budget 'banana-pancake trail'[4] is not an important component of the ideology as well as the economy of touristic consumption. This book attempts to add to the growing analysis of tourism's many forms (Crick 1985, 1988, 1994; MacCannell 1992; Urry 1990) and to place 'banana-pancake trail' examples in a wider context. Broadly, this context might be one in which it is found that 'in industrialised countries, tourism is frequently pushing out ... manufacturing, distribution, or extractive industry as the economic mainstay', while in other parts of the world 'the shift typically has been from an agrarian economic base to a touristic eco-nomic base' (Smith and Eadington 1992: 2), or, in still more general terms, a context in which small-scale economic and voluntary opera-tions (like budget tourism and Non-Government Organization — NGO — aid work) fit into a systematic global disorder. This 'fit' extends exponentially from cultural and even 'alternative' ideological produc-tion through to more blatant competition among capitalist powers to secure profit opportunities across the breach of First World and Third World relations, by whatever means necessary. I make no apology for telescoping the big picture here.

It is no coincidence that the increase in tourist arrivals in India provoked by the 'Visit India 1991' advertising campaign coincides with the period in which International Monetary Fund (IMF) and World Bank directed 'market internationalization' also rises. Debates over tariff protection, the (re)introduction of transnational food and drink chains — Pepsi and Pizza Hut — and massive development of tourism infra-structure in India can be fitted into much wider, but nevertheless crucial, international processes of global economic 'readjustment' and 'restructuring', often brutal. Gilles Deleuze, at about the same time that Said was writing *Orientalism*, listed important characteristics of this situation: 'the development of a world market, the power of multi-national companies, the outline of a "planetary" organisation, the extension of capitalism to the whole social body' and argued that 'at the same time, the means of exploitation, control and surveillance become more and more subtle and diffuse, in a certain sense molecular (the workers of the rich countries necessarily take part in the plundering of the third world)' (Deleuze and Parnet 1977/1987: 146) Only 'in a certain sense' would I agree that tourism, and especially 'Third World' tourism, is 'subtle and diffuse', but the identification of a 'planetary organisation' which extends from WB/IMF structures to advocates of 'alternative tourism' should not be missed. This is orientalism today.

So many travellers express an ambiguous uncertainty about their mode of travelling and its relation to codes of exploitation that they identify in their own practice, at the same time as they differentiate it from all they do themselves. The formula 'Yes, I recognize the contradictions, but I try to avoid them myself' is almost always a self-serving claim – a rationalization. At the same time, an intuition that this gambit is also inadequate completes a popular reflexivity that is not surprising given the difficulty of identifying and understanding the complexities of life within late-twentieth-century capitalism. The task of naming the dilemmas of our involvement in the abstract internationalisms of tourism, cultural difference, imperial exploitation, charity, capitalism, and so on makes it important to ask questions about the ways travellers name these things.

REPRESENTATIONS OF POVERTY

The inquiry into narrative politics, and the exploration of narrative alternatives any such critique might generate, provide the context in which to begin to rescind the definitional prejudices and privileges of the production of meaning controlled in the hands, and texts, of a narrow minority. Keeping this in mind is all the more important when it comes to working in contexts where power relations and positions are so clearly polarized, as they are with travel in the 'Third World', and with much anthropology. It has often been recognized that the privilege of researchers who are institutionally supported and enabled to produce text 'on' indigenous peoples does little to disturb such hierarchies.

This certainly has implications for a project on tourists working in a Calcutta street clinic, as many of the guests of Modern Lodge do. Part of the reason I have chosen to study the experience of travellers, rather than present a study of the clinic where they work, is that too often those with less power in a situation are made the subjects of study. Already the degree to which Third World tourism participates in a voyeuristic consumption of poverty is problem enough – this is at least sufficient to dissuade me from producing another patronizing text on the 'poor' and destitute. I do provide some detail about the street clinic in Chapter 2, and it would be important to ask in what ways the 'patients' of the clinic have less power, relatively less power, subaltern power in various contexts rather than others, not just when they are the 'recipients' of the 'aid' and 'care' offered in charity, and so on. These questions could be taken up in a study of the relationship between workers and locals in the clinic, but I am refusing such a project for reasons I derive in part from Gayatri Spivak's comment that auto-critical vigilance (for me, being a tourist, examining tourism and charity work from the subject position of Modern Lodge tourists) is better than to 'continue pathetically to dramatise victimage' (Spivak 1990b: 230).[5] Imperatives and injunctions may be offered: for example, Susan George has questioned the propriety of 'Third World' research. With some reservations – since things are sometimes more complex than she allows; there are also questions of access and resources and research grant priorities, etc., to contend with – I have tried to take up such suggestions with this study of the West in Calcutta:

> Meanwhile, not nearly enough work is being done on those who hold the power and pull the strings.… Let the poor study themselves. They already know what is wrong with their lives and if you truly want to help them, the best you can do is give them a clearer idea of how their oppressors are working now and can be expected to work in the future. (George 1976: 289)

Whether or not travellers to Calcutta are 'really' powerful oppressors might be questioned. Certainly my presence in Calcutta as a traveller offered me opportunities not available elsewhere, and so I produce a text that is also a confession. I hope it comes with a degree of reference and relevance to the people it is about. Texts are political, they are not autonomous, although their alienation from humanity on three sides – the writer, the reader, the subject – as abstract artifacts without responsibility, makes them often appear so. This is also how it is with the stock images of Calcutta, where representational fictions have come to be seen as real. Over and over, the objects of Western knowledge are reified in this manner. Stratton notes, however, that this is a contested terrain where the power to define, and the technological means by which this is achieved, is the basis of control:

> in an episteme where representation is privileged, the site of presence is always contested and power derives not only from controlling information but from controlling what people consider information to be. The site of presence and power now lies with people who are not only defined by ownership but by their control over information systems and systems of communication. (Stratton 1990: 26)

It is necessary, then, to listen attentively to the echoes of power in the 'systems' of this work on visitors to Calcutta. While the systems examined here are those employed by tourists *about* Calcutta rather than *between* tourists and Calcuttans, it is nevertheless obvious that power resounds throughout. This systemic dimension (and we should attend also to the geographical, visual and aural metaphors of this discussion) of the knowledge/power equation should not be ignored: in Calcutta, as one set of examples, the conversations, gossip, rumour, dialogue, discourse – call it what you will – of travellers in the Modern Lodge Guest House amounts to an apparatus of considerable influence. As examined in detail in the chapter on Modern Lodge, such an apparatus shapes and orchestrates opinions, experiences and perceptions of travellers in Calcutta.

HEIDEGGER AND MARX

All distances in time and space are shrinking. We now reach overnight, by plane, places which formerly took weeks and months of travel. We now receive instant information, by radio, of events formerly learned about only years later, if at all…. Distant sites of the most ancient cultures are shown on film as if they stood this very moment amidst today's street traffic. Moreover, the film attests to what it shows by presenting also the camera and its operators at work. The peak of this abolition of every possible remoteness is reached by television, which will soon pervade and dominate the whole machinery of communication…. What is happening here when, as a result of the abolition of great distances, everything is equally far and equally near?… Everything gets lumped together into uniform distancelessness. How? (Heidegger 1971: 166)

The theoretical apparatus of this work may seem opportunistic. This is attenuated, if at all, only by the possibility of gathering much of the culture theory to which I refer around a set of broadly Heideggerian and Marxist concerns. Throughout this book I have thought the issues through within the 'horizon' of a Marx-inflected Heidegger (no doubt a strange beast). Thrown together as they are here, diverse thinkers can be called upon in what is otherwise a dangerous project of theoretical tourism. The clutter and refuse of eclectic readings of other privileged texts – from Lévi-Strauss and Leiris to Bataille and Nietzsche and more – will, I hope, seem appropriately prompted from what travellers have said of Calcutta. Beyond this, there is little 'method' here, except perhaps what someone like Nikos Papastergiadis deems necessary in the 'absence of an established discipline' (Papastergiadis 1993a: 4) for studies which examine the dynamics of complex displacements such as migration, travel, identity and so on.[6] (I do not think it matters much that the only security of method here is what comes to hand.)

Among the book-production industry that is theory today, I have 'souvenired' some fashionable items. Prominent among these are the works of Heidegger[7]. There is a sense in which the importance of Heidegger cannot be charted except as a voice influentially speaking through all those who engage with questions of Being. While I have also 'souvenired' only a small part of Heidegger's oeuvre for my own purposes, the rumour of his questions in this work allows a frame within which a rather haphazard sampling of other theorists may pass under the banner of the 'secret children of Heidegger'. While I do not want to set out any detailed genealogy, I do think it is justifiable to link the varied works of Derrida, Foucault, Deleuze, Bataille, Virilio and Agamben to a (productively) distorted Heideggerian project.[8] It will be clear, I think, that this trinket-collecting of thoughts from Heidegger is hardly a philosophical investigation in his sense – too cluttered. My view is that this can be excused if Heidegger's work is combined within a Marxist project, although I will not provide an extended defence of such a mix here. Georg Lukács presents Heidegger as an exponent of what he called the 'cultural criticism of the bourgeoisie', which was wont to 'sublimate a critique of society into a purely philosophical problem' (Lukács 1968/1971: xxiv). I think this can be turned around.[9]

For this reason this work also claims the heritage of Marx. The legacy of his work is far too influential for anyone to approach in a totalizing and systematic way. The name-dropping above could also be linked here, along with writers like Spivak, Said, Castells, Soja and Clifford. Such lists are another form of sending postcards, telegrams, signs or curios. Nothing 'theoretical' in this work should be taken too seriously except in so far as it is useful along the way (yet again the travel metaphor). For my purposes, all these writers might be grouped together around a project: the critical analysis of discursive production – Foucault's archaeology of knowledge suggests the phrase. Whatever the status of superficial 'intellectual traditions' and scholarly star systems, I want to set out my work under the sign of both Marx and an analysis of processes of commodification and the world market, and Heidegger in so far as he was concerned with technology and the 'production' of how we live in the world.

There can be no question that the possibility of international travel and the associated industries of tourism, from ticketing to telephoto-lens sales, are conditioned by the uses of technology. As much of this work is explicitly structured around the framing apparatus of different technologies of perception, it is worth setting out a broad framework for what follows.

> Tourism is a visible result of the great waves of technology which have changed the social geography of the world since the nineteenth century. (Bhatia 1986: vii)

> Technological developments in transport have made it possible for millions of people to travel to far-away places which only a generation ago were regarded as being almost entirely inaccessible. (Bhatia 1986: 32)

The place of technology in the development of tourism could occupy much of this discussion. Marx was interested in the effect of transportation systems such as railways upon India, but I wonder if it was ever possible to anticipate the massive explosion of planetary travel which is now apparent. Heidegger comes close in the quote about travel and television above; he asks how it is possible that everything has now come together in distancelessness (Heidegger 1971: 166). The extent to which I wish to consider the technological has more to do with technologies of representation and perception, although I think it is necessary to show how conceptual matters are inextricably linked within the horizon of material technologies. This requires a brief excursion through the thought of Marx and Heidegger in a way that allows us to keep these general points in mind.

In *Capital*, Marx makes numerous suggestions which link intellectual production with the production of social relations and the sustenance of life. That the mode of social relations of late-twentieth-century capitalism must be grasped at a global level, encompassing also relations of tourism and media as extensions of more obviously economic relations between the First and Third Worlds, does not make specific technologies any less significant in the process. Marx wrote:

> Technology discloses humanity's mode of dealing with nature, the process of production by which we sustain our life, and thereby also lays bare the mode of formation of our social relations, and of the mental conceptions that flow from them. (Marx 1867/1967: 372)

Technologies of inscription and representation deserve special attention in so far as they are intertwined with social relations and ideology. The way in which technology is utilized has profound implications. In Heidegger's essay 'What are Poets for?', these implications are flagged in explicitly Marxist terms when he writes: 'technological dominion spreads itself over the earth ever more quickly, ruthlessly, and completely. Not only does it establish all things as producible in the process of production; it also delivers the products of production by means of the market' (Heidegger 1971: 114). This market then 'spans the whole earth as a world market', and 'subjects all beings to the trade of a calculation that dominates most tenaciously' (Heidegger 1971: 115). In Heidegger's 'Letter on Humanism', a new way of thinking about technology is called for within the horizon of 'a productive dialogue with Marxism' (Heidegger 1978: 220). He explains that it is 'necessary to free oneself from naive notions about materialism, as well as from the cheap refutations that are supposed to counter it':

> The essence of materialism does not consist in the assertion that everything is simply matter but rather in a metaphysical determination according to which every being appears as the material of labour ... the self-establishing process of ... production. The essence of materialism is concealed in the essence of technology, about which much has been written but little has been thought. (Heidegger 1978: 220)

Heidegger says that it is technology which 'renders beings manifest' (Heidegger 1978: 220), and so this has implications for the way Calcutta is 'rendered', the way it becomes 'manifest' for those who visit. The 'technological dominion' which governs travellers' experience in Calcutta can be explored by working through Heidegger's essay 'The Question Concerning Technology':

> Everywhere we remain unfree and chained to technology, whether we passionately affirm or deny it. But we are delivered over to it in the worst possible way when we regard it as something neutral; for this conception of it, to which today we particularly like to do homage, makes us utterly blind to the essence of technology. (Heidegger 1955/1977: 4)

Heidegger's method of questioning concerning technology is provocatively couched in the metaphoric domains of transport, geography and vision.[10] He asks about the essence of technology in a closely reflective way, concerned always to determine the direction of the critical task in order to bring to light what would remain hidden if the conventional paths of asking and answering questions were not challenged.[11] What Heidegger directs us to see is that technology is not something neutral that can be simply questioned; it is bound up with the ways in which we understand and use technology, and questions about technology. So, to begin with, as long as we do nothing but ask whether we accept or reject the technological, we remain hopelessly blind to any understanding.

In asking in a conventional way whether we might accept or reject technology, we remain within the horizon of a characterization of technology as instrument. This is the way in which we would understand technology as the making and using of machines, appliances, instruments – technology is a means towards certain ends. Heidegger suggests that we need to question technology not only in relation to it as a means, but also in relation to ends. What are the ends of the technological? Commonly, a technology, an instrument or a technique, is utilized in order to bring something to light – to make something, to achieve some end (as in material production, but also as with a technique such as questioning, which brings forth answers). It is this 'bringing to light' which interests Heidegger; an end of technology which is entwined with its essence is the work of revealing that which was otherwise unrevealed. For Heidegger this is a challenge to the way we understand the world itself; to the way the world is revealed to us in our understanding:

> The threat to humanity does not come in the first instance from the potentially lethal machines and apparatus of technology. The actual threat has already affected us in our essence. The rule of enframing threatens us with the possibility that we could be denied a more original revealing. (Heidegger 1955/1977: 28)

This rule of enframing is a difficult concept, but one which must be understood as essential to Heidegger's question concerning technology. The work of revealing does not simply happen in an unordered way; the means of technology do not work towards unordered or unconstrained ends; the ends of technology, however untechnological, are essentially bound up, enframed, by a certain, and specific, understanding of the world.

What this means is that, with the 'modern technology' of the oil or coal mining industry, for example, 'revealing' takes the form of a demand upon nature to supply energy which can be extracted by machine and stored. This entails an understanding of the land, in the case of coal mining, as that which reveals an ore deposit, which shall be revealed and extracted with the greatest efficiency and the least expenditure possible. The land is subjected to a demand of a specific type, and understood in a specifically related way – as a resource, as hidden and potential energy, as profitable. Enframed in a particular way, both with regard to means and ends conceived, the world takes on a character and is revealed in seeming truth as this character before any other way is possible. There is a particular world that 'comes into presence' through the frame of technology conceived in this way, and this world is dangerously subsumed to an instrumentalist and exhaustive exploitation (for the profit of some, rather than all). Are there not other ways, and other worlds, which might have been revealed?

The enframing of the dominant 'modern technology' of the mining companies must be examined in relation to the ideologies of the natural sciences which aim to comprehend nature as a coherent system of calculable forces. It is in this context that techniques of extraction, processing and development are able to proceed within a constrained horizon of efficiency, productivity and cost-effectivity, and where other issues, less calculable within the horizon of the natural sciences, cannot be revealed as 'real world' concerns. Enframing is the way the nature of the technology destines a certain world to be revealed rather than another:

> Everything, then, depends upon this: that we ponder the question concerning technology and continue to watch over it. How can this happen? Above all through our catching sight of what comes to presence in technology, instead of merely staring at the technological. So long as we represent technology as an instrument, we remain held fast. (Heidegger 1955/1977: 32)

In the end Heidegger goes on not so much to present an alternative way of viewing the world, because his position is more subtle than that, but to require that we ask, and answer, questions about the ways technology brings to light, or reveals, particular worlds in a much more determined, critical and reflective way. This is relevant especially for a work that will apply its critical insights to a politics of representation, a politics of meaning (of charity and of world tourism). Very near the beginning of *Being and Time*, Heidegger notes that the social sciences operate 'with definite preliminary conceptions and interpretations of human Dasein in general, even in first "receiving" its material, and in sifting it and working it up' (Heidegger 1926/1962: 76). Neither scientific psychology and sociology, nor an 'everyday anthropology', can provide us with 'proper access' to the phenomena we are studying. This reflection, then, is to be kept at hand as the enabling 'illusion' operating the 'technologies' employed in this work.

Another of the ways I want to use this sense of technology from Heidegger is to take technology as an instrument which brings something 'to light' and reveals that which was unrevealed. This is taken up by Virilio in *War and Cinema,* where he discusses 'machineries for seeing' (Virilio 1984/1989: 1) in a way that demands that the 'logistics of perception' (the book's subtitle) be rethought in terms of technology rather than unaided sight. I will argue along these lines when I come to discuss the structure of the camera in the latter half of this work. In any case, the ways in which the world is 'revealed' to us are conditioned by the use made of technologies which are instrumental in that revealing, and the ends – say, of the logistics of the commodity system – which that use of technology enables. In the cases I will examine, the modes of representation with which we are seeing Calcutta 'revealed' are largely determined by the categories of documentation and exposure typical of Western use of writing, recording and film in the Third World. These documentations and exposures obey already-established orientations to Calcutta. I argue that these orientations are best understood as specific manifestations of Western cultural and political imperialism, produced and played out within the appropriative and consuming framework of global capitalism.

When approached as a place to visit, Calcutta appears already inscribed as a site of exemplary experience and as something to be written in a before-and-after 'experiential' zone. Travellers come to Calcutta to experience, and hence to report on, something they expect to be extreme. Unusual and different from all other expectations and places – as a site of poverty, crowds, rickshaws, etc. – Calcutta is also a place that is to be seen and then left. Churchill said just this: 'I am pleased to have seen her, for I will never have the need to see her again' (this comment is variously quoted, and again interestingly inflected along gender lines). The hermetic seal of this city's framing resists any challenge, so that even alternative travellers and eco-tourists, volunteers, participant travellers and other traveller-expatriate forms do not deviate significantly from the established paths. For all the minutiae of travel guides, backpacker lore and gossip, literary imagination and snapshot voyeurism, it is striking how Calcutta is framed in such conventional ways.

With regard to film, the demand that shots be taken, and that they be replicable (fixed, true, saleable, showable), constitutes a particular way of viewing Calcutta, an acquisitive outlook which excludes other possibilities. The codification of Calcutta within the representative 'ends' of the technologies of documentary reportage, realist film and photography already means that certain other issues, less calculable or open to evaluation within the framework of such documentation, cannot be conceived or considered important enough to rate attention. Recognition of the narrow dimensions of documentary realism in photographic and cinematic approaches to the Third World invites challenges to established Western/touristic production, and to the unquestioned circulation of certain versions and evaluations or opinions about Calcutta.

For example, camera technology and its associated referents may be analysed with a number of interrelations: from the personal- and identity-effect level of everyday experience, to the global or world-system effect of these technologies. There is, perhaps, a link between a certain mechanic perception of the world and the world of commodities. Extensions of the body through mechanized frames of perception like the camera are closely related, at a level still difficult to 'recognize and name', to the alienation of a mechanized and formalized (impoverished) advanced capitalism, where all social needs are satisfied 'in terms of commodity exchange' (Lukács 1968/1971: 91–3). Another angle on this might examine the technological collapse of time and space which is now available for a dominant subsection of the world population (and its backpacking children). This truncating spatial–temporal effect ensures that the most 'remote' and 'different' experiences are entered into the exchange circuit of information capitalism as equivalences.[12] This is not to say that experiences are simply bought, but that the mediations of a global social hierarchy, based upon levels of technological development and attendant (often disguised, always contested) relations of production, provide the context for traveller experience in Calcutta, just as other experiences are drawn into the framing vortex of meaning in late-twentieth-century 'culture'.

An analysis tracing the implications of certain technologies of representation through their differential insertions into moments of economic and cultural significance carries problems and limitations which I shall try to indicate along the way. Nevertheless, even a partial development of such a project has its uses. Technologies of representation are major channelling factors which determine, to some extent, what kind of representations of Calcutta can be produced. The means of production here carries with it attendant world-views, socio-centrisms to be played out, an entire series and hierarchy of preferences and choices connected to the technological means of *re*production which it is my purpose to reveal.

It might be argued that for many Western observers, the dominant frame through which Calcutta, and perhaps India, is understood is first of all economic; specifically in a comparative mode which pays attention to the economic disadvantage of 'the poor'. This is too simple, but the 'rumour of poverty' is certainly present within the discourse of 'Third World' travel, and to a disturbing extent the 'poor' are a part of what is toured by tourists. Some travellers have referred to their medical and volunteer work on the streets of Calcutta with the ironic label 'sick tours'. The economic advantages for the First World traveller on a visit to India are great: beaches, cheap drugs, souvenirs and scenic temples are a bargain compared to other tourist destinations – say Europe or Australia. In addition to all this, the presence of comparative economic disadvantage can, unfortunately, be considered part and parcel of the cultural attraction of a Third World destination. Sometimes this attraction can be obscenely clichéd and sentimental, as expressed in snapshots of beautiful peasants ('They're so cute, let's buy a couple for the backyard', one brutally ironic postcard declared). Even among those who acknowledge the realities of economic disparities between travellers and toured, a degree of consumption of poverty is inevitable and can contribute to a maintenance of that poverty as subject of 'observation'. Technologies of perception such as the travel brochure, the objectifying camera, the cathartic guilt expiation of writing, the tour guide's explanations which refer to welfare and social programmes, and the knowledgeable analytics of academia, only insulate travellers from what may be otherwise more disturbing. (A small degree of disturbance can be part of the tour.) In many ways, poverty is a theme orchestrated by the technologies of budget travel too, as economic difference enframes almost all activity for the visitor to Calcutta. The constitution of Calcutta as a set of images of poverty and the exotic to be consumed fits neatly within a development narrative which offers affirmation to a Euro-American global hegemony while bringing otherwise threatening 'differences' of alterity into the commodity system as a set of equivalences.[13]

The rumour of Calcutta coexists with a mobile capital which chases all around the globe, making commodities of all it sees. The technological channels through which this rumour passes – the machineries of traveller perception, writing, camera, etc. – are the tools by which capitalism transmutes all culture, emotion, identity, into a form open to exchange.

As I will discuss in Chapter 3, Günter Grass suggests that international publishing is 'counterfeit', popular opinion often declares that travel guides are fabrications, reflexivity is rhetorical; others suggest that Raj history is bunk, Calcutta is a rumour and the Black Hole a fraud. What does all this mean for the study of tourist and visitor understanding, or representation, of the city? Will not all texts, including this, suffer from these deceits and more? Does not Heidegger's rule of enframing cancel all emancipative opportunity?

Possibly the most difficult issue about which to write in a social science study of tourism is the ways both academic work 'in the field' and various discourses of tourism participate in a complex construction of knowledges, cultures and meanings that systematically obscure possibilities of considering sociopolitical effects. Enframed as we are, in many ways this difficulty should be no surprise; in part it presents a paradox of attempting to write and understand things in ways that are antithetical to established and persuasive protocols of accepted understanding and writing. Further, even within these protocols, the place of antithetical writing is already inscribed and accommodated in a way that co-opts all (most?) challenges.

While the extent to which an exploration beyond accredited boundaries of scholarship can be achieved remains to be seen, a question which might usefully lead up to this impasse can be taken as a guide for thought that wants to traverse uncharted terrain: what is the possibility of thinking [about Calcutta] differently from the way we think of it now?[14] Asking such a question first requires some comprehension of how we do think at present, and then perhaps some search for that which is obscured. This question is then appropriate, in its suspicions of everything (some might object that this is a classical Cartesian manoeuvre, but it can also be defended with reference to Marx), for both the productions of the social sciences and the discursive productions of tourism. Everything that is written, said, constructed, meant, made, understood, opined or brought into existence in any way should be interrogated with this in mind. This interrogation itself would also be subjected to this critique.

I suspect that this should be a more central point, but for now it will be sufficient to note that I will return again to the issue of the status of my project and its intentions – why I only want to look mostly at Westerners in Calcutta (leaving Calcuttans to the Calcuttans), why I accept the accusation that I am guilty of 'staring at tourists staring at locals, and writing notes about it all' (Katie). In this discussion so far I may be also accused of a kind of transcendental absence – I have hardly 'theorized' my position; the ways in which I have been able to orchestrate the quotes and examples, the authority devices used to proclaim various 'truths', the privilege that allows me to write – on Calcutta, on tourists, on the city. I assume throughout that this will remain a problem, as I do not yet know how to explain all the contradictions of my position. I have been, and very much remain, a tourist in Calcutta – anything more than this will be dismissed as an arrival anecdote asserting presence. I have learnt much from Bengali writers, cultural workers, activists, academics, journalists and friends so that I can now never simply trace the influences, and I do not want these to be simply listed in an 'Acknowledgments' section before the text proper. I do have partisan views of the city, and of the ills and goods of travel and charity work which I will discuss as I go – I want to disenchant Calcutta somewhat; to show how some of the myths of the city are constructed; to argue from this constructed discourse for a critique of the imperialist burden of representations; and to recognize that although this critique is also constructed, the myths that might be made with it provide a more reflective travel/consumption/experience of the city than is otherwise available. So I want to begin, from Calcutta, a critique of travel that intervenes in its consumptions, its 'imperialisms', and further politicizes travel so that travellers recognize their imbrication with international imperialism, with the world debt system (not just the debts, but the whole deal), its structured inequalities and thefts, and with the horrors of the 'global world disorder' that is capitalism-as-usual. What sort of ethnography, then, and what changes to 'ethnographic' writing, is this?

While there is some merit, I think, in efforts to 'attempt to imagine and criticise the global capitalism which makes us a world community', it is also the case that these efforts amount to 'a way of thinking entirely in keeping with the centrality of the West in world history' (Lenaghan 1992: 30). I am concerned with the impossibility of avoiding the ethnocentrism which asserts the centrality of the West as well as the romanticism which idealizes the 'others' of that West. The danger is always the recruitment of 'Third World wisdoms' for the very 'planetary consciousness' that has fuelled the capitalist drive of this community – 'local knowledge' remains local only locally, and remains 'local' only if it is kept out of both books and shops, and social science does not do that. I have chosen to take the experience of Westerners as my example. My reluctance to make subjects, in this text, of Bengalis involved in the tourist trade, or of local authors, filmmakers or photographers, is partly a response to my understanding of the history of parasitic First World scholarly appropriation, and partly a consequence of, or convenience for, my touristic subject position. Now this is not just a convenient deceit. It was Peter Phipps who wrote that 'the "budget traveller" is best analysed as a subject position rather than a living, fully identified subject' (Phipps 1990: 1), and in this text there are very often tourist positions, not tourists, just as there might be local 'positions' – but not here, for good reasons. I choose, for 'political' reasons, to study my own (position). Yet 'not representing' Calcuttans does not mean that they are not 'here' in the text. In the Calcuttas put together in tourism, they even sometimes feature as proper names – authors, film-makers, politicians – but, as I have already wondered, would locals recognize themselves in this phantasmagoric tourist Calcutta? Perhaps this is *all* illusion.

The figures of deception, false consciousness, ethnocentrism, bad faith, alienation, prejudice, conceit and obfuscation feature in both the history of the social sciences and specifically in the areas of cultural studies, political science and history. On deception, Heidegger notes that this is the structure of knowledge: 'If one being did not simulate another, we could not make mistakes ... we could not go astray and transgress.... That a being should be able to deceive as semblance is the condition for our being able to be deceived ... the clearing happens only at this double concealment' (Heidegger 1971: 34).[15] It is very important to understand that this is also the structure of commerce. In a later part of this book, a similar 'double' structure in Marx – that of the commodity and the money form – can be considered in relation to the giving of charity, specifically of a coin passed to a beggar in the film *City of Joy*. This exchange is a key point which underlies the scene of aid work as well as the economics of tourism. Everybody needs that coin. Perhaps one way to grasp the significance of this scene in a way that resonates through all the themes of this work is to see this coin as a piece of technology that homogenizes. By extension, everything has a price, the trick is one of equivalence. This coin has a long history; it will be mentioned again and again – in the section on Lévi-Strauss, as well as in the sections on souvenirs and on the film *City of Joy*.[16]

Marx asks: 'are there not contradictions ... which are wrapped up in the existence of money alongside commodities? ... The simple fact that the commodity exists doubly, in one aspect as a specific product ... and in the other aspect as manifest exchange value (money)' (Marx 1858/1973: 147). A commodity may be exchanged because of its specific and useful qualities, but also because of its exchangeability. When a commodity is exchanged for money, money is different to the commodity, it is external, and codifies a social relation, determined not by its product qualities but 'abandoned to the mercy of external conditions [i.e., markets]' (Marx 1858/1973: 147). The act of exchange then takes on a double movement, purchase and sale, achieving 'a spatially and temporally separate and mutually indifferent form of existence, [and so] their immediate identity ceases' (Marx 1858/1973: 148). Then – and this is Marx's key point – 'Just as exchange itself splits apart into two mutually independent acts, so does the overall movement of exchange itself become separate from the exchangers, the producers of commodities' (Marx 1858/1973: 148).

This is a deceit by any reckoning (except by that of the capitalist). Marx's analysis of exchange and the commodity form (as opposed to the shackled orthodoxy of economic rationalism) allows us to take account of social processes within production. 'The rise of exchange (commerce) as an independent function torn away from the exchangers corresponds to the rise of exchange value as an independent entity, as money, torn away from products.' [Remember that Moorhouse was 'tearing' facts about Calcutta out of the place.] Marx writes: 'Exchange value was the measure of commodity exchange; but its aim was the direct possession of the exchanged commodity, its consumption' (Marx 1858/1973: 149). This is so for consumption which will satisfy needs, but the purpose of commerce is not consumption but circulation in order to recoup profit on the part of those who control production. Again, Marx summarizes: 'With the development of the division of labour, the immediate product ceases to be the medium of exchange. The need arises for a general medium of exchange.... Money ... the representative of all values' (Marx 1858/1973: 149).

The inequity of this is that when 'the product becomes subordinated to labour and labour to exchange' [labour is sold for money, the product's price is set by labour under the control of the capitalist], it becomes a matter of social and political circumstance, whether or not the product or its equivalent will return to the labourer. Since the capitalist is out to recoup that value which is produced by labour over and above the cost of that labour, the appropriation of labour inheres in the exchange of commodities, expressed via the money form. The gift of a coin in charity is a cruel mockery of a global system based on this unequal exchange. All calculations of charity, and of First World–Third World relations, must be understood within this structure.

> The social character of activity, as well as the social form of the product, and the share of individuals in production here appear as something alien and objective, confronting the individuals, not as their relation to one another, but as their subordination to relations which subsist independently of them.... The general exchange of activities and products, which has become a vital condition for each individual – their mutual interconnection – here appears as something alien to them, autonomous, as a thing. (Marx 1858/1973: 157)

This is the commodity form, which, in one example, appears as the souvenir, exchanged for a few coins, by travellers on the global circuit.

The circulation of capital is facilitated by just such substitutions. This must be understood in the context of what Spivak calls the 'irreducible rift of the international division of labour' (Spivak 1996: 128). This rift, in the broadest convenient terms, is between 'First' and 'Third' worlds, however interrelated and co-constituted these need to be for an adequate analysis (the First World in the Third and the Third in the First, etc.). Yet the broad parameters of this relation should not be underplayed, since at a time when more people than ever are 'travelling', it is telling that Spivak can note that exploitation is 'hidden from sight in the "rest of the world"' (Spivak 1987: 167). What needs to be done, then, is to attack this occlusion, which is consequent upon conditions of technological development − including an 'indefinite spiral' of relative and absolute surplus-value continually changing the 'technical composition of capital' (Marx 1867/1967: 622). What are Western travellers in Calcutta if not both witnesses, consumers and producers of the effects of a brutal global exploitation in which they are at one moment only minor agents, at another the prime architects?

No less illusory or dissembling conditions prevail in other aspects of tourism and travel − so much so that it is plausible to consider these areas as the most profoundly deceitful, and much effort has been expended in order to recognize and remedy these deceits: 'Don't get ripped off, don't take the text for granted, don't believe all you see, read or hear'. Yet for all this inquiry, and for all the critical faculties of the academy and all the street-wariness of the travellers and readers, it seems that little has been achieved towards comprehension of the politics of the illusions at play in these zones.

As will be accepted by those who follow the trails of these arguments, both the notion of culture and the notion of otherness are also deceits of a kind. James Clifford, for example, writes that 'culture' is a deeply compromised idea he cannot yet do without (Clifford 1988: 10). More specifically for this project, the idea of the city (say Calcutta) in the understandings of residents and visitors alike is illusory; as are history, difference, and perhaps all meanings in circulation. This is not to say that there is nothing true, or that there is nothing outside the text (which is a Derridean reminder of the importance of context, misunderstood often as merely a rhetorical claim about the textual mechanisms of illusion − this misunderstanding is taken up in a circumscribed way by those who would reassert the authority of the well-read teacher, and their critics), or that illusions and metaphors and deceits do not have their effects; that is exactly the point. What is at stake, and what has to be analysed, is the way these illusions take on their existence, their political context, and what this means for how we live, and (perhaps less importantly, but central to this work) how we write and understand.

Among recognition of these illusions, issues of representation and the authority of scholarly, as well as popular, commentary upon cultural matters are continually rethought with reference to notions of the authentic. In the context of an ever more pervasive commercialization of all parts of our lives and all corners of the globe, questions of nostalgia, the unique and the exclusive are articulated alongside celebrations of the hybrid (Bhabha, Said), the mixed and the intertwined, as well as cultural survival and maintenance. The commodity form allows an entire cargo cult of 'creative appropriation' and, with the systematic effects of a 'pastoral' desire, transforms culture into the stuff of coffee-table photo-books and pastiche slide-shows of exotic scenes. This allows, in the context of tourism studies, an opportunity to quote the most famous paragraph of Lévi-Strauss's oeuvre, regarding the ill-effects of the culture industry which so offended him in 1955:

> I hate travelling and explorers. Yet here I am proposing to tell the story of my expeditions ... Amazonia, Tibet and Africa fill the bookshops in the form of travelogues, accounts of exhibitions and collections of photographs, in all of which the desire to impress is so dominant as to make it impossible for the reader to assess the value of the evidence.... Nowadays, being an explorer is a trade, which consists not, as one might think, in discovering hitherto unknown facts after years of study, but in covering a great many miles and assembling slide-shows or motion pictures, preferably in colour, so as to fill a hall with an audience for several days in succession. For this audience, platitudes and commonplaces seem to have been miraculously transmuted into revelations by the sole fact that their author, instead of plagiarizing at home, has supposedly sanctified it by covering some twenty thousand miles. (Lévi-Strauss 1955/1973: 17–18)

The indignation of this quotation also carries a degree of irony and an inflection which draws the reader into the deceit that allows the author to repeat the crimes for which he berates others. It is seductive, and exactly the danger of a 'salvage' mentality of which Clifford warned us when he noted that Western scholarship appropriated 'others' in a variety of ways:

> In Western taxonomy and memory the various non-Western 'ethnographic presents' are actually pasts. They represent culturally distinct times ('tradition') always about to undergo the impact of disruptive changes associated with the influence of trade, media, missionaries, commodities, ethnographers, tourists, the exotic art market, the 'world system' etc. A relatively recent period of authenticity is repeatedly followed by a deluge of corruption, transformation, modernisation. (Clifford 1989a: 74)

Significantly, Clifford lists ethnographers alongside tourists as the myth-ologists of authenticity. Lévi-Strauss expresses this nostalgia; even when he was recognizing his mistake in imagining exotic countries 'to be the exact opposite of ours' (Lévi-Strauss 1955/1973: 47), he was brought up against the 'surprising' discovery (at a Paris luncheon) that colonists had wiped out most of the indigenous people in the region of his proposed study location, Brazil. On the back of this nostalgia and surprise, he understands 'the mad passion for travel books and their deceptiveness', since these books 'create the illusion of something which no longer exists but still should exist' (Lévi-Strauss 1955/1973: 38). What, however, 'authentic' Calcutta would be for nostalgics who prefer lost tribes and 'pristine' cultures is not apparent. The critique of the ways Western scholarship has 'salvaged' others in its books is important so far as it goes (Derrida's critique of Lévi-Strauss shows the lacunae of this anti-ethnocentrism: 1967/1978), but equally, the celebration of hybridity and seduction which some writers offer in its place might also be exposed as another well-funded recovery operation by the cultural insurance agents of monopoly capitalism – the very 'world system' which Clifford mentions but does not describe.[17]

Especially when he visited Calcutta, Lévi-Strauss was tempted by this salvage morality: 'I wished I had lived in the days of *real* journeys', he writes. He could then see the 'full splendour' of a not yet polluted spectacle. He asks: 'When was the best time to see India? At what period … for every five years I move back in time, I am able to save a custom, gain a ceremony or share in another belief' (Lévi-Strauss 1955/1973: 43). His 'salvage', however, is a resigned one; the alternatives are equally flawed, there being 'only two possibilities: either I can be like some traveller of the olden days, who was faced with a stupendous spectacle, all, or almost all, of which eluded him, or worse filled him with scorn or disgust; or I can be a modern traveller, chasing after the vestiges of a vanished reality' (Lévi-Strauss 1955/1973: 43). It is to his credit that he recognizes that he may also well be 'insensitive to reality as it is taking shape at this very moment' (Lévi-Strauss 1955/1973: 43), although this recognition did not modify his 'authentic' observations on Calcutta, to which I return in a later chapter.

For Fredric Jameson, taking up these debates from another angle, the problem with contemporary polemics about authenticity is that of the occurrence of a shift in emphasis from a morally and politically urgent critique to a strident but celebratory one (Jameson 1991: 198). His anxiety about the ways 'post-structuralists' might appropriate a critical Marxism and dialectical models 'hitherto associated with the

left' (Jameson 1991: 201) seems somewhat sectarian and simplistic —
and post-structuralism resists easy homogenizations at the very place
where authenticity and representation is questioned — but his suspicions
of the new turn in social science writing about cultural politics are
thought-provoking. In many ways politically urgent critique still remains
urgent, despite the proliferation of texts.

Of course this text proliferates too — it becomes an assemblage of
rumours. Perhaps this is because travel is fluid, because Calcutta sometimes seems to shimmer in haze or threatens to wash away as sludge in
the monsoon, because illusions always flicker at the edges of understanding. All this happens with a certain instability. A story forms out of
myths and legends, whispers, throwaway lines, clichés, sunset stereotypes, melodies, gossip, anecdote and conjecture. The city which
assembles itself for travellers in this ragged-edged way is one of trinkets
and souvenirs, misunderstandings and prejudices, as well as of curiosity,
communication and contemplation, of bustees (semi-permanent dwellings) and open streets (and sewers), of hotels and cafés, of *addas* (street-
corner talk/meeting) and institutions (elevated gossip), of bridges (old
and new) and tower blocks (both), of literature and comedy, graffiti
(words and images) and headlines, of drama, routine, excitement, and so
on, and also a bewildering array of political, social, economic and cultural
differences which cannot possibly, surely, be fused into a coherent
narrative even as I am attempting something of the kind, as an effort to
explain, from observation, participation and my own experience — those
dubious categories — the Calcuttas constructed for and by some of the
travellers who visit. It may or may not be Calcutta — it is certainly not
just the Calcutta of Bengal — but it does exist somewhere, of that I am
sure. That this city is to be made up of rumours and illusion is not
always recognized as the truth of Calcutta for visitors as they carry home
their authentic experiences. This, of course, is true for all who visit,
from the countryside and from overseas alike — for all of us, a city is
often a citadel of mystery. Whether it is the metropolis of the future or
of the long past — Gotham City or Troy — or of fantasy — Oz — or of
desire — the dream cities of the travel brochures — this rumourmongering
is the architect. Rumours are the stuff of the social.
    So where Trinh T. Minh-Ha has described anthropology as gossip,
there might be an opening for this book. Although her intention is
critical, it is one with which there could be hope for a renewal of the
kind of work social scientists might usefully pursue. Her reflections are

tinged with sarcasm, yet enthusiastic for the writing of explanation and narration:

> Anthropology is finally better defined as 'gossip' (we speak together about others).... This profuse, idle talk ... comes into being through boredom and the need to chat.... Scientific gossip takes place under relatively intimate conditions and mostly without witnesses; hence the gossipers' need to act in solidarity, leaning on and referring to each other for more credibility.... Gossip's pretensions to truth remain however very peculiar. The kind of truth it claims to disclose is a confidential truth that requires commitment from both the speaker and the listener (Trinh 1989: 68)

These gossipy stories that are told, then, remain in the realm of explanations; or rather: these stories are somehow valuable, however much we might doubt their exact fidelity to any kind of truth. Enthusiasm for the work of understanding, however circuitous and difficult, remains the chosen path of those who tell stories in the social sciences. And this very difficulty which is caught in the nexus of the taunt that science is gossip is one that offers us an opportunity. At the end of her book Trinh writes this out in a way that I would like to claim momentarily as an emblem of the kind of critical 'anthropology' and gossip I pursue, since I think it is true, and contradictory: 'Even if the telling condemns her present life, what is more important is to (re)tell the story as she thinks it should be told' (Trinh 1989: 150).

I am interested in what is at stake in the project of understanding, and I think this is more than a simple matter of gossip. Or perhaps it is a matter of the seriousness, and of the politics, of gossip.[18] The ways in which gossip, rumours, myths and legends are collected and reassembled are not without determinate effects. The materials from which Calcutta is constructed by the 'West' are organized and subject to the various controls that impinge upon publishing, travel writing, journalism and academia. These may be similar to those listed by Jacques Derrida in another context where he refers to an authority which 'would control and standardise [by] subjecting artistic discourses and practices to a grid of intelligibility, to philosophical or aesthetic norms, to channels of immediate and efficient communication' (Derrida 1992: 39). The project of tracing the ways in which various versions of the city are formed would be akin to that analysis which 'remains to be done' for intellectual production in general by way of new studies of the educational and editorial apparatuses right through to a 'mapping of new locations' (Derrida 1995a: 40). The questions to ask here would concern a 'reading effect', how it manifests through reading and writing devices, systems of promotion and censorship, publishing, publications, universities, schools

(I am paraphrasing closely here, but have in mind touristic versions of these manifestations) as well as clubs 'whether institutionalised or not – clans, cliques' (Derrida 1995a: 40) and through all manner of 'scribbles'.

Heidegger also mentions gossip and rumour – 'idle talk' in *Being and Time*, which Avital Ronell translates as 'rumour' (Ronell 1994: 21); Trinh equates idle talk with gossip, though these need not be the same. Heidegger writes of 'average' understanding: 'idle talk is constituted by just such gossiping and passing the word along' – a travel metaphor? – 'indeed this idle talk is not confined to vocal gossip, but even spreads to what we write, where it takes the form of scribbling' (Heidegger 1926/ 1962: 212)] Attention to these very serious scribbles should also not forget to take heed of the different rhythms and delays in the various apparatuses – the 'machine of being, the socio-political machine, the editorial machine (with its techno-economic norms of fabrication, distribution, stockpiling and so forth)', as well as 'the journalistic machine' which, Derrida notes, is only apparently the most important within marketing and reception but whose power, he suggests, may be more spectacular than effective (Derrida 1995a: 42). Add to this the theoretical machine with its systematic arrangement of discourses, procedures of selection and exclusion of concepts, all surrounding and producing concentrations around a name, a group, a school, a movement (Hmmm, *Derrida*™). All of this 'enumerates' the various categories that might be subject to an analysis – with their combinations, conflicts, contradictions and alliances – and could also be the model of what might be done to unpack the 'machines' that produce Calcutta. What in Heidegger might be called enframing or in Foucault power/knowledge (remembering Spivak's emphasis on the 'power to do' sense of *pouvoir* [Spivak 1993c: 40], and also remembering that H and F are not the same) is opened up in Marx as the commodity system, fetishized in the coin. Can these themes be combined?

The communications requirements of the travel industry and of journalism determine style as well as content, just as the protocols of gossip do – extravagances and speculations must be couched as fact; the rumour of the Black Hole is always to be presented as truth (is it?). This extends across a range of media; for example, Julie Stephens notes the importance of the underground or student press in the 'sixties' as having a role in the circulation of '*standard* ways of reacting to and interpreting experiences of India' (Stephens 1992: 100; emphasis added). It is not that there are no differences among these varied media, but the influence and confluence of certain 'styles' in which the 'conventional rumour of Calcutta' (Moorhouse 1971: 20) could be circulated across so many modes of communication, deserves recognition. Similarly, protocols and norms of style channel historical, anthropological and political science writing in quite definite ways.[19]

The double focus of this work is upon not only the deceits of social science and the authenticity or otherwise of touristic understandings of culture, India, Calcutta, and so on, but also the ways in which the critical capacities of these understandings, even the most reflexive and anti-ethnocentric of them, participate in maintaining a hegemonic series of fictions about the world. Travellers of all kinds engage in self-deceptions, even at their most enlightened moments of local rapport, just as do scholars, even in the ecstasy of their moment of publication, even in their scholarly authority. This authority is what is questioned: the authority of meanings, of interpretations, of the chance asides and incidentals, as well as the workings of style, the effects of certain metaphors and the orders, the comparisons and juxtapositions of images and expressions; all combined to generate various versions – none more absolutely true than another – of the city, of Calcutta, of India, and so on, which can be contested in order to assert other possibilities, other versions. Perhaps this could all be about the imperialism of meaning – the imperious attitude of our 'will to knowledge', which drives all visitors to Calcutta towards representation. It seems that everyone who comes to Calcutta is making representations of what they have seen. While my Calcutta begins from conversations with backpackers met in the city during the late 1980s and early 1990s, it is also produced in dialogue, as all understandings of Calcutta are, with significant technologies, texts, codifications and enframings. Although it can never become some kind of all-equal dialogue, with travellers or Calcuttans, it is an attempt to make sense of various experiences in a way that tries not to hide the contexts of that making-sense.

One of the difficulties obviously inherent in writing about travel is the tendency to slip into travel-writerly mode and simply 'report' on the exotic as if that reportage were not co-constituted within the various apparatuses that sustain writing – styles, disciplines, publishing, readerships. To do this, at the same time as to want to find ways to engage politically with the exploitation and inequalities of imperialism and colonialism of which international tourism is a major part, means that writing becomes fraught. As another circulating commodity, the potential of the cultural studies or ethnographic text to find any way to undo the double structure of commodification – what elsewhere might be called the deceit, or trick, of criticism – is slim indeed. The debt of this text to the contradictions in which it was made is extensive, and should not be easily resolved – one way, perhaps, to show some of the marks of these contradictions is to leave in the hesitations and experiments of finding a way to write this work. Or – still somehow prior, if not actually neatly separable into a research and writing temporality – to show some of the marks of how this project proceeded, on and off, over eight years. Such a task can never be completed, since the list of 'real-life' events that impinge upon the remaining text always exceeds the map of those events, even as the project enframes and enables them. Simultaneously recognizing the enframing of certain ways of writing, viewing, imagining, and so on, and recognizing constraints and conditions of commodification, deceit, illusion (metaphor, rumour, decay), there can be no straightforward rehearsal of older reportage modes of writing and research. I have not found it possible, or plausible, to pursue the kind of ethnographic-anthropology project that some might expect, some continue to valorize, some hold on to despite clear reasons to abandon the old scholastic ship. Nevertheless, the traces of earlier projects and paradigms, styles and forms, of writing culture remain. It is no easy task to imagine and execute a writing adequate to the circumstances in which it is produced, and towards which it wishes – I wish – to offer a transformatory project.

In more optimistic moments, I want to imagine that it is not utopian to begin the task of changing the possibilities of writing about Calcutta, about tourists, about charity and about representation. I want to do this in a way that leads towards an emancipatory politics capable of posing a challenge to the transnational circuits of capitalism as they are manifest in tourism and aid work, alongside other things, and I want to do this in a way that does not collude more than necessary in the commodification circuits that are the preserve of a broad 'international relations' context (feel-good cultural understanding, cultural relativism) and which are also the conditions which give this text life. This optimism is tempered by the likelihood of underestimating how this is a more complicated task than I have yet imagined. There are immense difficulties to be found by those who might wish to organize in this area. This is so whether the organizational task is contra-tourism activities or to raise questions within the charity sphere about the protocols of charity and aid. Any attempt to initiate a transnational political project that attends to local manifestations or, more intractable, semiotic representations that are local and mobile, or to the consequent inequities of the transnational situation, is necessarily premissed upon these difficulties. There is not enough here to show much more than the beginnings of such political work, yet it is possible to point to numerous examples where this work demands extension, where further research and criticism are called for, and where sharp questions and blunt admonitions can intervene and change the politics of representation, tourism, charity and Calcutta – at least for those few who visit. The shorthand version of this paragraph would be: Ah, but can you insert gossip and rumour into the round-and-round of traveller talk in a way which, while obviously not adequate to a project of global transformation, at least pricks consciences and upsets complacencies? (The consciences and complacencies of the group of alternative, volunteer, travelling backpackers at least.) Another rumour of this book is that it wants to give more than it can offer.

Because of the problems of deceit in these texts, I prefer Trinh's notion of gossip as a metaphor for social science, since to 'lend an ear to gossip already accepts either sympathizing with or being an accomplice of the gossiper' (Trinh 1989: 68). It is then easier to see the workings of power – for gain and, since gossips come unstuck through their betrayals, for loss – in the gossip's ever-mumbling, ever-verbose mutterings. Gossip may be a kind of flexible technology of equivalence and circulation, allowing meaning and 'rumour' to facilitate the continued production of an international bifurcation between subjected classes and consuming, capitalist, comprador ones. At the same time gossip is a tool for this work, the methodology of collecting these souvenirs of meaning. Social Science as gossip gently reminds us of the pretension and privilege of 'serious' texts in a context where I want to consider the workings of both 'high' scholarship and 'low' travel literature in the production of popular Western perception of Calcutta. The informal productions – the chatter of travel, the holiday snaps, the amateur videos – of all those travellers who are also often students, writers, academics and professors, and whose more formal intellectual work is taken ever-so-seriously by the academy in the form of essays, publication, lectures, deserves closer scrutiny. This chatter of tourism is impoverished only in so far as a privilege is accorded to the serious talk of social science on the very same topics. This is a question of undoing encrusted authority; the taunt of gossip reminds us to watch carefully over those texts that are authoritative, and those other texts that also have effects.

In Chapter 2 I report on the ways in which Calcutta is understood by Western visitors. The deployment of notions derived from a reading of Heidegger and Marx, as well as of Spivak, Trinh, Jameson, Clifford, Derrida, Deleuze and others, as I have attempted in this introductory chapter, begins to open up some of the 'technologies' which frame travellers' understanding and experience while they stay at the Modern Lodge. Based upon what they have said about the city, this next section also attends to a wider range of discursive production of the 'rumour of Calcutta', and serves as an elaboration of the main themes of this book: themes which appear later through other 'technologies of representation' (such as maps in Chapter 4, and cameras in Chapters 5 and 6) which are carried in the backpacks of travellers. What travellers bring to Calcutta is more than baggage, and entails a complex 'worldview' which must be seen in the context of a technologically complex international scene. Subsequent chapters will attempt to develop the workings of this complexity: in Chapter 2 by attention to 'gossip' and the specifics of experience at a particular site in Calcutta; in Chapter 3 I move on to read what has been written by visitors to the city, and the registers which govern representational peculiarities such as the fascination with garbage in Günter Grass and Dominique Lapierre; Chapter 4 explores maps of the city, and begins to link modes of representation to processes of travel in general and the circulation of meaning in a wider economy; Chapter 5 focuses upon photography and the camera effects which make representations of poverty, and perhaps garbage, and so on, photogenic scenes to be souvenired; Chapter 6 offers a close study of the screening of Calcutta by international cinema, specifically Roland Joffe's film *City of Joy* and Chapter 7 concludes with a look at the ways in which such technologies of representation frame Calcutta as a scene of impoverishment to be 'developed', by a charitable tourism, for the benefit of all – or not.

NOTES

1. At a much earlier seminar on 'The Cultural Profile of Calcutta' in 1970, a possible source for this notion may be found. Radharaman Mitra commented in the final session, in criticism: 'If you had made an effort to look at the full face of Calcutta you would have found not only diversity but varieties of contradictions in the city. Only one of her eyes smiles, the other is full of tears. It appears to me that the tears dominate her look with rare breaks in flashes of smile' (in Sinha 1970: 259). Mitra's comments were quoted verbatim in the introduction to the 1987 volume *The Urban Experience: Calcutta* (Sinha 1987: 9).

2. Gayatri Spivak writes: 'The study of colonial discourse, directly released by work such as Said's ... is an important (and beleaguered) part of the discipline [of cultural studies] now' (Spivak 1990b: 222), and there is no reason yet to call a halt to such historical muckraking – indeed, I'm all for it; the point is there is much of it about today, too, and Said's work could also release more contemporary studies.

3. Said has proffered a formulation of his work on Western authors writing in London but formed by their awareness of the colonial activity; what I am trying to do is similar with regard to Western visitors to the former sites of empire:

Instead of the partial analysis offered by the various rational or systematically theoretical schools, I have been proposing the contrapuntal lines of a global analysis, in which texts and worldly institutions are seen working together, in which Dickens and Thackeray as London authors are read also as writers whose historical influence is informed by the colonial enterprises in India and Australia of which they were so aware. (Said 1993: 385)

Perhaps it is significant that there are roughly as many second-hand travel guides as there are copies of Dickens in my local book exchange. I should also note that Said's use of the musical term 'contrapuntal' in the quotation refers to texts and institutions working together globally in the manner of two lines of a melody. The imperial brass bands of the Durbar may be what he has in mind but the tune is probably more discordant; the contemporary equivalent would be less grand; say the jingle of an American Express or Thomas Cook travel advertisement.

4. I have used this term to refer to the duplication throughout Asia of budget guesthouses serving touristic 'comfort foods' which are little different to the fare available in such places worldwide. Peter Phipps takes up this issue in a thoughtful study of Australian budget travellers (Phipps 1990: 16). A number of the ideas in this work were originally worked out at the Gnocchi Club, and here I am indebted to Nick Lenaghan, Chris Francis and Peter Phipps.

5. I realize I am stretching this quote out of context here; it was about the positioning of the 'postcolonial' teacher. It is no big deal to see that it is necessary to refuse the privilege of writing stories about so-called decolonized peoples. In another place Spivak quips: 'It is a bitter joke, the adjective postcolonial. It's not an enabling phrase. What I am witnessing as I learn more and more is that decolonisation is a hoax' (Spivak 1993b: 152). This does not mean she will lament her marginality; she rather, calls us to projects which make clear the circumstances and structures of this hoaxing.

6. In *Modernity as Exile*, Papastergiadis argues for a critical theory which approaches exile – which I read as relevant to both migration and travel – in an engagement with culture as 'zones of control and abandonment, of recollection and of forgetting, of forces or of dependence, of exclusiveness or of sharing, all taking place within a global history that is our element' (Papastergiadis, quoting Said 1989: 225). This critical theory then allows that it is '*with metaphor* that borders are both made and crossed, that memory becomes history, and that violence is named' (Papastergiadis 1993a: 27). But what is necessary is a detailed analysis of the violence-naming capacities of metaphor, the violence of language. Metaphor can be construed as an 'act of transportation' (Papastergiadis 1993a: 27) that carries meaning and defines zones, borders, selves and others. In its 'here-and-there migrant thought', *Modernity as Exile* begins to articulate metaphors with which to think against the violence of domination and exclusion: 'Shuttling between absence and presence, metaphor is the means for articulating action' (Papastergiadis 1993a: 27). A related point that raises the dislocation of the migrant as a metaphor for thinking the complexity of translation and the fluidity of culture may be found in Sara Suleri's *The Rhetoric of English India*:

To deploy migrancy as an interpretive figure is not at all to repress the crucial situatedness of cultures, or to suggest that colonial encounter can be reread only as an abstraction so slender as to be effete. Instead, it implies that the stories of colonialism – in which heterogeneous cultures are yoked by violence – offer nuances that cannot be neatly partitioned between coloniser and colonised ... the idiom of trauma itself requires a reformulation that can provide a slippage of trauma from apocalypse into narrative. (Suleri 1992: 5)

7. The German philosopher has been subject to much attention of late; gossip and rumour abound regarding Heidegger's relation to national socialism and the status of his 1933-4 period as Nazi Rector of Freiburg University. Lyotard (1988/1990), Derrida (1987/1989), Bourdieu (1988/1991) and others have commented on this 'issue', but the importance of Heidegger is not confined to these specific interventions in an emotive debate. For the journalistic reports, see Farias (1987/1989) and Wolin (1991). Speaking of Heidegger and the rerun of the 'Nazi controversy' occasioned by the publication of Victor Farias's book *Heidegger and Nazism*, Derrida noted:

> In certain newspapers and through a kind of *rumour*, one became aware of the violence of a condemnation. This condemnation claimed to teach, well beyond Nazism and Heidegger, the very reading of Heidegger, the readers of Heidegger, those who had referred to him – even if they had only asked deconstructive questions about him – still more those who were likely to take a continued interest him, even if it might be in order to judge and think, as rigorously as possible, Nazism and Heidegger's relation to Nazism. The gravest and most obscurantist confusions were being maintained, sometimes naively, sometimes deliberately. It was, not only but also, rather evidently, a question of banning the reading of Heidegger. (Derrida 1995a: 469; emphasis added)

8. Circumstantial evidence abounds. Michel Foucault said in an interview just before he died: 'I still have ... the notes that I took when I was reading Heidegger. And they are much more extensive than the ones I took on Hegel or Marx. My entire philosophical development was determined by my reading of Heidegger' (Foucault 1988: 250). Giorgio Agamben suggests that 'Like much of contemporary French philosophy, the thought of Derrida too has its basis, more or less openly declared, in that of Heidegger' (Agamben 1993: 158). Spivak (1993c: 34) makes a similar point when she discusses power/knowledge in a way that reminds me of Heidegger's concept of enframing – yet she wants to take some distance from suggestions of an 'affinity' between Foucault's 'power' and Heidegger's 'Being' as found in commentaries by Dreyfuss (in Spivak 1993c: 292). Heidegger, the 'West' and the colonizer, Spivak reminds us, should not be taken as monolithic homogeneities, and such lessons shake easy explanations as she reads 'Foucault in Derrida in the wake of a reconsideration of Heidegger' (Spivak 1993c: 45). Habermas also makes the point about the influence of Heidegger on 'post-structuralism', although in less generous terms. As for the influence of Marx on all social theory...

9. Bourdieu, however, suggests that the hagiographic appreciations of Heidegger's materialism (he cites Lefebvre's comment that there is 'no antagonism' between Marx's and Heidegger's historic vision, that 'Heidegger is quite simply a materialist') is insufficient to explain how Heidegger's thought could be reinterpreted for 'a new political context' (Bourdieu 1988/1991: 94-5) after the war. However, Etienne Balibar, in his recent work *The Philosophy of Marx*, has briefly returned to this relation between Lukács and Heidegger, and noted that Heidegger's *Being and Time* may, following Goldmann, be considered as a response to Lukács's themes: in particular, in his theory of social anonymity (*das Man*), which he sees as a characteristic of 'inauthentic' life, and later in his theory of the 'enframing of the world by utilitarian technology' (Balibar 1995: 69). It is exactly this part of Heidegger's work that I want to take up. Joanna Hodge also links Heidegger to Marx and Lukács (Hodge 1995: 83) and notes Heidegger's 'sympathy' towards Marx's analysis of alienation (Hodge 1995: 98), calling this an 'implicit agreement' and quoting Heidegger from the 'Letter on Humanism': 'the Marxist insight about history is superior to customary history' (in Hodge 1995: 97). She links Heidegger's view of technology to Marx's materialism, quoting Heidegger's sentence: 'The essence of materialism hides itself in the essence of tech-

nology' (in Hodge 1995: 97. I also quote this in my text, but from the English translation: Heidegger 1978: 220). Hodge notes that this 'proximity' between Marx and Heidegger would not be accepted by most Marxists. (For the cheap thrill of those interested in micro-Heideggeriana, for unknown reasons Hodge's reference to the key sentence is to Heidegger 1976: 337, but my copy of the German text has the sentence three pages later: 'Das Wesen des Materialismus verbirgt sich im Wesen der Technik' [Heidegger 1976: 340]. Archivists shall be deployed…)

10. In *Being and Time* Heidegger refers to 'the well-known phenomenon' that 'the whole stock of significations which belong to language in general are dominated through and through by "spatial representations"' (Heidegger 1926/1962: 421). Much of Heidegger's metaphorics of knowledge is concerned with the spatial, and its correlate visuality – and very often in terms of travelling. This is of importance throughout this book. In a recent discussion of Heidegger, Levin sums up: 'The will to power is very strong in vision. There is a very strong tendency in vision to grasp and fixate, to reify and totalize: a tendency to dominate, secure and control, which eventually, because it was so extensively promoted, assumed a certain uncontested hegemony' (Levin 1993: 212).

11. I am indebted to discussions with the late Dr Zawar Hanfi who took the time, over many late nights, to teach me to read Heidegger. I would also like to acknowledge Shirin Hanfi for her encouragement in the years when this book was only a 'notebook'.

12. Discussing the 'Megalopolis', Celeste Olalquiaga makes a point about urban yuppiedom which echoes here:

> Determined by exchange value, yuppie subculture homogenizes everything for easy consumption. Consequently, yuppies are the sponsors and most important patrons of the current 'ethnic pop' fad in clothes, food, and music, in which difference is not an attribute but rather a source of entertainment. This kind of ethnic diversity is but an extension of the homogenization that occurs in high technology: all signs are equivalent and therefore basically, although not ultimately, interchangeable. (Olalquiaga 1992: 32)

13. Suleri suggests that European writing about India might be read more as a symptom of terror rather than possession, whereby the 'unreadable' differences of India are transmuted into a fetishized 'intransigence'. Inscrutable India is the product of colonial fear of colonialism's own cultural ignorance transformed 'into the potential threats posed by an Indian alterity' (Suleri 1992: 6)

14. This is from Michel Foucault: 'There are times in life when the question of knowing if one can think differently than one thinks, and perceive differently than one sees, is absolutely necessary if one is to go on looking and reflecting at all' (Foucault 1984/1985: 8).

15. Going 'astray': Heidegger construes knowledge in geographical, even travelling, terms: 'thinking of Being is a highly errant and in addition a very destitute matter. Thinking is perhaps, after all, an unavoidable path, which refuses to be a path of salvation and brings no new wisdom. The path is at most a field path, a path across fields' (Heidegger 1971: 185). The path may lead to the clearing, but 'any path always risks going astray' (Heidegger 1971: 186).

16. *The City of Joy* was a book by Dominique Lapierre about a Polish priest doing charity work in Calcutta. In 1989 Rajiv Gandhi's Central Government gave British director Roland Joffe (*The Mission, The Killing Fields*) permission to make a film of the book. Despite Joffe's arguments that the film would 'project the indomitable spirit of the slum-dwellers of Calcutta' (*Telegraph*, 24 December 1989), the Left Front Government of Bengal withdrew permission later in the year on the grounds that

there was 'no need to show only the slum-dwellers to show the indomitable spirit of Calcuttans' (*ibid.*, 1989). Debates about censorship and freedom of information raged over the following months as Joffe refused to accept the decision and conscripted prominent Calcutta personalities to his cause. Coffee-house discussion turned often to the merits not only of the proposed Joffe film but also of other filmed representations of the city. I will discuss the book (Chapter 3) and separately (Chapter 6) the film, which starred Patrick Swayze, Om Puri and Shabana Azmi, and has quickly displaced all other texts as the way most visitors, and especially volunteer workers, now come to know and experience Calcutta. Much material for the film was gleaned from discussions with the travellers at Modern Lodge who are mentioned throughout this book.

17. It would be a separate but probably worthwhile work, which elaborated the scholarly history of attempts to describe this world-system. Writings by Wallerstein, Castells, Jameson and others are readily available on the bookshelves of university libraries and in fashionable theory stores, despite a decline of 'really existing' Euro-Marxism. Indeed, the proliferation of such studies appears as an option for many of those (ex-Eurocommunist career academics) who feel lost in the face of what they see as a decline in legitimacy (but which really requires heightened struggle) on the part of the European left. While I have relied largely upon old Marx, those who follow should not be ignored, and I thank Ben Ross for the reminder. This is not the place to attempt any evaluations of Left Front governments in Bengal: this is certainly beyond even those romantic communist visitors who souvenir government or trade-union red flags and perhaps read the *Economic and Political Weekly* (EPW) in their revolutionary tourism. It is also beyond the capacity and scope of this book; suffice it to note that it is widely accepted that the record of all left party formations in India has come in for criticism for neglect of the most disenfranchised sections (tribals, pavement dwellers, lower peasantry), and is to be understood in part as a failure of resolve, in part opportunist alliance with more 'advanced', and so empowered, sections, and in part a failure of the parliamentary experiment as a way of changing the system.

18. In another context Spivak, writing about Rushdie, does suggest that we can talk of 'gossip changed to rumour as vehicle of subaltern insurgency' (Spivak 1993c: 228). Here, I think, she has in mind the work of Ranajit Guha, where he writes of rumour as the 'register of political consciousness' during peasant uprising, and the 'media of its transmission among the subaltern masses in the countryside' (Guha 1983: 265).

19. In 'The Authority of Style' I argued that the ways in which anthropologists write were closely linked to the authority of their pronouncements. Debates on this topic seemed to revive anthropology during the 1980s, with ironic 'rejoicing for the end of anthropology' as well as new conventions which allowed 'anthropology-as-usual' (Hutnyk 1987; see also Hutnyk 1988, 1989 and 1990 for attempts to read anthropological monographs with this theme in mind).

TRAVELS IN CALCUTTA:

THE VIEW FROM MODERN LODGE

On the open rooftop of the Modern Lodge Guest House, some twenty-odd Western travellers sit on small stools, plastic chairs and upturned bins to discuss bowel movements. As happens once a week, these travellers — who are volunteer support staff with an organization providing medical assistance to destitutes and pavement dwellers in Calcutta — are led through the medical and social aspects of an issue of immediate concern to their work, in this case the causes and effects of bacterial infections, low-protein diet, unsanitary water and associated problems of sufferers with complaints ranging from diarrhoea to dysentery. This topic has a double significance for the volunteer-travellers, since unlike leprosy and tuberculosis, which are also present at the street clinics where they work, these bowel-related problems often afflict them. Not only do they deal each day with people, especially children, suffering from diarrhoea and dysentery among those treated by the Bengali doctors (and one, sometimes two or three Western ones), but many travellers themselves suffer from the variety of irritations of the bowel which are the lot of the visitor to Calcutta. (The old British sewerage system is now insufficient for the city's needs.) Indeed, across India, bowels are among the most commonly discussed topics for budget travellers, and it would be only a recent arrival who could say they had not participated in some very frank discussions over breakfast of their recent movements (my own experience since the mid-1980s carries related internal scars).

Volunteers are attentive to the effects of various bacteria and possible treatments for the 'patients' they see each day at the clinics. Among the several thousand who attend the makeshift street-side operation established in 1980 by Englishman Jack Preger — self-described 'nutter in

Calcutta' – perhaps one-third would be seriously inconvenienced by such problems. The speaker leading the discussion on the Modern Lodge roof is often one of the two or three trained nurses sent and funded by organized Western aid agencies or by means of international subscription. On other occasions this role might be taken by a traveller with medical expertise who has arrived, often with other intentions, in Calcutta under their own funds. Other volunteers without formal experience stay for months at a time. Many visit and work for only a few weeks. After each talk the weekly meeting breaks up for socializing, with a smaller group, led by one of the longer-term volunteers, moving aside to provide very recent arrivals with a short history, description and rationale of the project. Until 1994 the clinic was set up on a nearby street called Middleton Row or by the Hooghly river at Nimtollah Ghat. It provides basic essential medical and welfare support to Calcuttan street-dwellers. By 1992 a team of twenty-four Bengali doctors, another one hundred Bengali staff, and a floating population of sometimes forty Western travellers were working at the two clinics six days a week. I have deliberately not provided an ethnography of the clinics which shows the lifework of Jack Preger. I have tried to avoid what so many other writings and documentaries do: to celebrate the name of the founding doctor and interpret his work as only some heroic individual quest to save Calcutta single-handed. 'He's like a living saint', said one visiting nurse (reported in the Channel 4 documentary *34 Middleton Row*, 1987). Preger's work is arguably more sensible than this, and perhaps more humble; he works with a collective of local assistants and with a strong network of support. The clinics have over 80,000 people on record. Pedestrian, but nevertheless interesting, books on the work of Preger can be found (Meigh 1988; Josephs 1991). In recent years the organization has expanded in Calcutta, and overseas it is a formally registered charity operating with a significant budget equivalent to many middle-level Western NGOs. The travellers who work for this clinic (but also some others) are the subjects of this chapter.

The Modern Lodge rooftop is mentioned in Lonely Planet's *India: A Travel Survival Kit* as a good place to meet other travellers. It is a casual space where visitors have long gathered to exchange stories and information, and to get to know each other. The fact that one night a week it is now transformed, through the initiative of one of the clinic administrative workers, into an informal classroom does not seem too out of place in a very ramshackle environment.

The 'Modern' itself is a rambling establishment with dark corners, small simple rooms, crowded dormitories and a regular population which usually consists of French, English, Swiss, Australian and Dutch volunteers. Alongside them, there is a transient assortment of shorter-term travellers, not all of whom would be likely to participate in the work of the clinics, but who may be working at one of the centres organized by the religious order known through Calcutta's most internationally famous charity worker, Mother Teresa. Interesting though the work of Preger and others is, I think all the residents of Modern Lodge could tell stories which are instructive: about what they do, what they say of Calcutta, and how their experiences are mediated by backpacker-traveller, 'banana-pancake-trail', lore. This chapter shows that word of mouth, the say-so of a friend of a friend, and rumour and gossip, operate to orientate and produce experience for travellers. This discourse must be read as a text, or as the 'enframing' apparatus which makes Calcutta 'visible' in a certain way for those who visit. All the protocols of the clinic and of the Modern Lodge constitute the frame which throws up particular versions of Calcutta. There are other factors to be considered, but the main themes of travel talk are already set out here in the Modern Lodge: poverty, charity, how to get about in the city, give and take, how to behave (a being-towards-Calcutta), fashion, politics. The rest is an elaboration of the ways in which this being is formed and its somewhat awkward placement within global cultural consumption; awkward, since at times traveller experience provides a local critique of charity work which other NGOs and aid agencies would do well to hear.

BUDGET CALCUTTA

'I had to get away from the rat race, and here in Modern Lodge I'm plagued by rats, but I don't mind so much as long as they keep off my bed.' (Catherine)

Like so many of its counterparts elsewhere in the world, Modern Lodge is an unimportant establishment in the global scheme of budget youth tourism. Its significance as one of the most popular backpacker hotels in Calcutta is something else. While 'the *most* Modern' is not at all modern (as its 'pet' name suggests), there is a definite pecking order among the several cheap guesthouses catering for travellers in the Sudder Street part of Calcutta. A little off the traveller track of sandcastle forts, Taj Mahal, camel and elephant treks, temples and beaches, Calcutta does not host as many youth travellers as other major Indian cities like Delhi and Bombay. Nevertheless, a good number of travellers visit every year.

This 'ethnography' was made up of such people in such accommodation, as well as in the side-street tea stalls and coffee shops, and on
the Modern rooftop. These traveller spaces make up something like
what Bengalis call an *adda*: the 'scene' is marked by that conversational
tone that is often the *adda's* preserve. Anything can be discussed, references from all corners, citations here and there – and all quite incidental, it would seem, to daily concerns. So in a way this street-corner
society is not wholly uncharacteristic of Calcutta, although it is very
much travellers' Calcutta (an ethereal, yet real, echo). Amitav Ghosh's
character Tridib spends much of his time in *The Shadow Lines* at an
adda because 'he was happiest in neutral, impersonal places – coffee
houses, bars, street-corner *addas* – the sort of place where people come,
talk and go away without expecting to know each other any further'
(Ghosh 1988: 9). While a place like the Modern rooftop is not the
same thing, there is a loose similarity, and some travellers made the
link. Clinic '*adda*' topics have included: other locations where travellers
have done volunteer work; further problems of health and nutrition;
the perennial favourite subject and several variations on diarrhoea;
madness; eye transplants; the sewage infrastructure of the city; Bengali
language; and even the 'politics of representation'.

I feel no need to set out conventions of reportage here – yet for the
record, basic 'ethnographic' details about the Modern follow. Despite its
peculiarities, the Modern Lodge is paradigmatic of the 'banana-pancake
trail' (yet without the pancakes). As it is promoted by Lonely Planet's
India: A Travel Survival Kit, the Modern attracts a good number of
'average' travellers looking for cheap accommodation. In 1992 Modern
Lodge dormitory rooms could be had for as little as 20 rupees per night
(up from Rs8 in 1987), and rooms were offered from 60 rupees (Rs35
in 1987, approx £1). The establishment is run by a management group
(Messrs Roy and Sen until 1993) and a number of workers. The workers
are poorly paid, toil long hours, and are often working far from families
left in Bihari villages (the staff were on strike for parts of 1991 and
1992[1]). It is open year round, although during the monsoon period,
when heavy rains flood the streets and there are fewer travellers in
Calcutta, some beds lie empty or may occasionally be utilized by the
families of the workers. The Modern Lodge is the first to fill up in peak
traveller times, especially at Christmas, as Calcutta attracts a number of
Western travellers for the Christmas festival – celebrated with a good
deal of fervour in Bengal. The Modern's New Year's Eve rooftop party
is always well attended and rivalled only by the – now too expensive –
four-course Christmas dinner (with magic show, Salvation Army band

and a deadly punch) of the completely Raj relic Fairlawn Hotel (which gets a significantly glowing report in Lonely Planet – less deservedly). This hotel also features as a set in the film *City of Joy* and is now decorated with many stills from the film – a kind of Patrick Swayze shrine – and portraits of the British Royal Family.

Alongside such curiosities, what is distinctive about Sudder Street, and especially the Modern, is that many of the visitors who stay in this area for any length of time are those who do 'charity' work. These people offer themselves, for little or no payment, as workers in non-government clinics or institutions that serve street-dwelling destitutes and others of low economic status. Foreign travellers and volunteers in Calcutta are mostly middle-class youth (18–30) from the United States, the United Kingdom, Northern and Western Europe, Australia or Canada. They stay in the cheapest hotels, their rooms are basic and often shared or dormitories. Unlike those backpackers who pass through Calcutta for a day or two on the way to Darjeeling (for mountain views) or Puri (for beach and Bhang lassi), their stay may be anything from a few weeks to more than six months. Whether the primary reason for coming to Calcutta is to work for Mother Teresa or one of the other volunteer groups, or involved an unintended departure from a different 'tour plan' in India, the nomination 'volunteer' is the dominant identity taken on by most of the longer-term residents of the small hotels. A double significance related to the presence of these volunteers in Calcutta prompts interesting questions. Revolving around the meanings and motives of the designation 'volunteer' are possible explanations for why people do or do not visit Calcutta and related issues of reputation and representation of the city in various popular media.

There is little doubt that most travellers who engage in volunteer work in Calcutta stumble into it with not much more than general notions of commitment and charity. Questions of cultural hegemony, international and class privilege, and the extent of relative economic advantage are, at best, understood in a vague, not an analytical, way. What possibilities there might be for the promotion of more considered engagements with the complexities of visiting Calcutta are prefigured by a number of factors: (a) the insularity of traveller culture and traveller style; (b) the cultural and class background of Western travellers; (c) the hegemony of Western versions of Calcutta in 'traveller lore'; and (d) the hegemonic effects of the traveller 'gaze' and its representational technologies. Here I begin the task of considering these factors; the latter themes are subsequently taken up in detail.

I can offer descriptions of the kinds of people who come, and there are records available as to how many arrive at the Modern, and how long they stay, but these accounts have their limits. Is it sufficient to note that in 1989 almost 1,280 travellers stayed in the Modern? The average duration of the stay was one to two weeks, with just over thirty staying longer than three months (the fact that some travellers stay for a period in the Modern and then move to another hotel, or vice versa, means that these figures cannot be further generalized to indicate period of stay in the city overall). Just under half of the clientele were women, and women were more likely to stay longer, reflecting their greater involvement in volunteer work. Of the 1,280 some 300 were from Britain, almost 200 from France, 95 from Japan, 90 from Australia, 86 from Spain, 82 from Holland, almost 60 from the USA, 44 from Canada and fewer than 30 each from Germany, Austria, Belgium, Ireland, Malaysia, South Africa, Switzerland, New Zealand, Italy, Korea, Tunisia and Norway. (The Modern does not cater for domestic tourists; see below.) In 1992 these figures had increased significantly, owing in part to the impact of publicity from the Tourism Industry's promotional 'Visit India Year 1991' campaign. Total residents of the Modern reached 1,540, with a similar spread of nationalities − although British numbers didn't rise as much: 344; French rose to 270, Swiss to 80 (a fourfold increase), Australian to 139, and Japanese to 180.

For good or ill, I have not examined domestic tourism since the work of Tej vir Singh and others (Vir Singh et al. 1988) provides a local coverage. The fact that the Modern does not accept domestic travellers sometimes provokes concern, and has led to some fights between the staff or management and Western travellers who saw this as an unjustified restriction. On those few occasions when travellers have questioned the exclusionary 'foreigners only' policy of the Modern, a deep uneasiness has been signalled in Westerner–local relations. To account for this, it is necessary to refer to more than allegations of racism or various management intentions to minimize tourist 'culture shock', although these obviously apply. The desire, however, of Western travellers to keep their 'home base' secure, stable and safe, and most of all familiar, is achieved by ignoring the implications of the Modern Lodge rule. The management claim that the rule is for security and to exclude theft, but the constant vigilance and presence of several doormen seems to indicate that this is little more than an excuse for what, as Mr Roy (the manager), has said, has been a very successful crowd-puller for the hotel. The Modern is known among backpackers as a 'safe place', however, they are somewhat blind to the contradiction in this achievement.

Convenience is another factor which may explain the continued popularity of the Sudder Street tourist enclave in general. Although centrality does not seem sufficient to justify traveller tolerance of the 'hassle' of the area, which derives, though not so many tourists recognize this, from its reputation in Calcutta as a 'black-market' and 'red-light' zone.

> 'Outside of Sudder Street it's real India; the taxis even use their meters.' (Catherine)
>
> 'I have no idea why you people stay in that shithole.' (Jack)
>
> 'Of course it's a part of India, no more or less than King's Cross is a part of Sydney.' (Amanda)
>
> 'Why don't you people put ads in the paper and go live with a Bengali family? There are plenty who need the money, and you would learn so much more.' (Rajini)

Almost-plausible explanations are given for why volunteers do 'put up' with/at the Modern. First it is a space of refuge, from Sudder Street and from the informal tourist economy of taxi-drivers, rickshaw wallahs, hashish and smack sellers, pimps and other guides and service providers. Second, the Modern is a refuge of sorts from Calcutta as a whole, a room of one's own out of the bustle of traffic and people. But as a space apart, the Modern does not seem to fit into the urban 'chaotic' Calcutta of travellers' experience. Abdul, the day manager, rarely moves from his charpoy except to go and sleep in the shade after lunch; the rest of the staff work at what can never be called a leisurely pace in the heat of India, but at least without seeming hurried. A mischievous traveller once set up a punkah-style fan in the courtyard attached to the motor-energy of someone's big toe (you would need to have seen 'The Far Pavilions' or 'It Ain't Arf Hot Mum' to get the picture, twisted nostalgia aside). Except for the roof and the lounge, it can often be quiet. As a space apart, the guesthouse serves important functions for budget travellers. It is a site for 'reliable' exchange of information, for meeting like-minded travellers, for relating, confirming and redeploying impressions, and much more. Guesthouses serve as 'safe' space, not only as temporary homes for budget travellers, but also in their dislocated function as a kind of heterotopic space within a foreign city. The notion of heterotopia is one I take from Foucault following Kevin Hetherington, although I want to twist it a little. Reading Foucault, Hetherington elaborates heterotopia as 'sites of limit experiences', and in a sense the whole of Calcutta is such for a tourist. But further, heterotopic places 'are sites which rupture the order of things through their difference to what surrounds them' (Hetherington forth-coming), and the Modern may also be this. To go still further and equate the Modern with heterotopic sites where 'all things are displaced, marginal, rejected', and especially where such things 'become the basis of an alternate ordering ... offering a contrast to the dominant repre-sentations of order' (Hetherington forthcoming), would require the more detailed assessment which I, in part, provide here. 'Alternate ordering' of experience in Calcutta could be contrasted to the 'dominant representations' of ordered middle-class (mostly) Western metropolitan life, and certainly this description could be claimed as a parameter for backpacker life in the Modern. The point here is that the Modern can be contrasted to several quite different (and differently similar things). It is not home (and it is home-away-from-home); it is not Sudder Street (oh, but it is!); and it is not Calcutta (which is 'outside'), and so on. My argument above about enframing would allow such a flexible notion, but the point here is to note the separate/not separate hetero-topia that constitutes the Modern.

The Sudder Street area, despite the drawbacks, is a fascinating part of town. There are few opportunities to live in such close proximity to people who speak such a wide variety of languages. There is, first of all, the local Bengali, Hindi and Urdu – which an admittedly very small number of travellers learn, and do so with halting attempts to converse in a mixed version of what they take to be the 'vernacular'. With only a smattering of Bengali greetings or glossed Hindi-Urdu, a halting 'Pidgin' is the limit for Western use of local languages (This does not leave visitors incommunicado of course, since many Calcuttans speak English and/or another European language, and some 40 per cent of all publishing in India is in English). Thus the foremost 'technology' which might have occupied much more of this study than it does, and is the first technology through which Western tourists see Calcutta, is language. There are travellers from so many countries that the community is very much a 'polyglot' or 'heteroglot' mix of mostly English, but also French, Dutch, Belgian, and so on. Despite the prominence of English, hybrid traveller languages are an interesting effect of low-budget travel, with many jokes and plays on accent, and associated misunderstandings and mistranslations. While most visitors are European, the presence of Australian, New Zealander and Canadian accents adds to this mélange. For example, conversations with Christine were conducted in Hindi-inflected German because I don't speak French and she doesn't speak English. With variations and failures of language due to forced translations among different grammars, with minor nationalisms and hierarchies evident in subgroups, and with comic mistranslations – again a most popular storytelling theme recounts the vagaries of Restaurant Indian-English with classics like 'porge' instead of 'porridge' and 'mixed girl salad' instead of 'mixed grill and salad' – the linguistic diversity of the traveller's experience belies the homogeneity of their practice. Travellers are both similar and different.

As a hedging participant in Calcutta as a tourist, a traveller and a researcher in urban studies – among other subject positions open to me at various times – it became clear to me that the interstices within which I was placed as a visitor to that city were of more than biographical or local import. The focus of this book will shift from street level to the global in reflection of the 'double significance' of the volunteer position mentioned above (why visit Calcutta? how is Calcutta represented?). While at times my sympathy lies with the local-level experience of the traveller-volunteers, the limitations of that experience mediated through wider effects of a complex of neo-imperialist, commercial and discursive factors demands a questioning that takes on an internationalist perspective. Curiously enough, I want to claim that the possibility of such a perspective is grounded in 'idle talk' with people in Calcutta: writers, filmmakers, guesthouse proprietors, storekeepers, journalists, doctors, touts, and so on. The issues of representation and production of meaning, which are the core of my wider focus, owe as much to 'local' attentiveness and the suggestions and contestations of dominant representations of Calcutta by permanent residents and visitors as they do to the language and theories of semiotics, Marxism and post-structuralism in which I present my version. Much more could be said about my reasons for looking most closely at only middle-class 'Western' activity in Calcutta. It is enough to repeat at this point that I do not presume to comment in detail on Bengali or Indian productions about Calcutta, however fruitful such a study could be. Indeed, one of the points about this book is that the rumour-mongering of charity, Western NGOs and 'development' discourse (note that this is not the same as actual development) operates in a way that pretends to ignore, or is completely blind to, the organized and varied local 'Calcuttan' versions of the city, and responses to its problems. But can I ever so simply take a position in 'dialogue' with Modern Lodgers which is informed by other interactions, equally 'constructed', with other more 'local' Calcuttas? Bengali writers, publishers of small journals, photography and film students from Chitrabani film school, filmmakers and festival-goers, comrades and cadre, party literature and propaganda

– all the chatter that forms *my* 'other' version of Calcutta? Alongside interventions into Modern Lodge 'lore' through involvement in alternative 'tours' of the city and the contradictions and critical perspective of the clinic workers, the idea of any simple dialogue between visitor and Calcuttan, or between myself and either 'position' seems highly absurd. Things are far more complicated, and this remains the unresolved 'dialogue' of this work, this rummaging around in the gossipy fiction (a ficto-criticism?) of a global Calcutta apparatus.

The problem with the view from Modern Lodge is that it is always something of a 'verandah-view' – a term I take from Mary Louise Pratt, who uses it to describe colonial travel writers, imperial agents and the perspective of the administrators of empire (Pratt 1992: 221). Such a view is also that of Radcliffe-Brown (1922), interviewing Andaman islanders from the verandah of his hut for his 'classic' anthropological work. Many other ethnographic tentside scenes might be evoked (see Clifford and Marcus 1986: cover). While there may be no viewpoint exempt from this, that the Modern Lodge is the verandah made available for mass tourism is a wider critical point lying at the centre of this work. My attempt has been to look at representations of the city made explicitly from that verandah-place in which I, myself, dwell – (enframed by) the view *from* Modern Lodge – 'ideal place for foreign tourists' – as the shingle says.

ARRIVAL

A quotation from Michel Leiris links charity, wandering the streets, laughing, shouting, begging and the sound of my own voice in a manner that is perfectly surrealist and cannot be passed:

> 'Charity! Charity!' I am wandering through the streets of an unfamiliar neighbourhood, trying to catch a small dog who bears the name of this theological virtue. He was given to me by a baker; I was careless enough to walk him without a leash, and he ran away. A butcher (or some other shopkeeper) has already had a good laugh hearing me call after the dog that he has just watched race by. Shouting at the top of my lungs like some incensed beggar, I could very well be taken for a village idiot or for an escaped lunatic whom the police will swiftly move to arrest. Who cares. I go on shouting as loudly as I can, not only because I am so mortified at the loss of the little dog but also because I am drunk with the sound of my own voice: 'Charity! Charity!' (Leiris 1960: 169)

The predicament of this project is that it may be necessary, in order to explain or describe Modern Lodge, to enter into almost the same sorts of 'titillating' detail and anecdotal forms that characterize the Lonely Planet travel guides. I hope that this collection of trinket-anecdotes amounts to a different kind of guidebook, one which shows the markings of its construction in a way that allows a nod of self-recognition. If this work also collects and displays a 'Calcutta' of rumours and snippet-curios, it could also be subjected to its own critique (this is nothing new); the contradictions of this project at least include the possibility of a shared vulnerability.[2] Certainly the notes I took which tell the story of my first visit among those who live at the Modern and work at the clinic were framed in the Lonely Planet mould:

All travel diaries begin with airport scenes or taxi dramas, so who am I to claim an exception – whose passport foul-up, whose lost-luggage lament is this anyway? I remember cows and canals. It doesn't seem as crowded as I know it is, I don't have any feelings of 'exotic city crush', I am bored by the length of the drive from the airport to the heart of town. Tinsel town in tatters – Sudder Street, ten-rupee-a-night dormitories, Mother Teresa's volunteer camp. I'm a hit with the duty-free bourbon I've brought, I could be in a happy youth hostel anywhere except for the righteous indignation of a few guests in Room 1. Volunteers working their way towards heaven, balming their own souls with the soapsuds of leper baths? Well-meaning self-interest in the eyes of the faithful. I stare at parasites on India – not that I refuse to do volunteer work: I scrape a few wounds, I change bandages and beds; it's harder, however, to show the links between the capitalist world system and overwhelming charity. It's harder to refuse idealistic sincerity, no matter how naive. Justifying short-term commitment with atheism opposed to religious fervour and theorizing away the international corporate systems with the same smelly breath.

Third day or thereabouts, I taxi with a journalist I've met on some voyeuristic tour of the ghettos. On the way back from yet another 'slum' ('I'm sorry that I don't find them more depressing; why?'), she stops outside her homeopath (yes, hers: the possession of exotic services). I find the incongruity of West Coast American health fads feeding on 'mystical' India alongside the journalistic fodder of Calcutta – never 'really' fodder except in magazine articles – more shocking than anything else. Mother T says her help is but a drop of water in a bucket, but who is holding that bucket? Obvious answers to obvious questions: you just get in and scrub. Hopefully the wound will heal. No infections? Well, the chances are not too bad so long as it's kept clean. Douse everything with Dettol. My hack-taxi-tourist-'correspondent' corresponds to nothing more than a tired repeat of boring sensations. She has these little categories into which she can place the various volunteers. Dinky little questionnaires and dinky little forms, tape-recorder, pencil and notepad. She has a ready-reckoner kind of mind, fitting responses into the major categories: 'those that are doing good works', the 'religiosie', 'those that are running away from something', 'those that are looking for something'; ah, the readers.

We arrive at a next-to-last stop – directly after an orphanage full of one hundred beaming faces; outside on the street some thirty 'urchins' were not so well fed – and at this stop I part decisively and with relief from journalism. The questionnairing is going on again, and the respondent is answering with a serious tone: 'Yes, I'm here in India helping the poor, I'm trying to get in touch with cosmic harmony, uncoil the kundalini at the base of my spine...', etc., and the intrepid globetrotting newshound is writing it all down! The glib send-up is never broken, the journo thinks it's real, but I am rocked inside with laughter along with the volunteer, trying to hold a straight face at the scam. A sense of having found people, a sense of familiarity. It is by this roadside in the centre of town that I chip in my share of the fare – forfeiting the last item of my little tour. She goes on alone, oblivious to the jester's role in which, in a delicate reversal, she had been cast. I never see the article.

The ways in which journalists and travel-guide writers write seem so easy. Always now, especially in Calcutta writing about friends, the anxiety of beginning to write about others, even when they are near, dear and very much just like us. It is difficult to escape the dilemma once it has been made visible; again and again: how to write? And once there is reading, the co-constitution of these two makes the anxiety something of a nostalgic one. The only time you can worry about whether to write or not is before writing, and therefore before reading, as the two are inseparable. Perhaps the morality of reading should be questioned just as carefully as the strokes of the pen or keyboard – but this is a kind of censorship we wouldn't want, preferring instead to require our writers to be moral and leaving the inevitable omissions and inclusions (a kind of censorship, anyway) to the haphazard whims of circumstance, coincidence, the vagaries of promotion, distribution, recommendation, and so on and on.

In *The Predicament of Culture*, Clifford writes with fascination about Leiris as surrealist and anthropologist (not necessarily unconnected roles), and describes his defence of a 'rigorous subjectivity' in his African ethnography/journal. He describes Leiris's sense of duty to write everything, to record 'the course of a dream or a bowel movement – along with observations of the locale' (Clifford 1988: 170). I wonder if the haphazard and fragmentary nature of such work isn't in danger of becoming the latest clone in a series of prescriptions on how to write the 'good' ethnography. Too many prescriptions in an already overly prescribed project. Polytextuality as the new protocol; should every word that is said be recorded in some attempt to prove fidelity to the real?

Way back in 1954 Graham Greene wrote of his travel notes and his 'diary written in pencil', and 'a number of photographs taken with an old vest-pocket Kodak, and memories, memories chiefly of rats, of frustration, and of a deeper boredom on the long forest trek than I have ever experienced before – how was I, out of all this, to make a book?' (Greene 1980: 49–50). This makes me think that the inclusions and exclusions of a travel guide are more coherent (in a stream-of-consciousness way) than academic texts (with all their careful intentionality) can now ever be.

Yet experience of India is hybrid, multiple, mixed-up and simulated all at the same time. For some travellers it is possible to spend a great deal of time in India and still not see the Taj Mahal. Perhaps, though, they will have sent off a picture postcard of it. Among Modern Lodge travellers, the fashion for postcards becomes a competition to develop a series of 'readymades' – a restaurant menu, an Indian rum box cover, a mosquito coil packet sent to a friend who had contracted malaria in the Punjab. These quirky postal pranks remind me that Muecke said that tourism narrative demands texts no bigger than postcards (1990: 131).

All the efforts of the last few years to theorize the hybridity of culture seem to amount to so much justification for the same old sins, the same old scenes. Anthropology, especially in India, covers pretty much the same old ground, includes the same themes and, I imagine, makes the same exclusions – of course it is not surprising still to be caught within these productive institutional entrapments. Calcutta is so hard to write about but so much is written. Readers of recent ethnography are unavoidably familiar with the logistics of such a dilemma; in another context I might have written about the verbosity of the anthropologist paralysed by the problem of how to write ethnography today, given that anthropologists have begun to recognize (only to forget, to proclaim in order to ignore, to refer and defer) the inbuilt imperialisms of their productions. None can be unique in this: the productive crisis of cultural difference has also inspired many pages of travel literature and many pages of travellers' diaries, and filled many aerogrammes, postcards and letters home. I wonder if this bears any more attention.

To write is often a privilege (as a consequence of politics), and to do so instead of pursuing those – albeit not always successful, useful or justifiable – practices of aid called charity is fraught with problems. The Preger group tries to intervene in local lives as little as possible, has no religious affiliation, tries not to impose a foreign logic or set of values (although in this it must fail; it is said 'to run as haphazardly and miraculously as any properly Indian concern might' [Marcia]), and offers only what it can to cure leprosy, tuberculosis and other ailments under guidelines set out by the World Health Organization. As volunteers who have worked there often say: 'It's still charity, but...' There are a number of contradictions to be explained here; I think the volunteer who described her work as 'putting Band-Aids on lepers in the hope of stopping capitalism' (Julia) sums up all that makes me suspicious about charity work in this clinic. Even as some of them do recognize and articulate an understanding that the problems of Calcutta are the result of old history: the legacy of the Raj, partition (not one, but two), floods, famines, wars, and on and on; and even as they sometimes recognize that there is little they can do about this in Calcutta, there is something that intrigues me in their continued, and repetitive, efforts. Still, it seems that one of the most positive consequences of having a bunch of middle-class backpackers work on the streets of Calcutta has been a reasonably high rate of politicization which these travellers take back to their homes – many of them have taken up some form of activist community work upon their return to London, Toronto, Baltimore, wherever. Explanations which point to how a lack of guilt at having a good time in Calcutta perhaps mixes with other frustrations do not seem to be enough. 'It's so dumb that we can't do more for people but have all this energy to play soccer on Sundays' (Rachel). Feelings of stupidity, which come with the realization that 'working for the poor' implies all sorts of problems and inbuilt assumptions or prejudices, combine with the opportunity to observe the contrast between Calcutta and home to allow travellers to see their homes anew. Can it be said that as a catalyst for re-evaluations of liberal charity (and it is more than this), the clinic is worthwhile?

What am I to decide about volunteers' responses to lepers? If the clinic wasn't there they would hardly see so many, and if there were no Mother T or Lonely Planet, Calcutta might not be portrayed as being so poor. The structure of tourist responses to lepers can be unpacked into constituent parts, such as an amazement that the lepers keep going at all – an amazement that has more to do with the distance between a volunteer's life and health and that of a leper – for it is not really so surprising that these people want to live. Similar things can be said about the volunteer reaction expressed in comments like 'They can teach us so much about how to be happy' (Heidi) – such lessons and appreciations are noteworthy only across the significant chasm between First World volunteer and Third World leprous body. What also needs to be taken into account in this is an unproblematic location of the potent sign of leprosy here in the Third World city. More and more, this takes on a geopolitical orientation, the global hegemony.

For me there is no better way to do this than by working through my own obligations at this site – why Calcutta? Why leprosy? Why write? And this is a streetwise question from another Indian metropolis; in Anand Patwardhan's film *Bombay, Our City*, a pavement-dweller confronts the camera with the question of how an intellectual's documentary could ever really help her desperate position. In a review of this film, Vishwapriya Iyengar writes:

> A woman asks the director for a place in which to hide her face during the four months of monsoon. She belittles him by saying he can't even give her shelter. She accuses him with cynical candour that he is taking photographs of the poor to earn a name for himself. She tells him since he cannot do anything for them he should not take the photographs. (Iyengar 1987: 65)

This prompts further questions, since the sequence is shown in the film, becomes a 'scene', encrypted; Iyengar thinks this through:

> Anand's almost casual inclusion of the scene is pertinent at a time when poor people resent being questioned about their situation and ask why they should be questioned. It is a fundamental question which not only a depressed and downtrodden people ask when violated of their last bastion of dignity – the privacy of their lives, but a question which an enquirer of people's lives asks at a time when such details and images have become dead nerves of facts and academic commodities. (Iyengar 1987: 65)

Spivak, also in Calcutta, once said that she had been 'forced to perpetrate' a volume of essays – what a dastardly crime! And of course I wonder, too, why we keep trying to be better at this textuality. Why do we keep straining with this shit? In a toilet in the Modern Lodge I read graffiti which said: 'When the bottom falls out of your world, come to Calcutta and watch the world fall out through your bottom'. Derrida, quoting Artaud, notes that our works are waste matter that cannot stand up by themsleves. Excremental point; and this, too, just the page after Artaud refers to the 'black hole' of his birth (Derrida 1967/1978: 181). This 'Calcuttan Artaud' will say that 'writing is all trash' (Derrida 1967/1978: 183).

REPUTATION

Calcutta is an extraordinary city, an urban monster carrying contradictory images broadcast far beyond India's frontiers: clichés, myths or realities to which one cannot remain indifferent. (Racine 1990: xxxi)

The reputation of Calcutta figures high on the list of reasons given by travellers in India for visiting or not visiting the city. With few exceptions, people have preconceived notions about what to expect, and they judge accordingly. Even those who express an open attitude to the city and come 'just to see what it's really like' (Janet) cannot say they have no expectations – indeed, it would be almost impossible, and undesirable, for there to be any notion of writing Calcutta on to 'a clean slate' (Janet). The main themes revolve around notions of poverty, overcrowding and urban decay – tracing the emergence of these representations would require a thorough survey of immense historical and literary productions over the past three hundred years, taking in sources as diverse as the records and experiences of the colonial administrators and officials of the East India Company, the works of a wide range of authors from Rudyard Kipling to Amitav Ghosh, as well as travel literature, government reports, forms of mass media and a host of other communicative practices which can be said to impact upon the ways individuals think of the places of the world. Plainly, anything other than a highly selective sampling would be exhausting and near-impossible.[3]

The views of those who stay at the Modern are interesting because they are those of visitors who have not stayed long enough to become 'acclimatized' – 'You can't get used to this city' (Peter) – and yet they are not completely subject to the dictated 'impressions' of promotional or academic literature and received opinion: 'Try not to make assumptions' (Gail). Many of the travellers who stay for more than a few weeks in the dormitories of Sudder Street guesthouses *do* express a healthy disregard for the stereotyped and superficial presentations of the Lonely Planet guide and books such as *The City of Joy*. This is not to say that budget travellers have any more or less insight into some kind of 'real' Calcutta than others; nor that their impressions could be any more authoritative than those of Calcutta residents (although they sometimes claimed such arrogance), or of the scholars and dignitaries who gathered to comment on Calcutta at forums such as the Calcutta 300 seminar or conferences at the History Institute. Such travellers are heavily influenced by the literature and other media they consume before, during and after their visit. Reproduction of the metaphorical register of this representation circles back upon itself, and more often than not experiences in Calcutta are informed and understood in terms derived from already received versions of the city. Moreover, discrepancies of representation give (for visitors, at least) greater weight to European representation than any local code; priority goes to the famous visitors to the city: Kipling, Malle, Günter Grass.[4]

Poverty is possibly the major foreign trope of Calcutta; from the works of academics and filmmakers, from the tracts on the city by travel writers and the backpacker guidebooks, through the subjects of snapshot photography, to the comments of aid workers and short-term visitors. That the reputation of Calcutta in this regard is largely supported by the international reputation of Mother Teresa should not be understated. In addition to this, there is the undeniable and quite visible economic hardship of those who live on the pavements of the city, and the effects of successive waves of migration from the countryside after floods, famines and wars. The continued destabilization of the regional economy can be traced back to the partitions of Bengal and the lingering effects of the Raj and British colonization, as well as centre–state hostility (Congress versus Left Front) and the ever-hungry interventions of global capitalism, to which Calcutta and its people are subject. In such a context it should be no surprise that the city has its share of 'the poor'. But there are those who would question attempts to single out Calcutta as 'more impoverished' than other places. It is not a far-fetched idea to suggest that the Mother-Teresa-enhanced version of Calcutta's poverty has implications and explanations which go beyond the immediate material conditions of those who live on the streets and in the bustees; attention only to 'the poor' amounts to aiding and abetting the interventions of Western 'international care' delivered across the development divide with little systematic reflection on the political relations which underpin and enable this (patronizing) charity.

The exemplary status of poverty in Calcutta has to be understood as a function of this international reputation, revealingly noted by one traveller:

> 'Calcutta is famous for its poverty – one of its tourist attractions, and it doesn't have many. Yet it doesn't seem as bad as some other cities – sure, there's no area that doesn't have bustees or street-dwellers, but...' (Mary)

In another Indian city a conversation between two travellers suggested much about the importance of reputation in determining itineraries and opinions:

'Calcutta – terrible place.' (Rob)
    'Have you ever been there?' (Rachel)
    'No, but I've read about it, and I've been to Bombay.' (Rob)

Whatever the status of descriptions and opinions of Calcutta, 'the poor' as a category of human existence deserve more thoughtful consideration. Such a homogenizing category cannot provide much analytical value, and its invocation suggests a literary gesture towards images such as Dickensian London, or an unfounded evocative comparison with television images of 'the starving millions in Africa'. The category of 'the poor', as used by some Westerners, can have very little reference to people at all, as a traveller doing volunteer charity work explained while discussing other workers in Calcutta:

'I don't think the term "the poor" means much. It's not about people. An Irish nun working at Mother Teresa's talked about the "beauty of the poor", and even though she meant well, it's as if "the poor" are forever there and will never change, will remain forever "beautiful", and always poor.' (Kit)

Other references to poverty are appropriative in different ways. One volunteer said that people who suffer are there to 'keep us compassionate', reminding us not to become indifferent, 'which would be the worst form of living death' (Samantha). This volunteer did not understand 'how people can commit atrocities without a twinge of guilt at the sight of suffering'. Questioned by another volunteer, Samantha recognized that her views implied that those who suffer are offered as a kind of 'compassion register' for her benefit. The debate that ensued revolved around accusations of misunderstandings of her motives, the unfair attribution of an 'uncaring' attitude on her part and a lack of recognition of exploitative relationships. While this was not the intention of the observation – that 'the poor' were not there to provide a moral reminder to the Western traveller – the displacement of this argument onto the terrain of caring attitudes and action is important. It revealed again that investment in notions of poverty and suffering on the part of Western volunteers often had more to do with their own interests, values and motivations than with the interests of those that they purport to defend.

There were those who were able to recognize Calcutta's poverty in some sort of context, where the 'myths about Calcutta poverty are true', and the 'horrid and extreme things in Calcutta' (Hannah) were recognized as similar to things found in other cities. These had become 'epics' in the stories told of the city.

A somewhat different orientation came from another traveller who had worked as a volunteer for many months. Despite some rather unsupported 'explanations' of the caste system, he gained vocal approval from the group who heard his justification:

> 'We owe a debt to the poor – since like the Brahmins who profit from the structures of caste, we in the West have profited from the Third World – our debt then takes the form of intervening in the system that keeps the poor poor.' (Mitch)

The problem with this is that there is no guarantee that the interventions of Western charity workers will not simply reassert the patronizing relationships which reinforce the inequities which Mitch identifies in both caste and India–West relations. The debt remains.

The 'truth' of Calcutta, of course, is also a question of privileges, and some authors have noted that among the dangers of acceptance and tolerance of illusions is that in which suffering and distress can be dismissed as illusion only by those with the luxury to do so (Hanfi 1988: 27). Increasingly, issues of representation are recognized as important in the cultural politics of evaluation and opinion about places, people and things. Reputations are closely linked to representations and to the distribution of value-laden images among varied groups of observers, in varied locations, with varying degrees of opportunity to challenge, confirm, or contribute to the circulation of these images.

While a great majority of travellers carry with them images and evaluations from popular Western media about the city, there are a number of visitors whose experience displaces the main tropes and realigns opinions about Calcutta in interesting ways. One traveller explained her repeated returns to work in Calcutta with a curious reference to one of the prevalent afflictions suffered by children who live on the streets. Referring to the city, she said: 'It gets under your skin like scabies' (Sue). Perhaps rumours are contagious. Many of the volunteers who are second- or even third-time visitors become enamoured with the place: 'If you stay just two days it's horrid, if you stay longer you get to love it' (Dieter). The days fill up with 'routines' and recognitions which change surprise into familiarity. Some expectations dissolve, while other prejudices are confirmed. 'Everyone is disappointed that Calcutta is not more difficult' (Suzie). The cyclical nature of routine works in a number of ways to sustain the traveller in a strange environment. Habits form quickly to enable the sorting and editing of the hundreds of things which would otherwise demand attention – decisions to ignore something or other, to postpone, to omit, a repertoire of devices, conscious and unconscious, to *reorder* experience: 'I expected something more from the black hole, and I still find it a little strange that it's not a nightmare, it even seems somewhat normal. Well, not normal, but capable of seeming normal once you have got your routines sorted out' (Will).

Conventionally, volunteers are doing charity work, and so they can be expected to have some strong ideas about the value of their work and their 'mission' in a 'Third World' city. In all likelihood, these expectations could be confirmed through interviews with volunteers in Calcutta working for Mother Teresa or other religious groups, but many of the travellers in the Modern Lodge display a healthy disregard for such expectations. Many refuse to work for Mother Teresa, preferring the Preger clinic for a variety of reasons – the one most often expressed is 'lack of structure'. One nurse was notorious for her comment: 'It's the only hospital in the world where you can tell a stubborn patient to get fucked and get away with it' (Mary).

Much more could be written about the clinics and those volunteers who show a certain nonchalant ambivalence towards their activities. While there is no obvious open conflict between these 'philosophically different' groups of volunteers (at the Sunday football contests between the religious and non-religious groups, of course the non-religious team wins because the others are morally bound not to cheat), the Modern Lodge and the Paragon Hotel next door seem to attract more Preger workers than 'Teresa-ites'. The Salvation Army Red Shield guesthouse on Sudder Street and the YMCA and YWCA are different in this respect, although over time fashions shift and, largely owing to the transience of traveller-volunteers in Calcutta, the occupancy rates of each of the hotels fluctuate. In any event, during most of the period from 1988 until 1996 'the Modern' was the preferred home of long-term Preger volunteers and other travellers, many of whom made comments about Calcutta that did not always conform with expectations and conceptions that could be derived from popular media and opinion. While it may not be grounds for a valorization of travel, the scathing contempt of some volunteers for the sentimentalism of charity in the Swayze/Joffe *City of Joy* film, or in the Mother Teresa form, is striking. Perhaps the self-critical irony and humour of tourists *against* Lonely Planet protocols give grounds for a re-evaluation of the hegemony of traveller style. It is true that the Preger clinic works with a somewhat different orientation to that of the Mother Teresa order. An evaluation of spiritual motivations among what, in any case, is not a large population might also consider the international 'image' (and adoption programme) of the Mother Teresa outfit as an affect in representations of the city as a destitute child.[5] Within the horizon of charity operated in both organizations, however, it is difficult to imagine Calcutta in ways other than as a site for benevolent aid.

Other travellers – non-volunteer or semi-volunteer – at 'the Modern' and at other hotels are important too, in terms of traveller influence upon each other through information sharing (tips, competitive bargaining, storytelling) conversations, peer pressure, and so on. The complexities of relationships in even a small hotel (70–80 beds) are such that the traces of opinion formation, development and change would be unchartable even if they were not predetermined by complicated and contradictory preconceptions. The coexistence of the regular myths, prejudices and stereotypes with a decidedly 'anti-myth' orientation among some travellers and volunteers indicated something that could be marked as more than a conventional 'range of opinions' among a given population. At the same time, it would be wrong to attribute too much significance to, or to simplify, the 'scepticism' with which some travellers treated generalizations about Calcutta. Similarly, a haste in allocating influences and determining sources for this critical orientation while the mass media of the world remain unruffled in their continued acceptance of the common mythic tropes of Calcutta – as most crowded, most impoverished, most filthy city. etc. – would be unwise. Even as I note that it is common to find that Modern Lodge 'guests' do not trust mainstream comments about Calcutta, even if they have no ready access to alternative literature or imagery (nor do they seek it out), it is, in part, their non-formalized irony and scepticism which most intrigues me.

THE SURVIVAL KIT

Increasing numbers of young people all around the world are participating in tourism. People in their teens and twenties tend to be more venturesome and willing to travel to places all over the world. They also use means of travel which perhaps the older person would not favour, such as hitch-hiking, and staying and eating at youth hostels, or other low-priced accommodation. Rising standards of living, technological improvements resulting in increasing productivity per worker, increase in leisure time with decrease in work week, longer vacations, changes in the age compositions of the population, the increasing levels of educational attainments, better communication, increased social consciousness of people relating to welfare and activities of other people throughout the world, and the shrinking of the world by fast jet travel have combined to produce great interest in travel. (Bhatia 1986: 57–8)

In his discussion of world travel and the 'power of travel to increase understanding and appreciation' (Bhatia 1986: 58), Bhatia refers to a complex number of factors which combine to make travel worthy of attention. While many might question an overly optimistic evaluation of travel in terms of increased understanding – it is rather, at best, a 'mixed blessing' (see Crick 1989: 39) – a positive evaluation of tourism views it as 'a profound, widely shared human desire to know "others", with the reciprocal possibility that we may come to know ourselves' (McKean 1989: 133).

Many may call it escapism. Indeed, there is much doubt as to how far the desire to know others governs the activities of the traveller. Certainly 'foreign tourists' in Calcutta seem to do a good deal of avoiding 'others', and while the reasons for this should not be automatically assumed to have to do only with ethnocentric prejudices, there is cause to doubt the more romantic evaluations of the 'togetherness' and understanding of 'travel'. Backpackers in Calcutta do have numerous difficulties to contend with – that the city is not the easiest place to live in is attested by many Bengali writers, too – but the reasons why backpackers 'stick together' may be more adequately explained in terms of identity and the sense of community they develop among themselves in Calcutta, and more generally in India.

Western travellers to Calcutta are not a homogeneous group, although by far the largest number fit quite closely within the stereotypes of youth backpacker. The backpacker is not, as the popular mythology might suggest, so much of the same ilk as the hobo or the Kerouac-style 'beat' traveller of *On the Road*, carrying 'home' in a rolled blanket on their back, or living out of a car – some kind of turtle existentialism – but is very much someone who has left 'home', usually for a finite time, and often between the end of a period of formal education and the beginning of work or higher studies. The relationship of the backpacker to home *is* mediated by images such as that of Kerouac, and of the exile and the hobo, and notions of escape and adventure, autonomy and self-sufficiency; but for many backpackers the adventure trail is so well worn that departure can only be a sanitized and temporary break. Notions of *rites de passage* from anthropologists like Van Gennep (1960) or Turner (1974) may be useful in making sense of some aspects of the departure, but equally notions of exploration and adventure, the appeal of difference and the exotic, the marketing of foreign destinations, and the dynamics of international transport and tourism development would have to be taken into account. In many ways these matters can be better explicated with reference to shared strategies of a middle-class Western version of 'survival' which is an overt part of the make-up of traveller identity in India. This is recognized by Lonely Planet and its commercially successful, strategically named *Survival Kit* travel guides, protecting against imagined dangers and differences of a threatening world.

Despite national differences, the world community of backpackers make up a distinct set of travellers over against tourist-class categories. Yet as Nash points out, travellers stick together and 'begin to build a familiar social network involving people from home' (Nash 1989: 45). Backpackers develop rituals, rites of inclusion and exclusion, and markers of status in common with all groups. It is significant, if mundane, I think, that backpackers identify themselves as being very different to other kinds of tourists, especially those who stay in expensive five-star hotels.

While the Modern Lodge is the most popular of the budget accommodations, it is tiny compared to the three or four comfortable up-market hotels catering for wealthier and older tourists and wealthy middle-class Indian nationals. These four- and five-star accommodations are, of course, out of the price range of the budgeting traveller, and they provide the standard of service and luxury that could be expected from a similar-quality hotel in any city. Straddled along one side of Jawaharlal Nehru Road (Chowringhee) is the best example of such an establishment: that off-white beast the Oberoi Grand, with all its marble, plush carpets and huge staircases, its ballrooms and swimming-pool. Colonial splendour. It was in this luxury that the director Roland Joffe and movie star Patrick Swayze stayed when they were making *City of Joy* in 1990–91. In contrast, the hotels of Sudder Street are more famous for bedbugs, mice and rats (although backpacker folklore suggests that the self-filtered drinking water in the Modern or the Paragon is safer than that served in the Oberoi café).

Apart from the very occasional 'dress-up' to visit the Oberoi disco, such locations are not part of the map of the budget traveller in Calcutta. Traveller concerns revolve more often around places like cafés and chai stalls, English-language movie theatres, markets, the Telephone Bhavan for calls home, the General Post Office for letters from friends, and perhaps the Foreigners' Registration Office for visa extensions after three months. Any longer-term visitor to Calcutta will know the location of these places, and which tram or bus you need to get there.

Information like this is shared haphazardly and informally along the backpacker routes in India. Recommendations about where to stay, what to eat, how to get a cheap air or train ticket, the best buys in silver jewellery, silk, hashish or kaftans – India-wide – or muffins and chocolate brownies, best Indian rum, or bookshops – in Calcutta – make up a large part of traveller conversation in the coffee-houses and chai stalls where travellers congregate. These informal exchanges of information constitute and confirm the norms of backpacker identity. The success of the Lonely Planet guidebook series comes from the documentation of this kind of traveller talk in its 'chatty' style – the fact that few visitors to India now come without this *Survival Kit* is testimony to the importance of such talk, and the idea or 'ordeals' of survival in what for many is a difficult country. The fact that the survival kit has not silenced such talk, and that a significant number of long-term travellers discard the thing after the first months, since much of its information is quickly out of date or considered biased, is incidental to its continued significance. A sale is a sale. Even if the survival kit remains in the bottom of the backpack for the whole of the journey after the first week in India, or if it comes out only as a quick guide to bus, train and guesthouse locations – its attempts at potted histories of regions and sections on 'things to see' and 'what to buy' are soon dismissed – its continued sales and resales in the Western traveller market are an indication of the depth of the 'survivors'' trail of tourism in India. The guidebook is still among the few in any way useful ones available for the subcontinent, despite its moments of unthinking racism and its commercial agenda. It does assist in demystifying (or sanitizing) some of the less 'home-like' or unfamiliar, but necessary, mechanics of travelling in India. It is the first 'machine' through which traveller experience in India is produced.

The importance of casual talk and information-sharing – not always correct, sometimes wildly exaggerated – among travellers is not diminished by the Lonely Planet's phenomenal success. That the *Survival Kit* points to the roof of the Modern as a storytelling and meeting place is interesting, as Lonely Planet's productive force is founded upon a steady stream of correspondence from some of those same travellers. Curiously, a self-deprecating passage in a recent Lonely Planet Guide publicity brochure advertises itself as 'the most important item of luggage next to toilet paper for a trip to India' (1993 brochure). (It is on this same roof that I have heard various different versions of the weird death of Lonely Planet publisher, and millionaire, Tony Wheeler: a sports car accident in Africa, a bus over a cliff in Nepal, under the foot of an

elephant in Thailand and pierced by the tusks of a wild pig in Highland New Guinea. As far as I can establish, at the time of writing,
Wheeler actually remains alive and well, working from his office in
Melbourne. 'He is Nosferatu, Vampyros, the Undead – a smart business
man'. [Peter].)

Storytelling, after all, is a traveller's medium. 'Ninety per cent of travelling
is talk' (Catherine). Some of the most interesting ways in which Calcutta
and India are (re)constructed for travellers is through their own stories.
Often these stories are offered in a 'more-knowledgeable-than-you'
routine, including embellishments of reality; consequently they have a
good deal of entertainment value. There are certain themes which continue to be recycled in traveller-frequented chai stalls and cafés; retellings,
in truncated form, of religious epics such as the Mahabharata, the story
of Kali and the foundation of Calcutta, and three minute distillations of
the Ramayana or similar; tales of 'weirdest' India and specific characters
met along the way; (boring) stories of endless bus or train journeys; and
tales of amazingly good food, drugs, guesthouses, or completely 'un-
touched' villages that 'no one has ever visited ever' (Heidi).

There are stories worth retelling, although the skill of some of the
traveller raconteurs wandering around the banana-pancake trail may well
be difficult to reproduce on paper. Tall tales or true? One of the most
popular came from a German traveller who brought to Calcutta a series
of (scratchy) photographs of what he called the Naga-babas: mystics
who practised the art of stretching their foreskins by attaching weights
to their pierced ends. My incredulity was not reduced by the presentation of what could have been fabricated photographs of men lifting
tourists off the ground with the aid of their foreskins, which they held
by the end while the stretched portion – some several inches – was
wrapped around heavy metal bars. Truly weird. I am assured, however,
that this is true; subsequently published coffee-table picture books appear
to confirm it. Other tales of mystics such as that of the sadhu outside
of the city who declared one day that he would stand on just one foot
for seven years, and had attracted a group of followers who attended to
his needs, had become classics – no doubt they will find their way into
the Lonely Planet Guide in due course.

Can these stories illustrate something more about the representation
of India and Calcutta? Perhaps the fabulation of the city? Of the subcontinent for those from abroad? Invented as a mystical dreamscape,
India is located in an esoteric geography that has been largely renounced
by the secular West[6]. Among longer term Modern Lodgers there are

efforts to 'appreciate' cultural life in India that offer a slightly different take on Indian travel clichés. Among volunteers, after some prompting, there have been attempts to set up Bengali and Hindi classes, and some travellers gained a degree of (five-sentence) fluency that was much appreciated by local people. It is almost a truism of the tourist circuit that learning a few local words adds authenticity and rapport to travel, although this is perhaps overestimated. Other longer-term volunteers, especially in the 1992–94 period, took up the Buddhist-ashram-Bodh Gaya path, which seems still more illusory. Yet others were learning instruments such as tabla, sitar and sarod. Another learned dancing: Amanda, a clinic adminstrator, did not, at first, think it necessary to learn any Bengali, but relented after some prompting. Within a month of getting settled in Calcutta, she also wanted to learn tabla drumming, guitar, classical Indian dance, go to an ashram, shave her head, live in a cave and adopt a child (obviously not all at the same time).

In an expensive large-format hard-cover two-volume publication called *Calcutta: The Living City*, coinciding with the 300th-anniversary celebrations of Calcutta, Sukanta Chaudhuri writes: 'Few modern cities have bred so many myths as Calcutta. By "myths" I do not mean falsehoods, but myths in the social or anthropological sense' (Chaudhuri 1990: xv). As I have argued, Calcutta is already overdetermined with meanings for everyone who visits – a host of preconceptions and expectations, illusions and knowledges. Indeed, it should be no surprise that the public image of Calcutta could have been considered as a site for a structuralist analysis *à la* Lévi-Strauss. The fact that the noted anthropologist visited Calcutta in the 1950s is mentioned by French commentators such as Jean Racine (1990) and Gaston Roberge (1991), alongside their calls for a mythic analysis of the city. Lévi-Strauss does not provide any suggestion that his theoretical studies of American mythological systems could be transported to urban terrain (there are hints that he thought not), and the invocation of his name with reference to Calcutta has had more rhetorical importance as a kind of authority marker for claims that Calcutta is mythological than it has as the opening of a fruitful research development. However useful such a gesture is, and to whatever extent the city is indeed 'mythic', cannot, I suspect, be evaluated solely within the gamut of the structuralist methods of Lévi-Strauss. What can be taken from this invocation, though, is the idea that the 'host of preconceptions and expectations, illusions and knowledges' that informs opinion about, and perhaps experience of,

Calcutta can be taken to have some systematic characteristics which can be elucidated.

This 'mythologique' study of Calcutta is not, then, the primary intention of those who invoke the name of Lévi-Strauss, since authority claims are usually counter-claims to some other authority. Racine and Roberge wish to challenge the dominant 'myths' about Calcutta. Presenting different myths as replacements, and the possibility of a kaleidoscopic routine of myth and counter-myth – in this case amounting to a 'politics of representation of Calcutta' – was recognized much earlier by Nandy in *The Intimate Enemy* (1983). Nandy's blunt challenge was that those who would not like his 'myths' of India would be obliged to create better myths, and it is this contestation of meanings – largely absent in the calculations of Lévi-Strauss in the Americas – which gives the force to the creative experience of some visitors to Calcutta today. Some sense of obligation emerges here also: in consideration of this project, and the dilemma of 'knowing' the 'real' Calcutta, one traveller, Suzie, offered a remark on what I was trying to do which anticipated exactly this thought from Nandy: 'You will have to write anti-myths of Calcutta'. It may be too convenient to present this as a more advanced position, where recognition of a dominance of some myths does not dictate a search for 'truth', nor a contestation through presentation of other myths, but demands a kind of deconstruction of prevailing myths and their working effects without positing some authoritative non-mythic awareness. But the effort to reveal the political contexts in which certain 'truths' about Calcutta are produced and circulate, and whatever potentially progressive character can be found in the experience of *some* of the travellers and volunteer workers at the Modern Lodge, is contained, I think, in this distinction.

What else do the guests in the Modern discuss on that rooftop? As so many of the Modern's clientele are volunteers at the Preger clinics, it is very convenient that the rooftop provides space for the weekly volunteers' meeting. The information session initiated in 1990 dominates discussion only once a week and, as it is not a decision-making forum, much time outside the meetings is devoted to clinic-related gossip. While the weekly meeting is the place where some formal discussion of people's expectations and opinions about Calcutta occurs, there is a conscious effort by longer-term volunteers and administrators to dispel some of the more obvious illusions about the city in casual talk. It is also true that some prejudices are confirmed, and certainly the availability of some rather conventional postcard representations of street children – sold to raise funds and promote the clinics – codifies certain stereotypes. The formal structure of the meeting ensures that someone leads a talk on an issue of relevance to the clinic, but it is the follow-up 'idle talk' among members of the group and new arrivals which forms and confirms opinions.

There are many opportunities for travellers to get together to talk. Endless – and circular – discussions on the morality of tourist charity work seem to indicate a particular preoccupation. The viability and applicability of the kind of charity work performed by travellers in Calcutta is measured against an awareness of the ways such work is contextualized within the international situation. 'We are the front line of imperialism in many ways, but someone has to help these people, and we can do it' (Gail – see also Janet, quoted below in Chapter 7). The co-existence of a moral crisis with a pragmatic and sympathetic urgency continually expressed in this self-checking commentary effectively sums up the view of many.

Debates about the morality of giving to beggars are a good example of this, sometimes leading to confusion and contradictory positions. Travellers argued the pros and cons of what was an everyday concern in Sudder Street and its surroundings. A general consensus was never apparent, but the influence of recommendations to avoid 'encouragements' did emerge. The relations of charity workers to beggars illustrates many of the contradictions of being a volunteer in Calcutta, as expressed, for example, in another scene involving passing out coins:

'Is it decided that we shouldn't give money to beggars? Giving only food, or giving nothing at all while we are volunteers seems crazy when, in some kind of overly generous gesture at the end, we will give all our possessions away.' (Ian).

Undecidability remains here. There are some volunteers who will give only to the very old, some who buy food and sometimes insist on seeing it eaten (due to suspicions that it will be sold); some volunteers have their 'favourites' – an old rickshaw-puller, who gets few customers and sits at the end of Stuart Lane (off Sudder Street), gets a rupee from Peter each day, and so on. While it is difficult to judge the proprieties and protocols of these scenes, much can be discerned in the travellers' attitude to locals about the travellers' 'psychology'. Not that I want to posit that these discussions of 'morality' *explain* much, but it seems to me that talk of morality presupposes a subjectivity that sees itself as separate from the world upon which it acts as an independent ego in ways that make sense in terms of the Heideggerian point about the ends of the technological cited in Chapter 1. I am less interested in the self-exploration exercises of volunteers and backpackers than I am in the ideological messages that underwrite their representational activities. Biren Das Sharma has pointed out that what is offered in the *City of Joy* film, as with many other narratives about India by Western visitors, is the message that 'with just a little help, or push, from the *developed* world, India would be able to succeed, rise up, etc.' That this 'message' appears repeatedly can be seen most explicitly in Joffe's film, but it is also frequently expressed by other visitors and in the Modern Lodge rooftop discussions – and it appeals to a wide audience who are attracted to notions that even the poorest of the poor can be aided by the good conscience of the magnanimous West, which gives them the push-start they need. 'We are here to begin a self-help programme for these people; it's a statement; we are helping them here today' (Mary – video 'Dr Jack's' 1991). The correspondence of such views with the structural adjustment policies and programmes of the World Bank and International Monetary Fund should not be lost. With such broad questions in mind, the ways these travellers 'place' themselves in relation to Calcutta becomes more significant, less innocent:

> 'It's a question of what you have to do – you have a moral obligation to help people in need, but at the same time you have a moral obligation to provide this help with respect for local cultural values.' (Tim)

> 'Can you ever really know these "local cultural values"?' (Olivia)

In this exchange, notions of morality and culture seem to have a fairly popular 'common-sense' character. The absurdity of this discussion is that 'local cultural values' of Calcutta already boast a rich history of resistance and self-reliance. Knowledge of this, however, is not readily 'souvenired' by those on the budget-traveller circuit.

The trope of the market commodifies everything for the tourist. Bargaining structures relationships, and India becomes one enormous colourful bazaar. The comparative financial security of even the traveller with a well-considered – albeit tight – budget still seems to transform everything into the evaluative framework of money. Travel could be seen as a training ground for unabashedly extravagant consumption as travellers bargain and calculate what for them are the most minute amounts. The evident financial security of the Western traveller attracts – not unexpectedly – repeated requests for assistance from beggars and street children. Traveller responses vary from the granting of small requests, through strategies (condoned by the Lonely Planet guide) to curb 'excess' such as only giving a rupee or two on every second morning, to complete refusal and sometimes expressions of anger. The persistence of some beggars, especially those who mill around the tourist establishments, becomes too much for less tolerant travellers. Others become skilled at ignoring requests, or favour the most abject. Some travellers are taken by boisterous children demanding piggyback rides as well as ice creams, chicken biriyani and rupees. It is often those in the most need who are least able to utilize the established avenues, forms and protocols of tourist begging. It is also certain that the few returns that beggars gain from tourists amount to only a very minor improvement in their material circumstances.

The market turns to a kind of carnival where begging competition for the infrequent acknowledgments of tourists is most congested. Outside the India Museum on Chowringhee, begging blends into a kind of alternative theatre, ranging from chalk drawings on the pavement to more surreal performances. The sometimes dismal effect of this was described in detail by one traveller:

'I only like the beggars who provide a bit of a show, more than pathetic asking for rupees. Like the boy who buries his head in sand in a hole in the footpath outside the museum. I'm more inclined to give money for that rather than for some half-convincing expression of misery by someone who minutes before was arguing with a neighbour or playing with a child. The kids who run across the road to drop before you and twist their legs up under them are almost worth the show – it's theatrical – but of course the real cripples and the really abject don't get a look-in.' (Will)

This situation borders on the callous, where recognition of a problem seems to lead to the most inequitable of possible responses. The commercialization of all things within the tourist economy permits travellers to experience India as a market sideshow.

And the market as a site of consumption offers other metaphors, the meat section of New Market suggesting to one traveller-volunteer, William, that Calcutta was a 'raw' city, cut to the flesh, clear to the bone: 'there are no compromises – the city is raw – it's difficult to deal with its fantastic and immediate honesty' and William continued, curiously: 'Even the lies it tells you are true, even the rip-offs are sweet, you've got to appreciate this.' Calcutta is also described as a kind of cannibal: 'feeding on the countryside, swallowing whole families, sucking them in at Sealdah station, the city's jaws' (Sam). Calcutta also 'absorbs travellers into its teeming mass like a giant snake'. Evocative of the city's favourite goddess, Kali, who wears a garland of skulls in fearsome regalia, the place 'chews people up and spits them out on the street as bones' (John). Travellers, of course, are not wholly consumed in the same ways, and may indeed be considered somewhat irrelevant to the city's commercial diet. In a taped interview, the presence of foreign tourists was considered insignificant:

> 'It wouldn't be any different if Westerners didn't come, the city doesn't have any mechanism that specifically deals with us tourists, it just folds us up into itself as it does with every other group. However different, however rich or artificially ragged – I mean those who dress up after some image of mystic India – however various the types of tourist, they don't seem to stand out in Calcutta. The city eats them up, consumes them – it digests everything.' (Andrew)

The metaphorical registers of travellers' Calcutta are sometimes most bleak, and, for some, time spent in the city can be depressing and an ordeal. There have been suicides inside the guesthouses of Sudder Street, although perhaps fewer than could be expected. At times Calcutta can be far too much, and the available images articulate a kind of despair:

> 'My version of Calcutta seems as ominous and dark as I feel – rats and sewers, a brewing, hovering monstrosity lurks the streets. The terrible stoneman from the *Telegraph* newspaper stories [the so-called stoneman who, over a period of six months or more, attacked sleepers on the streets in the small hours, smashing their skulls with a rock] killing destitutes under Howrah Bridge – all this imagery of destruction and decay suits my temperament, my resentment.' (Michael)

Much remains to be understood about the ways in which we justify our actions to ourselves, and travellers are no different from other communities in this. The conventions of the banana-pancake trail provide confusion-minimizing familiarities, as does the sense of closed community developed in the Modern. Volunteers have their roles already defined to some extent; there is little demand upon them to invent their own cultural spaces and responses to what they find unfamiliar: 'The worst thing about travellers in India is listening to them moan about what a bad time they're having – prats' (Catherine).

Among the most important ways in which the rooftop discussion sessions determine traveller experiences in Calcutta are the directives offered by longer-term volunteers on 'how to behave'. Introductions to the clinics usually begin with recommendations about modest clothing, no shorts or singlets, no loose-fitting tops and no jewellery. Bringing valuables like cameras, passports or wallets is discouraged, and a request is made that volunteers 'not enter into any financial transactions with local people' (Amanda). These recommendations are justified with reference to rare incidents of stolen passports and travellers' cheques, but restrictions such as that on cameras are more complex. In some ways, this restriction invites volunteers to anticipate thefts by the recipients of clinic services, thus confirming a prejudice most common in guided tours: 'Hang on to your handbags as we walk through the market, stick together, watch each other and look out for pickpockets' (tour guide, Calcutta 1988). At another level, the restriction on cameras at the clinics limits the number of images taken of people in distress – many examples of these have found their way into the Western press – and allows some minimization of opportunity to take advantage of the photogenic aspects of poverty.

Discussion of etiquette in the orientations of volunteer workers shows evidence of ample good intentions and optimism in ideas, though perhaps sometimes also overenthusiasm. Not all volunteers are interminably inclined to discuss their motives for working at the clinic, and in comparison to the piety of some of those who worked with Mother Teresa, this reluctance – which was often simply a matter-of-fact casual modesty – was refreshing. Nevertheless, enthusiasm of intention was not always translated into deftness of practice, and was a source of friction at times. Perhaps because people did not stay long enough to carry plans through, and partly because they were unsure of their place, there were complaints that new volunteers seemed to wait to be told what to do. There was an expectation that volunteers would follow the injunction to 'get in and do what you could see needed to be done', but I think this often presumed a degree of familiarity with the clinics that was the exclusive domain of longer-term volunteers. This meant that a good deal of talk sometimes accompanied a lesser degree of activity. New ideas, and reinvented old ones, were continually discussed, allowing one volunteer, Anil, to exclaim: 'It's all very well to talk about what ought to be done, but when do people get around to doing it?'

COMMUNISTS

The rooftop of the Modern can also be the site for working out the 'identity' of Calcutta itself. Discussions of the city and of traveller activity are not solely about personal identity – things are multi-dimensional. Symbols orient experience, and are the material from which identity and understanding are hewn. Among the most obvious (textual) productions that appear on the streets of Calcutta are the symbols of communism. Communism is often an 'event' in the city, and a point of discussion among travellers. Not far from the Modern Lodge, an impressive statue of Lenin stands by the bus exchange: rallies of sometimes half a million people gather in the Maidan Park and red flags adorn many buildings, including some of the cheaper restaurants where budget travellers eat. From the Modern it is a short walk to the Indian Coffee House, which is known as a centre of Marxist discussion for some of Calcutta's university students, and alongside which is a CPI(M) publishing outlet occasionally visited by curious travellers. While it would be an exaggeration to stress this, among the longer-term visitors to the Modern interest in communism – however superficial – is a significant part of the tourist experience of the city.

The red flags of the communist parties remain highly visible in Calcutta, providing a source of some surprise to many visitors and becoming a cult fad in the Modern Lodge. While guidebooks like *Survival Kit* do mention, in passing, that the state of Bengal has enjoyed communist rule for many years, this information is probably not sufficiently prominent to counteract the mental baggage on this score which travellers bring with them to the city, a baggage which amounts to variations on the theme of 'communism is dead' gleaned from campaigns by the Western media empires who have celebrated the demise of the 'Eastern bloc' and the USSR, mixed with a general lack of familiarity with the notion that cities could function and people could (still) live under a stable communist administration (we could, of course, debate deviations and mistakes…).

'So, you're a communist then?' (Nigel)
'Aren't you?' (John)

Expectations do not match experience; even the trappings of daily life offer visible differences; visitors to Calcutta have to make some re-adjustments. Some are taken aback by the prominence of hammer and sickle symbols painted on street walls; some enjoy, as a kind of exotic theatre perhaps, the rallies and marches that sometimes clog the city thoroughfares; others are drawn into discussions of the merits of communist and socialist policy on the basis of articles they read in the daily papers about interparty debates. If communism is dead, it is quite a surprise that so many travellers spend so much time photographing its flags and symbols, reading pamphlets and articles, and securing red flags as souvenirs from rallies, trucks, buildings or party offices. But for the media glee with which the 'triumph of the new world order' was promoted in the early 1990s, and the leakage of this 'end of the Cold War'/end of communism slippage into people's preconceptions, this surprise should not have been too great, since more alert media-watchers have noted that the 'collapse of the USSR', and of the Eastern European communist states, is merely a setback for a 'sausages-and-three-veg' form of communism, specific to a certain part of the world. Other parts of Asia (Vietnam, China, North Korea, Nepal) and other nations in Africa and the Americas (Cuba), very much open to budget travel, are forgotten, so that the assumptions of international tourism and privilege can be illustrated once again as European events are Eurocentrically transposed to signal the end of communism worldwide. Lonely Planet successfully manages survival kits for China and Vietnam.

Awareness of communism among the travellers who stay in Sudder Street is not necessarily comprehensive, and is often little more than an amalgam of impressions and somewhat modified stereotypes.

'I'm not that aware of any communist aspect amongst the people even though there are lots of red flags and from reading I know that the communist government has achieved some good things like land reform and high literacy rates, but...' (Albert)

Travellers' experience of Bengali communism is of considerable interest, since many have not visited a communist-ruled city before. This provides a distinct contrast with their home experience, and much can be learnt about travellers' own views from their observations of this aspect of Calcutta. There were some who thought that 'only a communist revolution can save Calcutta from the ruthless plunder of big business and local and foreign elites' (Christian), and then there were those who thought that 'communism can't work because people are inherently greedy' (Bronwyn). Between these two poles – each of which implies some degree of unease about the nature of life under capitalism – other travellers and visitors to Calcutta expressed a range of opinion that shows how something called 'communism' can be understood, misunderstood, picked up and consumed like a souvenir, and discarded in a wide variety of ways.

Against most conventional responses to the city, those predisposed towards leftist politics could find Calcutta inspiring – 'Yes, it is a communist city, I love the red flag – there is still hope' (Françoise) – while the beginnings of reassessment of previously unexamined preju-dices could be discerned: 'I thought communism was really bad and full of thought police, but all I have seen is traffic police and they have absolutely no effect whatsoever' (Harriet). Some found the whole experience bewildering, or were led to a recognition that they had much to learn: 'I have no idea what I'm doing here surrounded by all this stuff I don't have any reference for – politics, religion, language…' (Wendy). In many cases visitors who stayed more than a few weeks came to have quite complicated views on the pros and cons, and various versions, of Indian communism:

> 'The ruling party – CPI(M) – has a good record but doesn't seem to be doing much about the city. The non-government communist groups like the Naxalites have complaints that the CPI(M) has sold out to the industrialists, the trade-union groups seem to agitate all the time on wage issues and all of it is mixed up with people trying to make their few rupees a day to survive. The CPI was reported in the paper to have abandoned Lenin and Stalin in favour of nationalist heroes like Mahatma Gandhi, while the CPI(ML) still supports Mao Zedong. You can learn lots of things about communism here because it is debated all the time, but I don't think the place runs along communist lines, even after so many years of communist government. I don't think anyone really runs it. How does it run?' (Daniel)[7]

More unusual responses to the question of communism in Calcutta included the suggestion that communism could never work because it didn't have a spiritual dimension – 'It's a beautiful idea but it leaves so much out' (Amanda) – and a curious mind/body split appraisal from a stoned traveller: 'Are these people communists? My heart is here in Calcutta, but my head says no because it's a communist state' (Wayne). A more sober assessment concluded that 'what the communists have achieved in Bengal is amazing, but it's not enough. Communism doesn't solve all the problems' (Frances).

> 'The communist leaders are just as corrupt as our ones back home, at least according to the papers. And aren't they all politicians? The only real communist activity I have seen are the red banners outside restaurants that are closed. Here the workers and trade unions have set up their own cooking facilities and sell food outside, which I think is terrific.' (Lucy)

CHARITY WORK

'Problems' are often a dominant theme in discussions of visitors to Calcutta – Western middle-class predispositions, the reputation of the city and contrasts of poverty with wealth seem to determine a 'problems-and-answers' framework within which visitors respond to, and try to make sense of, Calcutta. As one 'answer', communism is a factor to be considered, but as a large proportion of visitors to Calcutta, especially budget travellers, become involved in, or come specifically for, volunteer work for charity organizations that are explicitly *not* communist,[8] there is little scope for elaboration. A few volunteers who have worked at the Preger clinic would describe themselves as communists, some have become communists while working there, but by far the majority believe in a kind of liberal mission: 'We have to do something to help these people'. The work of Mother Teresa, and more recently that of Preger, has focused international attention on the 'problems' of Calcutta in a way that eclipses more analytical responses with a glossed global media profile. In the process, the question of what might be communism's role with regard to the problems of the city seems to have slipped off international screens. For their part, communists, not surprisingly, look unfavourably upon the activities of Western charity organizations in Calcutta, although the international prestige of Mother Teresa, and international support for Preger, have been marshalled by local supporters to counter obstacles to their work.

Some volunteers who had worked for extended periods in Calcutta experienced (minor) bureaucratic difficulties with visa extensions. The hassle of gaining extensions beyond three months was thought by some travellers to be a CPI(M) attempt to restrict long-term volunteers from working in the city. Volunteers were cautious about police and government: 'We can't get involved in politics because volunteer work is sensitive. The communist government doesn't want us to draw attention to the problems because it gives an excuse for the Western media to bag out Calcutta' (Neil). Inevitably, volunteer work does raise political questions; whether this involves the debates about how the 'poverty-stricken' reputation of Calcutta is being used by charity organizations as a kind of advertisement to attract funding for a worldwide franchise – as some critics have claimed of the Missionaries of Charity and of World Vision – or whether it simply means a failure to consider alternative 'solutions' to the problems: any participation in charity organizations must be considered political. Volunteers did sometimes say as much: 'Whatever we do here has its contradictions, and I don't think handouts and charity are ever going to do more than keep things the same – change has to be a self-help, grassroots kind of thing' (Olivia).

This last kind of view indicates some reflective thinking among volunteers and travellers that would perhaps not be completely opposed by local communists. Indeed, many travellers who do volunteer work in Calcutta become alert to wider global processes in the course of their stay. 'What's good about volunteer work in Calcutta is not that it "saves the poor", but that it shows us that the problems are not just local ones. Volunteers can't just go home to their regular jobs – something has to be done on a worldwide scale, and in our own backyards' (Lisa). And: 'It's good that some people are made more aware of the intricacies and politics of these issues in Calcutta. Its a shame that it can't happen more often and to more people at home, but at least some of them will bring some new ideas home with them and – so long as they don't get mixed up with too much New Age hippie stuff – this will be a good thing' (James).

A common criticism made of Western development workers in general is that they often advocate 'revolution' in the Third World but rarely do anything revolutionary in their home countries. An attitude that was not uncommon among volunteers in Modern Lodge was that the work they were doing 'was only a maintenance measure' (Gail), and that any solution to the problems of Calcutta had to do with factors outside the city such as the role of the National Government, the international marketplace and other wider contexts. While volunteers felt that they must do something, and some did not think what they did was of such significance: 'It's not romantic or idealistic at all, we just do our little bit' (Ingrid), there were many volunteers who did romanticize and idealize their work. In Calcutta, the ways in which they might intervene in more global issues was not readily apparent: 'The problem is that things must change on a world scale, not just in small corners like Calcutta' (Ingrid). Another traveller who had done some volunteer work expressed some of the contradictions of this work when she complained: 'How can there be a people's revolution when they are continually treated to handouts from volunteers and aid workers?' (Elaine). There is a point to be made here about the role of NGOs as a stopgap anti-revolutionary and counter-revolutionary placebo.

The issues of international context and local conditions, of course, are questions of importance to the communist movement, and it is interesting that views held by some visitors and volunteer workers converged with the positions of the Indian communist parties on at least one point, and led to activity which addressed several of the themes discussed above. After reading newspaper reports and both CPI(M) and CPI(M-L) literature on the IMF and World Bank plans for the Indian economy, a small group of long-term travellers in Calcutta produced a critique of charity work which showed ways in which Western volunteer workers could take up activity in their home countries after their return from India (Some members of this grouping were not volunteers; some were working with Preger, one with Mother Teresa; one was an observer). Under the slogan 'Charity is not Enough – isn't it about time we started tackling the causes of poverty and not just the symptoms?', a leaflet was produced for travellers outlining what they might do to put pressure on Western banks to cancel the huge foreign debts that countries like India had been placed under, and on the basis of which the IMF and World Bank were directing the Indian economy. The leaflet quoted sections from pamphlets from the CPI(M) and CPI(M-L), and was based on literature from both parties and a booklet from the 'World Development Movement' which had started a campaign calling for cancellation of Third World debt.

Included in the leaflet – which was handed out to travellers in the Sudder Street area, as well as outside the Oberoi Grand – was a quotation from a CPI-ML publication outlining the Communist Party's criticisms of IMF–WB imperialism in India:

> Domination by imperialists has meant not only drain of wealth from India to foreign countries but they have also strangulated industrial growth. In league with their compradors–big bourgeoisie, they have dictated the level of production, technology used, and controlled technology upgrading and research. Their continuing sway has been ruining the national bourgeoisie. The Indian industries serve not the needs of the Indian people but secure maximum profits to imperialists and compradors. (CPI-ML Political Resolution of Party Congress, adopted 16 April 1992)

By identifying locations in Western countries where travellers could focus campaigns to force banks to cancel 'Third World debt' – even though this was only a part of the problems of Calcutta, and it was soon recognized that the call had to be to cancel not just the debt but the whole lending/dependence system – it seemed that this group of travellers had found a way to bring solidarity work away from charity, and charity support organizations, to something seen to be more substantial at 'home'. Whether the numbers of travellers that could trouble the banks – by cancellation of credit cards, by refusing to use travellers' cheques – was significant or not, this activity was articulated as an avenue for 'politicized' volunteers to take their politics 'home'. That cancellation of debt would not ultimately change the logic of the capitalist system was not considerered – the leaflet produced was, inevitably, the subject of a rooftop clinic meeting.

READING THE MODERN

Although only a percentage of travellers manage to shake off the anti-communist prejudice (which seems to be a correlate of a pro-charity sensibility) and bring politics home from their travels, in the final section of this chapter a more common connection with home can be explored. Even in the middle of the city Calcutta circulates back towards the West via writing, and a prominent part of traveller experience is mediated through its forms. Letters, for example, are important in terms of reminders and links with home, and are brought to the rooftop to be read. As a substitute for talk with parents, siblings, friends, and as a topic of conversation – 'I got four letters this week', etc. – they should not be ignored. Letters are a structuring experience in physical and emotional registers. Just getting to the Post Office to collect letters from home entails a crowded bus journey or a long walk through the centre of town, passing Lenin's statue, the famous rat-park (where vendors sell bread pieces for feeding the hundreds of rats who live in the corner of the Maidan), alongside the Great Eastern Hotel (where Kipling and Somerset Maugham wrote) and by the Writers' Building, the administrative centre of Bengal. In some ways this walk could provide a tour of the main 'mythic' characterizations of Calcutta: the rats to signify poverty, as Günter Grass might have it; the Great Eastern to remind us of the days of the Raj, and British illusions of glory; Lenin to indicate the promise of communism in Bengal; and the Writers' Building to ensure its demise through the impediments of a juggernaut bureaucracy.

Mail from home is a prize which makes exile less painful, which is a public marker of a connection outside the immediate clutter of Calcutta, a recognition that something called 'home' has some purchase on one's identity – an apparatus linking the traveller to a world outside Calcutta. The arrival of letters, since they are often few and far between, is almost cause for celebration for some travellers. Excitement is often publicly expressed, as if this connection to home must be emphasized through articulation within Calcutta, among the Modern Lodge population. News from home is shared, letters are sometimes read aloud in the dormitories, postcards are displayed above beds, and the non-arrival of letters is cause of a silent pain: jealousy. It is very much the case that the stamp of home, and the promise/reminder of a future return, is marked on the arrival of letters, just as the stamp on the passport is the marker of arrival from the home country. Letters 'in' serve a number of connections. 'All letters are like written voices, heard not remembered, whispered into your ear from afar' (Birgid). Some travellers write a lot of letters, and this aspect of connection to home has a more complex set of meanings. Both documentary and restorative, indicating presence away from home, but also keeping a space open in the memory of those who remain at home – the simple formula of this is the claim 'Remember me, I'm out here in Calcutta...'

Postcards achieve this most efficiently, and sometimes creatively. In addition to the curios travellers made into postcards (which I mentioned above) were: the top of a 'Taj Mahal brand' tea box, a candle packet from 'Raja Candles' and beer placemats from the 'Rambo Beer Bar'. Stamps and addresses were fixed to these – one series of eight different badly printed shots of Howrah bridge was sent as a narrative in parts, it being unclear as to whether the bridge or the printing was meant to represent Calcutta. In conventional accounts, the bridge comes to stand for Calcutta (it was used in the promotion shots for the *City of Joy* film), but there are more ways to read these cards. Naomi Schor quotes a postcard manual: 'Postcards have shown, and continue to show, it all' (Schor 1992: 203), but it would be well to recall Derrida's lesson that the unsealed or open face of a postcard is just that which makes it more likely to be encrypted with secrets (Derrida 1987: 185). Derrida also points out that the 'guardians of tradition, the professors, academics, and librarians, the doctors and authors of theses are terribly curious about correspondences' (Derrida 1987: 62).

Postcard curios and other incongruously collected images tell something of the offbeat orientation of some Modern Lodge travellers. As a pastiche of heterogeneous elements, Calcutta appeals to a sense of surreal humour. Newspaper headline clippings attached to postcards decry the Calcutta news: 'Two fatally wounded in ice-cream riot' and 'Last standing Calcutta traffic light collapses near hospital road'. A form of kaleidoscopic information overload is apparent. For one medical student on university holiday this became a 'melody of forms, besmirching pure categories in complicated and seemingly transgressive blends and blurs': a poetically overdetermined way of describing the spectacle. Michael, the volunteer who wrote this in a letter to Modern Lodge after returning to Melbourne, had said earlier that the best thing about Calcutta was the mixture of items for nostalgia. He was fascinated by 'sixties watches, fifties films, forties motorcycles and cars', and a host of other icons of world culture somehow jumbled together without care for their temporal location.[9]

Yet fifties movies and forties cars don't seem as important for the Indian experience of some travellers as the sixties drugs which prevail in some sections of the banana-pancake trail. Calcutta itself was described by guesthouse rooftop smoker James as 'an LSD trip without the drugs'. Such confused modes of thinking (or lack thereof) were responsible for numerous ridiculous perceptions of India. Gita Mehta's book *Karma Cola*, on the hippie-spiritual exploration of India still proves relevant when one considers the activities of a great many of the middle-class Western travellers on the circuit. In Calcutta, the 'drug scene' is perhaps a little less visible than it is in other parts, possibly because the hashish available on the street is often inferior to that available elsewhere, and because the 'quality' consumable drug in the area is heroin, with which Western users are usually more discreet. Drug use and a kind of wide-eyed spiritual quest often go together among budget travellers in India, and while the west coast and the far north – places like Pushkar, Jaisalmer and Manali – are among the most popular locations for 'heads', Calcutta is not without a number of them. An attempt at a serious interview with Gabby, a very stoned traveller in a coffee shop, was abandoned in laughter – by all present – when India was described as 'a spiritual Disneyland', and as being 'like a brontosaurus' because it was 'thin at one end, Kashmir, fat in the middle, Bombay to Calcutta, and thin again at the other end, Madras'. A serious study of this discourse might nevertheless find some threads of coherence and continuity among the representations of such travellers. The incorporation of aspects of Indian philosophical and spiritual concepts into traveller understandings (some would insist that these are misunderstandings) is a recurrent theme.

The letters and postcards of travellers can serve an exhibitory function which might be best described by the rather tacky intent of the message 'Having a great time, wish you were here', which is associated with the postcard. The 'wish you were here' phrase also works as an authority claim which, as much as the foreign postmark, indicates to friends and relatives that the traveller has been, or is currently at, some – usually picaresque – location. The scenes on the front of the postcard may have little immediate reference to the experiences of the writer, whereas the formula messages of the cardboard side may be more resonant with the common loneliness of the traveller. Not all travel is about meeting people, laughing, sunsets and romance. The glossy façade of tourism shows nothing of the psychology of absence and displacement which is also a part of foreign travel – the loneliness and alienation of the traveller (singular) is as much a part of the scene as the happiness of the travellers (plural).

From a postcard:

> We visitors will never know Calcutta; and even this is not saying much; it hardly distinguishes the city from any other on the travellers' trail. We each make a subjective map, negotiate imaginary paths across an unknown whole. What? Where? Who? There are more than 20 million answers for Calcutta – home of the world. It is not the surprise that everything said about Calcutta is interpretation which should occupy you, but rather be surprised that Calcutta

could be approached any other way. It is not news to find that the city floats
on a swamp of metaphor – the drains overflow. (postmarked 1988, Calcutta)

If writing postcards and letters, and chatting on the roof of the Modern,
are part of the production of traveller identity in Calcutta, then there is
also good reason to consider reading as a metaphor for Calcutta too.
This anticipates the next chapter by noting that among those material
objects that travellers accumulate in Calcutta, as elsewhere, books have
great significance. Collecting books, reading, the 'pleasures of the text'
(in social science folklore this means Malinowski reading Conrad in his
tent, and Kurz up-river making notes in the margins of *An Inquiry into
Some Points of Seamanship*), is a part of travel. Sudder Street and Free
School Street have a number of bookstores frequented by backpackers,
and a regular trade in second-hand novels sustains some of these. Among
travellers, too, there is an informal exchange, and one North American
traveller was somewhat successful in operating a book exchange out of
cardboard boxes in one of the rooms of Modern Lodge. But, College
Street and its hundreds of bookstores is the booklovers' tourist attraction by far. Crowded into a small block adjacent to Calcutta University
and surrounding the Indian Coffee House, bookstores spill their wares
out onto the streets. The abundance and variety of books cannot be
adequately described – from medical texts to political pamphlets, and
including hundreds of volumes not readily available outside Calcutta or
India. College Street as book utopia is rivalled only by the Book Fair,
of many hundreds of stalls, held in the Maidan every February. The
Modern Lodge office also has its own traveller book exchange full of
dog-eared novels and esoteric texts.

Travel literature is readily purchased in the various bookshops
available to backpackers, and this material comprises a considerable
percentage of backpacker reading matter. Much can be learnt from
such material, and not just about India: travelling tales may have always,
and everywhere, been accorded a certain status – sometimes more,
sometimes less respected as a way of knowing the world.

The visitor to India is influenced by a range of writings as diverse as
those of Eric Newby (*Slowly Down the Ganges*), Allen Ginsberg (*Indian
Journals*), Somerset Maugham (*The Razor's Edge*), and Vikram Seth (*From
Heaven's Lake*).[10] Taking into account more critical evaluations of travellers in India, such as texts by Gita Mehta (*Karma Cola*), and David
Foster (*Plumbum*) to take an Australian example, it remains true that, in
a very haphazard way, a range of 'identities' are made available through
these texts from which travellers can draw 'role models'. There can be

no doubt that, in contemporary 'travel literature', travel operates in powerful ways to shape identities, experience and the 'self' of the traveller, as well as to influence – even determine – what a traveller can 'know'. Guidebooks and travel narratives make up one of the most widely read 'minor literatures' of capitalist culture. Less authoritative in the institutions than sociology or anthropology, yet with great general authority in popular culture, this diverse category of knowledge, with all its locations, cultures, languages and peoples, deserves closer analysis. The processes are never simple, and it would not do to consign traveller identity to texts, adding a few guidebooks and films, since identity formation – however much it may be constituted in an abstracted literary/media or semiotic zone under contemporary capitalism – is always an amalgam of many things. Rooftop critical evaluations intercede. What can be done is to point to some of the motifs, trends and dominant themes, which operate in the various formations of traveller identity found in books. This chapter has attempted to do this with regard to a discrete set of travellers in a discrete time and place, although any comprehensive evaluation of the various 'technologies' of identity formation in such a zone already seems too complicated a task. There can be no attempt, beyond the obvious generalities, to prescribe easy explanatory codes for these wider matters. The next chapter attempts nothing more than this by looking more closely at the textual 'sources' – Günter Grass's *Show Your Tongue*, Dominique Lapierre's *The City of Joy*, travel guides, tourist literature and official publications – that contribute to the formation of traveller news of Calcutta.

CODA: ILLUSIONS

'For better or worse, Calcutta will remain a symbol of the future' (Roland). Some travellers insisted that 'Calcutta was not India' (Fiona). But neither could it be easily imaged as India's future, because its kaleidoscope included a historical nightmare known as the 'black hole'. Others indicated that Calcutta was simply exaggerated India, an idea that was also held by those who had not come:

> 'When I told people at home I was going to India, they looked at me in disbelief, and told me of the horrors there. When they found out I was going to be in Calcutta for a month they were aghast. They get these ideas from TV.' (Amy)
>
> 'It is an experimental place – take mud, people, cows, buildings and heat and stir it all up with the books of Marx and statues of Lenin .'(Peter)

As a cipher Calcutta is always about to dematerialize in traveller talk – where whole cities are evaluated and references have disappeared in the haze, having become invisible, it is as if they were never there. Perhaps Calcutta vanished for us as soon as a collection of its descriptions began. In another version of the city, it is not a black hole, but a matter of intensities of light and sound, where the locations are film sets and voicebox – image drifts and audio-circuits, subways and vistas, a landscape full of signatures and gossip, postponed and delayed, and relayed throughout the looping media circuits of an ideological Calcutta that has shifted from its geographical moorings. This is Calcutta as a universal cipher – you can never leave the city, the train never pulls out of Howrah, you are stuck at Sealdah, an interminable journey which recurs and recurs.

NOTES

1. The Modern was awash with the red flags of the Centre for Indian Trade Unions (CITU) and hand-painted slogans which read 'Immediately settle the workers' charter of demand'. The management had made some improvements to workers' conditions, and wages were doubled (which was still not much), but while this had been accepted for a period, there was a further strike late in 1992, and by early 1993 the Modern had closed for a long period before being sold. During the last months of the strike some volunteers made a placard which read 'Immediately settle the tourists' charter of demand'! – a moment of harmless irony in the eyes of travellers, but one which, for obvious reasons, was not approved of by the workers, nor by the hotel management. In 1994 the Modern was operating with almost entirely new staff, but pretty much the same business-as-usual conditions. In 1995 and 1996 the dormitories were closed, but Preger clinic volunteers still filled many of the rooms.

2. Koepping suggests that a trickster redeems all through a winking self-deprecation like this; a complicity whereby the audience identifies itself in the figure of the jester who is as wise as a ruler, but remains also a fool (Koepping 1989).

3. Several interesting volumes appeared to coincide with the tercentenary commemoration of Job Charnock's arrival on the site of present-day Calcutta in 1690. A short review essay by Partho Datta (1992) entitled 'Celebrating Calcutta' covers the most readily available publications. The excellence of this review is my excuse for not listing background literature here, and this is also my excuse for leaving the extensive material on tourism and representation which is also relevant to this project to Malcolm Crick's bibliographical review in *Chai* (1988), his *Social Analysis* article (1985), and his book (Crick 1994). Crick's work on guesthouses in Kandy, Sri Lanka, also offers the model for this presentation of life in the Modern Lodge. I read an early draft of his book while I was at the Modern in 1990.

4. Grass visited the city for six months in 1987, amid some controversy. During a Calcutta seminar he declared: 'God shat, and there was Calcutta.' An almost audible tension was only somewhat covered by his quick addition: 'But when God shat bricks, there was Frankfurt.' Grass produced a book of sketches and stories soon after his visit (Grass 1989), which I consider in Chapter 3.

5. Mother Teresa is the international sign of poverty in Calcutta. Any consideration

of the effects of this sign would displace the specifics I want to explore here with regard to Modern Lodge, Preger volunteers, backpackers and representational technologies. A basic biographical study of Mother Teresa is that of Navin Chawla (1992). A not quite so sycophantic portrait can be found in a short essay by Christopher Hitchens (1992), where 'M.T.' is seen in a less than charitable light: leading an anti-abortion campaign – 'propaganda for the Vatican's heinous policy of compelling the faithful to breed, and of denying where it can the right of non-believers to get hold of birth control'; 'as a kind of paid confessor to the Duvalier gang' in Haiti; laying a wreath on the tomb of Enver Hoxha in her country of birth, Albania; and, as reported in the PBS documentary 'Other People's Money', accepting millions of dollars and use of a company plane from businessmen implicated in the US savings and loans rip-off. Hitchens described M.T. as a 'hellbat', a 'dangerous sinister person', a 'leathery old saint' and the 'ghoul of Calcutta' (Hitchens 1992: 474). Hitchens made this the subject of a half-hour polemical television show and a thin book in 1994–5, in which he claimed to be the first to dare criticism of 'Mother' (though there are some questions to be raised about his debt to Aroup Chatterjee, who also has a study of Mother planned). There have been other critics. To select only one from Calcutta, what comes first to hand is most appropriate for this study: Jack Preger's position on Mother T directs concern towards the Calcutta Corporation which tolerates her presence in the city. My view is that this is somewhat misplaced and I would want to suggest that it suits wider international interests to have Mother Teresa perform the function of symbol of human virtue. Nevertheless, Preger's analysis comes close:

> it suits the Corporation of Calcutta to have a place like Kalighat [Mother T's 'home for the destitute and dying'], where they can dump many of their destitutes. Many will die there and many will die unnecessarily. Nobody in Mother Teresa's order would ever dream of turning round and saying, 'My God, why don't they do something about it, why don't they build some homes or start some factories?' – they never say that – they just say how beautifully he or she died. Which is all nonsense, quite apart from being socially regressive. What actually happens is that when people die they get this contraction of the face muscles called *risus sardonicus* – this sardonic bitter smile ... It's this smile that is misinterpreted by Mother Teresa and her novices as some kind of proof that these poor, wretched people were somehow happy when they died. (Preger in Josephs 1991: 142).

6. Ashis Nandy's discussion of secularism in India entails different connotations to the meanings I have in mind here, see Nandy (1985), and Miller (1992) for an excellent commentary on Nandy's work.

7. Alphabet soup?! CPI = Communist Party of India; CPI(M) = Communist Party of India – Marxist, the dominant partner in the ruling West Bengal Left Front coalition; CPI(M-L) = Communist Party of India – Marxist-Leninist, often called 'Naxals' after the armed uprisings which began in the late 1960s in Naxalbari in West Bengal and now numbering several separate groups (People's War Group, Maoist Communist Centre, etc.), the CPI (ML) group most often referred to here is TND = Towards New Democracy; there are various Marxist trade-union and student groups affiliated to any of the above party organizations. And most of these groups produce various pamphlets and papers which are sometimes read by budget travellers and visitors to Sudder Street.

8. I realize that this whole discussion begs the question of what communism is. So many volumes have been devoted to tedious micro-debate over definitions that I want to steer clear of the whole thing with this glaring essentialism. For what it's worth, the versions of communism that appeal in my reading are derived from CPI

(M-L) TND and CPI (M) literature in Calcutta, the texts of Marx, Lenin, Mao, Gramsci, Adorno and Lukács, and the Communist Students group in Australia (especially Angie, Ben, Cass, Hazel, Marcus and Andrew), and, as a counter to any dogmatic orthodoxy, occasional dips into the work of Antonio Negri (1988, 1991) leavened with Bataille (1976/1991). The most readily available introduction to Negri was important for this book in its early stages – the pocket-sized (traveller edition?) correspondence between that author and Félix Guattari, called *Communists Like Us* (1990). For Bataille, see *The Accursed Share*, vols 1–3. What a terrible confession it is to leave this issue in such disarray, but Communism is still to be defined, and it is not necessarily the same as rule by communists.

9. Said refers to 'a new relationship with the past based on pastiche and nostalgia, a new and eclectic randomness in the cultural artefact, a reorganisation of space, and characteristics of multinational capital' (Said 1993: 392) as being the features of the postmodern. To this Said would add a Jameson-like addendum to capture a 'phenomenally incorporative capacity, which makes it possible for anyone in fact to say anything at all, but everything is processed either towards the dominant mainstream or out to the margins' (Said 1993: 392) – again his margin is undifferentiated.

10. Seth's *From Heaven's Lake* (1983) is a tale of travels in Tibet, but it is much more widely read in India since Tibet is largely closed to tourism under the Chinese annexation. His 1992 effort *A Suitable Boy* has enlarged his fame (and wallet) well beyond the traveller market.

WRITING CALCUTTA:

TRAVELLING WITH LÉVI-STRAUSS

AND GÜNTER GRASS

The next chapters look at more formal technologies of representation, such as the book, the map and the camera. Inevitably such technologies are bound up with the themes that have already been discussed. While Jonathan Crary may note that 'codified and normalised ... systems of visual consumption' (Crary 1990: 18) might not share a singular or continuous evolutionary history (Crary 1990: 26), I think the ways in which a 'politics of poverty' in representations of Calcutta can be *re*hearsed both through the casual discourse of the travellers in the first sections and the staid tomes and flat prints of those that now follow means that it is neither possible nor desirable to demarcate strictly between the machines which produce, and consume, the rumour of the city. It is no accident that the words of travellers continue to inter-ject throughout these pages on more formal enframing devices.

DEMARCATIONS

In the preface to *The Intimate Enemy*, Ashis Nandy suggested that 'the concept of the modern West' had been generalized 'from a geographical and temporal entity to a psychological one' (Nandy 1983: xi). The complexities of this statement are many; the argument of the book invokes the idea that the 'West' has been internalized in India, to a degree, incompletely. The 'West' is the intimate enemy of the title, but the intellect itself is also this enemy, the self too. As a category of mind, the geography of the West fragments into a myriad of locations, representations, citations. These are, of course, hugely homogenizing categories – India, West, mind, spaces, representation – and Nandy, too, would abandon them, after he has used them to make his points, to write his 'alternative myths', about India. In a declaration which can be read in several ways, Nandy claims that India is not the non-West; it is, rather, India, since the non-West is a construction of the West, at least in part (Nandy 1983: xii). I think this provides a usefully compacted way to get into a discussion of what has been written about the Western city of Calcutta: its historical records, its promotional literature, its fiction and 'fact', which all might share this ambiguous schema.

Much has been written on Calcutta. A city of books – far too many to survey. What I want to do here is look at how several prominent Western visitors to the city have written about their experience. This chapter looks most closely at the famous visitors; such as Claude Lévi-Strauss, Günter Grass and Dominique Lapierre, each of whom came to Calcutta from Europe, from 'the West'. Visitors to Calcutta who bring their own city with them as a category of mind. I will place these writings alongside more populist writings on the city such as the very 'Western' travel guide and 'survival kit' from Lonely Planet, and some of the promotional writings of the Bengali government.

I can try again to describe the city: if Nandy's formula is to be taken as a starting point, Calcutta, then, will also not be the non-West, but Calcutta. It is a city intimate with the West, and yet oppositional to it. Calcutta is in some ways the least 'Western' of all cities. Not only is it on the east coast of India, its status as the antithesis of 'Western' cities is inscribed everywhere (usually under the sign of poverty or overcrowding); it is also considered by some in India to be more resistant to 'Westernization' (see Srinivas 1962) than any of the other major Indian cities: Madras, Delhi, Bombay. It was said to be the most glorious city of Empire, and it was – as so many have repeated – Kipling's 'city of dreadful night'. It can be twinned with the rise of industrial capitalism and that most Western of cities, Manchester – and yet antagonistically so, since the Manchester mills were the downfall of Bengali weavers – just as it is opposed to the paradigm of modern cities, New York, despite being compared to it as the image of New York's future (Theroux 1991: 109). It was the 'centre' of British rule of India until 1911 (when the capital was moved to Delhi), it was the port through which flowed the untold wealth that the East India Company extracted from the subcontinent; it was the font of the British Raj. If the history of the last three hundred years were to be written from outside Europe, Calcutta's importance would possibly eclipse that of London. It is also in Calcutta that the Indian nationalist movement has its origins: arguably, then, the independence of so many other colonies can be traced to this place. It is said by many to have been a

British city, it was designed by British architects, the East India Company and Raj officials – yet, despite common opinion that it was British-built, the city was very much a product of Indian labour, built by Indians who lived and worked there, under the Raj and after, and who were always in the numerical majority. Since there can be disputes over its material construction, it should not be thought unusual that representation also becomes an issue.

In a recent review it was noted that 'books on Calcutta could at least fill a few library shelves even though most of these only serve antiquarian interest' (Datta 1992: 87). It seems there is something of a gap when it comes to studies of contemporary Calcutta – in any case, in English – and the prevailing historical circumspection could only be enhanced by the Calcutta 300 commemoration volumes which, as Datta points out, were mostly old stuff. Contemporary Calcutta, however, is often captured in essay collections, of varied quality – some very good – and in occasional monographs, photo albums and works of fiction. What I want to do now is not so much to survey the archive of written Calcutta as to examine the ways in which travellers read their path into the city. This might mean that I will not so much look at books *on* Calcutta, but must take up the task of analysis of the work of visitors *to* Calcutta who, though perhaps mentioning Calcutta, and in some cases devoting whole books to Calcutta, have written primarily *on* themselves.[1]

CLAUDE LÉVI-STRAUSS

Halfway through *Tristes Tropiques*, Lévi-Strauss describes his 1950 visit to Calcutta. He arrived at Calcutta airport mid-century amid a torrential downpour, and was quickly whisked away to his hotel. From here he describes the city. Lévi-Strauss's contribution to scholarship can hardly be questioned, but for all the erudition and learning of his other writings, his impressions of Calcutta are disappointing. In a few brief pages he presents the city in ways which will be continually repeated in the travel literature and popular histories I want to discuss in this chapter. A rather long but 'representative' passage illustrates all the major themes:

> we are accustomed to associate our highest values, both material and spiritual, with urban life. But the large towns of India are slum areas. What we are ashamed of as if it were a disgrace, and regard as a kind of leprosy, is, in India, the urban phenomenon, reduced to its ultimate expression: the herding together of individuals whose only reason for living is to herd together in millions, whatever the conditions of life may be.[2] Filth, chaos, promiscuity,

congestion; ruins, huts, mud, dirt; dung, urine, pus, humours, secretions and running sores: all the things against which we expect urban life to give us organised protection, all the things we hate and guard against at such great cost, all these by-products of cohabitation do not set any limitation on it in India. They are more like a natural environment which the Indian town needs to prosper. To every individual, any street, footpath or alley affords a home, where he can sit, sleep, and even pick up his food straight from the glutinous filth.... Every time I emerged from my hotel in Calcutta, which was besieged by cows and had vultures perched on its window-sills, I became the central figure in a ballet which would have seemed funny to me, had it not been so pathetic. The various accomplished performers made their entries in turn: a shoeblack flung himself at my feet; a small boy rushed up to me, whining 'One anna, Papa, one anna!' [an anna is a small coin; this theme again] a cripple displayed his stumps.... And then there were a whole host of minor players: men who touted for rickshaws, gharries and taxis. There were as many vehicles as one could possibly want, only a yard or two away, waiting in line by the pavement.... Not to mention the multitude of merchants, shopkeepers and street-hawkers, to whom one's advent brought a promise of Paradise, since one was perhaps going to buy something from them...

A single obsession, hunger, prompts this despairing behaviour; it is the same obsession which drives the country-dwellers into the cities and has caused Calcutta's population to leap from two to five millions in the space of a few years; it crowds refugees into stations, although they cannot afford to board the trains, and as one passes through at night, one can see them sleeping on the platforms, wrapped in the white cotton fabric which today is their garment but tomorrow will be their shroud; it accounts for the tragic intensity in the beggar's gaze as his eyes meet yours through the metal bars of the first-class compartment, which have been put there – like the armed soldier squatting on the footboard – to protect you from the mute supplication of a single individual, who could easily be transformed into a howling mob if, by allowing your compassion to overcome your prudence, you gave the doomed creatures some hope of charity. (Lévi-Strauss 1955/1973: 134-5)

This is, I think, the lowest point of Lévi-Strauss's work. While he may describe what he sees, his failure to consider the context, to account for his own blind presumption, his Eurocentric and arrogant 'horror', his all-too-swift consignment of suffering people to a hopeless 'doom', is enough to condemn him. Even allowing for the special circumstances of Calcutta so soon after partition, this description is, tragically, a representative example of those which continue to be promulgated by Western visitors at the present time. In a few short paragraphs, the reductive gaze of Lévi-Strauss, from his hotel balcony and first-class carriage, condemns the whole city as a slum, as a kind of generalized leprosy, as chaos; human beings are characterized as a meaningless herd of millions; these 'millions' eat, sleep and live amongst filth; whining for a spare coin, nurtured only with dreams of Paradise (if the anthropologist buys some trinket) or the forlorn 'hope of charity'. All these are exaggerations, embellishments, hyperbole and fabrication. The work of visitors who invent falsehoods and mythology under a reeling personal and cultural disorientation contrives to gloss such concoctions as 'reality' – as they have witnessed it with their own eyes – rather than as the perspectival apparitions they must, in the circumstances, be.

In a short essay after a visit to Moscow, Jacques Derrida identifies two 'risks' of travelogues: 'The first is that of selectivity', and he describes a '*récit raisonné*' as a 'narrative that, more than others, filters or sifts out the supposedly significant features – and thus begins to censor' (Derrida 1993c: 197-8); and the second stems from the first: '*raisonner* also signifies, in this case, to rationalise ... active overinterpretation' (Derrida 1993c: 198). These two risks of perspective and ordering selection are the themes of this work which take up Derrida's call (his is not the only call of this sort) for a 'systematic reflection on the relations between tourism and political analysis' at a time when tourism has become highly 'organized'. Derrida writes – with Walter Benjamin in mind, but also perhaps Lévi-Strauss – that such an analysis 'would have to allow a particular place to the intellectual tourist (writer or academic) who thinks he or she can, in order to make them public, translate his or her "travel impressions" into a political diagnostic' (Derrida 1993c: 215). The politics of travel literature remains to be unpacked.

CONTESTED REPRESENTATIONS

'The black hole idea has a squalor-ridden ring to it that sends shivers down the spine of the most intrepid of travellers.' (Fiona)

Travel literature is possibly the most important source of information about Calcutta for all the travellers I met. There is no doubt that travel guides are influential, although the entries in guides like that of Lonely Planet – *India: A Travel Survival Kit* – are mostly glossed from other texts like Geoffrey Moorhouse's *Calcutta: The City Revealed* (1971), a book which is itself cobbled together from less well known sources which complement the author's two short visits (1983 introduction). If the Lonely Planet says that Calcutta has 'become an international urban horror story' (Wheeler 1987: 311), then is it a confirmation to hear this repeated in the cafés and guesthouses frequented by tourists? Also worthy of note are the ways in which highly evaluative opinions about the city are circulated by these texts throughout the world. Moorhouse senses some of this, even as he contributes his share of 'truth' to the 'conventional rumour of Calcutta' (Moorhouse 1971: 20):

> The truth is that almost everything popularly associated with Calcutta is highly unpleasant and sometimes very nasty indeed. It is bracketed in the Western mind with distant rumours of appalling disaster, riot and degradation. The one incident in its history with which every schoolchild has always been familiar has been called the Black Hole of Calcutta, and nobody who knows the place can ever have been surprised to learn that one of the most vicious weapons ever devised by man, the Dum Dum bullet, was invented and produced in a small arms factory within a rifle shot of that splendid new airport. The very name Calcutta is derived from a symbol of fear and evil. (Moorhouse 1971: 19)

Moorhouse later retells the received British version of the story of the Black Hole with an added proviso that 'there is reason to believe that some of it is fabrication' (Moorhouse 1971: 45), although he does not elaborate upon these reasons. Since the story of the Black Hole must be told here as well, it can be in a critical version: Marx calls the incident a 'sham scandal' (Marx 1947: 81). In an extensive collection of notes made on Indian history, Marx comments that on the evening of 21 June 1756, after the Governor of Calcutta had ignored the order of Subadar Suraj-ud-daula to 'raze all British fortifications' in the city:

> Suraj came down on Calcutta in force ... fort stormed, garrison taken prisoners, Suraj gave orders that all the captives should be kept in safety till the morning; but the 146 men (accidentally, it seems) were crushed into a room 20 feet square and with but one small window; next morning (as Holwell himself tells the story), only 23 were still alive; they were allowed to sail down the Hooghly. It was 'the Black Hole of Calcutta', over which *the English hypocrites have been making so much sham scandal to this day*. Suraj-ud-daula returned to Murshidabad; Bengal now completely and effectually cleared of the English intruders. (Marx 1947: 81; emphasis added)

Marx also reports on the subsequent retaliation against and defeat of Suraj-ud-daula by Lord Clive ('that Great Robber', as he calls him elsewhere [Marx 1853/1978: 86]), and Clive's 1774 suicide after his 'cruel persecution' by the directors of the East India Company (Marx 1947: 88). Not long after Moorhouse produced *Calcutta: The City Revealed*, Iris MacFarlane brought out her study, *The Black Hole, or The Makings of a Legend* (1975), in which she contested the received version of the event and argued that the importance of 'the non-event of the Black Hole of Calcutta' (MacFarlane 1975: 20) is 'only in the use to which it could be put afterwards' (MacFarlane 1975: 19). Six months after the alleged event only a single report had emerged, and this in the context of a new British campaign. Certainly we can understand that the manufacture of an atrocity against British authority could be used to justify retaliation, and the British response to their ousting from Calcutta – Clive's attack known as the Battle of Plassey – instituted what even Macauley had to call 'a reign of terror' (MacFarlane 1975: 249). That this image continues to exert its influences today requires more careful analysis than Moorhouse can provide. His uncritical repetition of the received British version is typical. While he discusses the Dum Dum bullet in his intro-duction, it takes a further sixty pages before he bothers to note that the vicious bullet was invented by a *British* captain to kill Afridi tribesmen (1971: 80). Moorhouse's quick etymological history of Calcutta evokes Kali – as always, total anathema to British sentiment: 'She is Kali the Terrible and she is propitiated with daily sacrifice, as well as with flowers. When the Thugs strangled a traveller, they knotted in one corner of the handkerchief a silver coin consecrated to Kali, to give them a better grip' (Moorhouse 1971: 20) (does he offer this as advice on how to deal with travellers, perhaps? or journalists?). It is Moorhouse, not Marx, who is recycled in the Lonely Planet guide.

What kind of Calcutta is it that the travel guide promotes, when it gives the directions to Job Charnok's mausoleum and the site of the Black Hole? The repetition of given perspectives from popular histories provide a shorthand of selected highlights of a glorious past which partici-pates in the sanitization of history. Travel guides today remain overly generous to the British Raj and relatively silent on the tragedy of partition, the politics of weaving, or the terrible famines and the failure of the British administration to respond to them. Nothing, either, of the gains of contemporary Calcutta – instead, only the sensations of the most extreme Naxalite actions.[3] Travel guides actively reinforce the idealized viewpoint of the Raj for visitors, by encouraging site-seeing of an explicitly ideo-archaeological kind. Travellers are provided with enough clues to find a rather insignificant old plaque near the Post Office which marks the site of the alleged Black Hole. Similarly, the obscurities of the earliest European gravestone and the burial place of Charnok are recorded, but no information directs the visitor to see the statue of Congress and wartime leader Netaji Subhas Chandra Bose, or that of Lenin standing by Chowringhee. Only the glories of the Raj, and eccentricities like the Marble Palace, are made the subject of these historico-treasure hunts. The sightseeing activities of travellers who follow the advocations of these guides (West Bengal Government Publications do seem less un-even) give spectacular support to a sham version of Calcutta's history.

Histories of the British Raj available to visitors are sanitized, despite the bleak imagery of Kipling, colonial wars, and malarial infestation. The British Raj is remembered, and its histories are written, in terms of grand durbahs, elephant hunts, Victoria memorials and the romance, *Stürm und Drang*, of Empire. This kind of history has been challenged many times, and yet the stereotypes and myths, like some fabulously monstrous Sunderbans tiger, keep rearing their ugly heads. Although they are less readily available in hotel and backpacker bookstores, it is nevertheless possible that attentive visitors can find local texts. Global and commercial circulation systems conspire to make such texts less popular than Moorhouse, yet when they are sought out it is revealing that the productions of the Calcutta administration express a guarded optimism:

> Calcutta is the city that leaves no-one indifferent.... A gigantic melange of mood and style, culture and politics, industry and commerce.... There is so much to see in this *apparently* confused and incredible city. Turn where you will and a thousand images assail the eye. A million people from every corner of India stream across the massive Howrah bridge. (Promotional Pamphlet 1992; original emphasis)

> The city of Calcutta conjures up images of a sprawling urban conglomerate, bursting at the seams with population overload, and with basic civic amenities under severe strain. It would, however, be less than fair to this 300 year old city if one were to take this sort of cursory view without seeking to appreciate the long train of events leading to the present state of affairs. To probe the historical roots of the city's maladies, one needs to hark back to the days of colonial rule whose legacy continues to burden Calcutta even today (Government of West Bengal 1991: 111)

West Bengal Chief Minister Jyoti Basu (CPI-M), writes in a Department of Tourism brochure that Calcutta 'requires today a lot of renewal', yet he invites tourists from other states and abroad to visit this 'great city noted for its social interactions, political struggles, cultural activities and progressive movements' (Basu 1985). His position as leader of a Marxist party currently introducing privatization and capitalization may add a certain irony here as he continues with epithets like 'great metropolis', 'profoundly attractive despite its limitations and inadequacies', and 'always alive and alert'. So that Calcutta is bound up with all 'our hopes and aspirations, struggles and tensions ... experience tells us that this city casts a deep impact on all tourists because of its tremendous vitality' (Basu 1985). Equally evocative, and now gendered, evaluations are offered from the Professor of Economics at Calcutta University:

The afflictions Calcutta has suffered since independence are of gigantic proportions.... She [sic] made no exception when hordes of uprooted people from East Pakistan flocked to her to strain her miserably meagre resources. With no attention, no sympathy forthcoming from anywhere, she absorbed them.... But that was no end. She was in for further deprivation and humiliation. Her desperate appeals, particularly in recent years, for resources and concern from the nation went unheeded, occasion after occasion. She met the challenges and indignities by scaling newer heights of forbearance and she is still building.... There are straws in the wind to indicate better days ahead, there need not be any further concern about a declining hinterland.... State domestic product touched a growth rate of 7.5% in 1988-89.... Thus there is an excellent possibility of a significant generation of employment.... Calcutta can now set off on a fresh note. (Roy 1991: 109–11)

This optimism, however, can be tempered; again from the promotional pamphlet we can read: 'No logic of history or geography has ever applied to Calcutta. Its charm and fascination defy analysis' (Promotional Pamphlet 1992).

Defiantly, then, more analytical observers can recognize contemporary dilemmas and historical and geographical causes, while looking at a wider context:

Historically, Calcutta, a colonial metropolis, has been an impoverishing city rather than an enriching one. The role of Calcutta has been that of impoverishing the countryside and of fattening itself at the latter's expense. In the seventeenth and eighteenth centuries, the East India Company, and in the nineteenth century its successor the British Government, exploited the whole of eastern India with Calcutta as its suction base ... while one thinks of the problems of Calcutta, the more fundamental problem is one of resuscitating rural West Bengal, Bihar, Orissa and Assam. (Mitra 1990: 59)

Mitra contextualizes images of Calcutta as the site from which the wealth and riches of India were plundered and exported to Europe. As I have already signalled, the point of my work is to examine how available literature and the experiences of tourists doing volunteer work in the city fit into this zone. In contrast to Mitra's less widely available views, the significance of the various glossed 'generous' histories of the Raj – as consumed by tourists – should not be underestimated.

LAPIERRE'S CITY OF JOY

A prominent example of the way a sanitized history of the British Raj circulates is the success of Lapierre and Collins's book *Freedom at Midnight* (1976). This text is generally accepted among Indian historians as overstating – to say the least – the heroic deeds of pukka British officers and the 'indomitable' and charismatic Viceroy Louis Mountbatten. The book is explosively sensational and makes much of Mountbatten's efforts to oversee a smooth transition from colony to independent nation. The book does not detail Mountbatten's terrible failure in this, preferring instead to hint at sexual liaisons between Congress leaders and Edwina Mountbatten, the Viceroy's wife. Across India travellers read this as the most convenient English, German or French narration of the Independence period. Another Lapierre blockbuster is among those that have caused great concern in Calcutta in recent years. In *The City of Joy*, the French author further lionizes the British Raj when he manages to describe Calcutta as an 'area of political exoduses and religious wars such as no other' (Lapierre 1985: 31) and of dreadful famines, partition, and war, without mentioning the responsibilities of the British in these matters.

Lapierre begins by calling Calcutta a 'mirage city'; it is 'one of the biggest urban disasters in the world – a city consumed with decay' (Lapierre 1985: 31). He does not mention the British until after he has described the:

> crumbling facades, tottering roofs and walls eaten up with tropical vegetation … some neighbourhoods looked as if they had been bombed. A rash of posters, publicity and political slogans, and advertisement billboards painted on the walls.… In the absence of adequate refuse collection service, eighteen hundred tons of refuse accumulated daily in the streets, attracting a host of flies, mosquitoes, rats, cockroaches and other creatures. In summer the proliferation of filth brought with it the risk of epidemics. Not so very long ago it was still a common occurrence for people to die of cholera, hepatitis, encephalitis, typhoid and rabies.… In short, Calcutta was a dying city. (Lapierre 1985: 32)

Having weighed all that garbage (eighteen hundred tons – how did he weigh it?), and after he has prepared his list of rodents and diseases, Lapierre comes to the contrasted British Raj period, where he can eulogize the 'prestigious past' of this metropolis. The discord with Bengali writings on Calcutta could not be more obvious. The tone – even when it mouths obligatory critical facts – is the stuff of heraldry:

> until the departure of its last British governor on August 15, 1947, Calcutta, more than any other city in the world, had epitomized the imperial dream of the white man's domination of the globe. For nearly two and a half centuries it had been the capital of the British Indian Empire. It was from here that until 1912 its governors-general and viceroys had imposed their authority on

a country with a population greater than that of the United States of America today [why this comparison?]. Calcutta's avenues had witnessed the passing of just as many parading troops and as many high society ladies in panquins or barouches as the Champs-Elysées of Paris or London Mall ... George V and Queen Mary had processed in a gold-studded carriage between two rows of Highlanders in Scottish kilts and white spats ... [and on and on...] (Lapierre 1985: 33–4)

Although familiarity with the volume among expatriates and budget travellers in the late 1980s was significant, and despite these glorious passages, Lapierre's book has not had a good press within Calcutta.[4] In the absence of any other easily accessible recent texts on the city for tourists, Lapierre's popularity among tourist-market book traders was greater than anywhere else, and in the Sudder Street area copies could often be seen in the hands of newly arrived visitors. Beyond the tourist 'ghetto' little good was said about it. Jack Preger wrote a critical review, as did Jesuit film-school head Gaston Roberge; both Europeans condemned the author for cheap sentimentalism, misplaced emphasis and glaring errors of fact. Bengali critics were even less generous, and popular opinion came down firmly against the book when even the Pilkhana residents, about whom Lapierre had written, refused an offer of part of the royalties from sales. Tempest explained that 'the governing board of the main community organisation in Pilkhana', which Lapierre renamed City of Joy for his book, 'unanimously rejected a donation of nearly $400,000 from the author on the grounds that the book was an "exploitation of poor people"' (Tempest 1987: 19). Despite this, the book remains in print, is available in bookstores throughout the world – sales boosted by the film version – and in general can be said to be one of the best known Western texts on the city.

Not every traveller accepts the 'veracities' of the text. One Modern Lodge resident commented on Lapierre's book: 'Every tourist is reading *City of Joy*. It's so stupid and romanticized, and next they are going to make a blockbuster film here of it. Who will profit from that? Western cinema chains and video stores mostly, and all to reinforce the stereotypes of poverty' (Adrienne). A Calcutta newspaper article complained that tourist interest in poverty in Calcutta was mainly attributable to Lapierre's novel (Tempest 1987: 19), and *The Statesman* carried an editorial which declared: 'Despite Calcutta's reputation, its long-suffering citizens never really thought that their city would one day figure on the tourist map of squalor' (in Tempest 1987: 19).

While more considered explications of the predicaments of Calcutta are sometimes available, so that some visitors come to different conclusions, this is quite rare among mainstream tourists. It was Adrienne who was first to mention a Bengali writer – Mahesweta Devi – when I asked travellers to list their favourite Indian authors. Significantly, Mahesweta Devi's stories have been made most popular in the West through the efforts of Gayatri Spivak (Spivak 1987; Devi 1993). The most often-mentioned 'Indian' authors amongst travellers in Calcutta were Salman Rushdie followed by V.S. Naipaul, both these foreign-resident writers mentioned far more often than Tagore, R.K. Narayan, Mitra, Manto, Bandyopadhyay. Few others were named.[5]

What is interesting is that evaluative representations of Calcutta, like those of Moorhouse and Lapierre, now circulate in an ever more internationalized economy, where the global order and national 'identities' are, in part, played out in a zone dominated by media and 'information'. Knowledge of cultural differences within the global order is now gleaned from the accounts of foreign correspondents, travel writers and tourists – and perhaps occasionally historians, anthropologists and political scientists. Control over and dissemination of meaning today is in the hands of a relatively privileged sector predominantly located in the 'First World'. This point should be considered alongside Gramsci's suggestion that 'ideas and opinions are not spontaneously "born" in each individual brain: they have a centre of formation, of irradiation, of dissemination, of persuasion' (Gramsci 1977: 192). At the same time, as Gramsci also indicates, there are other circuits of meaning, counterhegemonic articulations, which are more difficult to discern, yet also in circulation. Suggestions which challenge the received versions of cherished illusions such as that of Calcutta are often overlooked. They remain 'subaltern' even among historians. Another example of a more sympathetic account of the city, which also goes some way towards an explanation of its 'bad press', may be gleaned from Mukherjee's 1986 A.L. Basham lecture, published as a small pamphlet in 1987. After reviewing nineteenth-century literary views of the city, Mukherjee suggests that the earlier splendid palatial view of Calcutta gave way to a gloomy countenance – city of dreadful night – not because of insanitary conditions or intolerable climate, but because the growing antiimperialist agitation in Bengal 'threatened the illusion of permanence' (Mukherjee 1987: 23) of the imperial administrators. This, he offers in an aside, perhaps remains the reason why contemporary tourists avoid the city. He does not elaborate, but the linking of the reputation of Calcutta to the fortunes of the Raj in the face of emergent Bengali nationalism would fit well with the work of groups like the Subaltern

Studies collective (Guha 1992), and would be a useful counter to the platitudes of much Western writing.

Today, journalism and tourism (notably Western journalism, Western tourism) have overtaken a world in which these discourses were previously complemented (or complicated) by a world of explorers, missionaries and traders. Increasingly the internationalization of markets, communications and military organizations provokes a reconfiguration of thought about relations of domination, of cultural and meaning production, and of the ways in which people caught within these interstices of power construct their worlds. Mary Louise Pratt uses a notion borrowed from Spivak to describe the ways travel and exploration writing made a 'domestic subject' of colonial encounters for European readerships. 'Writing produced "the rest of the world"' through signifying practices which 'encode and legitimate the aspirations of economic expansion and empire' (Pratt 1992: 3). This 'domestication' of the colonial encounter (the word 'encounter' evokes Talal Asad's excellent book on the relations between anthropology and colonialism, as well as the euphemistic use of the word by police and journalists in the Calcuttan press to refer to incidents where, often unarmed, 'Naxalites' are killed by police fire) is not only directed towards the 'readers' who sit in the metropolitan libraries; it is also the case that travel itself is made a domestic subject by such writing, so that travellers who write do not ever quite get up from their reading chair (armchair anthropology).

Graphically illustrating the dynamics of the new world information order is the way travel literature and the travel industry correspond with a huge, many-tentacled writing machine. This machine writes Calcutta for every tourist from various scraps of information circulated through books like those of Moorhouse, travel guides, traveller talk, the advice of agents, journalistic snippets on the documentary news and other information sources. Among all this, the written versions of Calcutta are arrayed as a cut-up text for new visitors to reconstruct within determinate rules.

GÜNTER GRASS

The writing of travel guides need not be elegant; it is, after all, a functional convenience. (The best guidebooks are tough, well-bound, stitched and sturdy – able to survive at the bottom of backpacks, thrown around, spines cracked, well-thumbed). To a greater or lesser extent travel guides are part of a literature which serves a dual purpose: to provide detailed practical advice for travellers; and to describe. Michael Taussig finds that writing is fascinating because of its ability to be the means of transportation to other places: he wants 'to estrange writing itself, writing of any sort, and [to] puzzle over the capacity of the imagination to be lifted through representational media, such as marks on a page, into other worlds' (Taussig 1993: 16). Using this facility of 'marks on a page', guidebooks and popular histories like that of Moorhouse convey what they have to show readers in simple terms, and promise no more. Lapierre's book is a 'blockbuster', and is described in promotional ravings as just the sort of 'transportation to another world' that Taussig notes. Perhaps more complex are those works with pretensions towards literature.

Links between urban studies and surveillance can be made in a variety of ways. Guards posted at the fortified walls of the castle, the census of the city residents which follows from mechanisms of defence from the plague (Foucault 1977: 205), and so on. Those who visit Calcutta to perpetrate a text – and it seems that at any one time there are several visitors attempting to write books on the city in addition to those filling diaries and journals, and writing many letters home – are part of this vast writing machine whose transcription process can be understood as surveillance. When Günter Grass travels to Calcutta he writes, and draws, in a way that emphasises the spectral quality of his writing. He observes and transcribes what he sees through his sixty-year-old eyes.

Grass has written several books that include sections on India. In *The Headbirths Are Dying Out*, he describes an early visit to the country, but seems more concerned with the fortunes of some German sausage carried to Singapore by friends. In a later novel, *Flounder*, which purports to be a history of Planet Earth, he devotes fifteen terse pages to Calcutta. Writing in the guise of one of the earliest visitors to India, Grass provides an array of stereotypical pronouncements. The most volatile of these, and perhaps the one which betrays the greatest arrogance, is his line about God shitting and Calcutta appearing (Grass 1977: 186; see Chapter 2 note 4). Prefigured in this earlier novel are also all the themes of the major work he has devoted to Calcutta, *Show Your Tongue* (1989), including the anecdotal explanation of the significance of showing tongues – after visiting the Kali temple Grass asks why Kali's red tongue lolls out, and is told that it is through shame after a frenzy of destruction and mayhem. Grass links this to the image of mothers dipping baby pacifiers into 'brackish sugar water', for reasons that are unclear (I mean Grass's link is unclear, my guess is that he is

horrified); things he sees are continually cross-referenced to mythological curiosities. There are other themes in *Flounder*, such as anger at
poverty, refusal to ignore the slums, and insistence on the moral imperative to 'do something' rather than write a book about Calcutta.
However, he writes. His best suggestion, because it is mischievous, is
that the United Nations be transferred to Calcutta. Yet the ambiguities
and self-deprecations should not convince everyone that Grass's attitude
to the city is genuine, despite his rhetorical or stylistic placement of
himself, as narrator, in the position of first-ever Western visitor. Grass is
not the first to see the city, and his portrayal of a 'crumbling, scabby,
swarming city, this city which eats its own excrement' (Grass 1977:
181) adds very little to the compendium.

For all the ambivalences of *Show Your Tongue* – fictional, anguished,
hypocritical, well-written – there are passages which cannot be ignored:
'the strangeness becomes familiar – and remains strange. Forget the
twaddle about art. Do decay with a broad brush, with the edge of the
pen, with crumbling charcoal' (1989: 90). Why is it that even he, with
an established and successful individual 'literature' to his name, still holds
the pen differently in Calcutta? He writes with difficulty; in fact now
he draws – with crumbling charcoal, horrid bleak black scenes, rats
and poverty. He (rightly or wrongly?) ignores the intellectual life of
Calcutta, which to him seems irrelevant amidst the squalor. He sees
the squalor, visits the garbage dump. Would it be more interesting to
ask Grass – rather than other visitors – how he came to see Calcutta
this way – he, a famous writer, writing pretty much the same things as
any other visitor, any tour guide? Stock representations and expectations flow through him into the sentences of his book. He writes as a
voyeur:

> Everything, especially the underbelly, is to be shown to us: through rear
> courtyards – garbage everywhere, stopped drains, open sewage – into the
> courtyard of the university clinic, the largest in the country, we are told. In
> front of the lecture building the untouchables who work in the morgue are
> bivouacked in raggedly tents. For several days now, the airconditioning in the
> morgue is out of order. (Grass 1989: 91–2)

And the combinations of garbage and airconditioning, universities and
death, reek with questions revealing not so much the underbelly of
Calcutta as the anatomy of Grass's view. Always the garbage fascinates –
Lapierre weighed it to the ton, Grass goes to school in it (the book is
dedicated to the Calcutta Social Project, an NGO which runs a school
for children who work in the dump):

I spend the afternoon drawing people in garbage.... After three months, Calcutta begins to gnaw. Yet the sketching and recording do not abate, even when eyes have grown tired and dry from all the openly spread-out misery.... Yesterday, late, when driving home through streets lit only haphazardly, a greater number of sleepers. Or is it just that we, our eyes trained now, see them everywhere? Many are hard to spot, lying by walls, in niches. Unlike the sleepers filed head to wall, in family rows. (Grass 1989: 47)

He has sorted and filed his sleepers, those 'dumped' on the streets, and is now training his eyes to find those who are out of order. This surveillance project will find poverty 'everywhere', and describes Calcutta over and over as the squalid site of garbage. In this project people themselves are addenda; after an evening with unnamed Bengali intellectuals, Grass then observes the sleepers on the pavements, and writes: 'The soles of their feet show for identification. Our nocturnal small talk about Calcutta's future is refuted, as it were, by footnotes' (Grass 1989: 10). He does not seem interested in discussions with local activists, preferring instead to describe only what he sees – a visit to a sociologist whose team, researching the living conditions of rickshaw-pullers, is given one paragraph; while his earlier visit to the Queen Victoria Memorial fills three pages. At the home of the Bengali sociologist, Grass eats 'fish, rice, mashed lentils, and over-sweet dairy dishes', and writes: 'our museum visit doesn't interest the sociologists. That history is counterfeit. People have other problems' (Grass 1989: 15). Recognition of counterfeit, however, does not mean that he should not describe the memorial. Indeed, what he has to say is worthwhile, he laments the meagre offerings to the history of the independence struggle – a photograph of Gandhi, another of Netaji Subhas Chandra Bose, and little else – but it is revealing that he has nothing to report from his discussions with local activists.

He writes from on high:

From the roof, a panoramic view across the labyrinth of houses and huts, through the thicket of TV antennas and laundry, as far as Howrah Bridge, which vaults above the river between two great pylons and is considered the city's emblem. Now, toward evening, smoke rises toxic out of chimneys, courtyards, and windows. The pavilion on the terrace is crowned by a mutilated angel. I draw. (Grass 1989: 74)

The panorama, the labyrinth, Howrah Bridge, toxic city – all the conventions of representation for Calcutta are there for us to see. Indian cities are continually glossed this way by Western writers. Kate Llewellyn does the same in what would be almost plagiarism if it were not so clearly the convention, and here she is describing Delhi:

Smoke, fumes and a grey haze hung over everything and people lay like bus accident victims asleep in rows on the ground while cars, buses and people streamed past. It was an operatic set from hell. (Llewellyn 1991: 5)

I must accept, that I can only look at India. (Llewellyn 1991: 21)

Grass does not talk often; his authorial persona is mute. I think this is not so much to do with his being German – after all there are many German-speaking Bengalis, and his English would be sufficient – but is, rather, a consequence of his intellectual voyeurism. He sets out further tasks for his writing project. One is to 'follow a single cow for a day' in order to be able to describe 'how she grazes on garbage, is an island in traffic, how she lives in the shadows, is fleetingly a resting place for cows, how – late now – she watches over the sleep of pavement dwellers' (Grass 1989: 90). (It is interesting that Grass has often identified with animals rather than people – the rat, the flounder, the cat and the cockroach feature as authorial identities in his writing. What does this mean?).

Grass seems frustrated and furious. So why, I wonder, was he compelled to subject himself to this 'ordeal' in the city? He makes it an ordeal, and produces a book – is this the equation? Suffering for his art? Just what is at stake when one feels the urge to produce a text – when one needs to write? What sort of necessity is this? The cathartic activity of the author who must write what he sees and tell it how it is? Grass is subject to the same singularities of perception and perspective, even as he claims, and is claimed to have, the higher status of 'literature'. Echoing Lévi-Strauss, he writes: 'What is India? An occasion for publishing handsome picture books in colour or black and white. The legacy of the British Empire' (Grass 1989: 87).

When Grass does listen to Bengalis, he is shamed into recognition that his 'empire' – that of publishing – is interested only in 'Third World' exhibitionism:

I hear the complaints of Bengali writers. The 'Indian Week' during the Frankfurt Book Fair was a fraud. Invited and trotted out, they had been merely used for show. Some splendid art books were sold, yes, but no large publishing house was seriously interested in the literatures of India. I am shamed by these complaints, not merely because they are justified. (Grass 1989: 54)

Part of Grass's shame, perhaps, is that he, too, is able to sell an art book. His book carries some 56 sketches, and might be described with the same words he uses to condemn the exhibitionism of the Frankfurt fair: 'as garish, as exotic as possible, with just a touch of political involvement' (Grass 1989: 54–5).

Immediately after this comment, Grass includes a brief description of a Mrinal Sen film which, not accidentally placed in this narrative, shows that India, too, has its hypocrites. Upon the arrival of more sketching materials, he travels to a crematorium to watch and draw, and be watched while drawing:

> three fires are burning; one has burned low, the corpse turned to ashes. Down toward the Ganges, the courtyard opens to scenery through which pass thinning swathes of smoke. Simultaneously, the chant of young men around a new fire, and the forsaken corpses once the cremation draws to an end. Occasionally someone adds wood or shoves a charred piece – is it a body or a branch? – back into the blaze. The slightly sweet odour. (Grass 1989: 55-6).

The observer at the cremation, again a voyeur, makes no comment at the propriety of such invasion. (At which I am surprised: I, too, ignorantly went to stare at the ghat – only to be chased away very quickly by vigilant attendants. Why do tourists like to hang around with the dead? I would never go to funerals for entertainment at home.) Afterwards he attends an orchestral recital: 'A lost, obscene evening' (Grass 1989: 56). The obscene here is not the European orchestra, but the fact that in the next sentence Grass values more highly his drive home, which provokes reflections 'on pyres, sleepers in shadows, vigilant cows' (Grass 1989: 56). These thoughts are more than repetitive; they are the raw materials which circulate through the conduits of international publishing to provide material from which ever more orchestrated versions of Calcutta are collaged. These daily diary moments of Grass's cathartic writing are also produced for readers, produced and marketed in coffee-table-size hardback glossy covers, within a global economy in which meanings circulate and reinforce the stereotypes of Calcutta as a city of cows, garbage, sleepers and ghats.

Does cathartic writing work? Is it the 'action' Grass seeks? The status of enunciative statements of problems needs to be evaluated alongside the fragility of comparisons which enter into the global market – they are so easily appropriated. A Bangladeshi guide, Daud, takes Grass into a decaying 'Indo-Victorian' palace, now crowded with refugees. Daud 'should be depressed' (Grass 1989: 75) since he is to be deported, and because of the state of his countryfolk living in slum conditions. He is not depressed, but hopes Grass can help. Grass counsels him to 'write about it' (Grass 1989: 76), but there is no evidence of any book

from Daud. Does Grass's publishing house offer Daud a contract; what
kind of audience would be available, interested, attentive? And to what
end? Writing it out may sometimes be cathartic, but there is no indication that this can be generalized, universalized. Perhaps the erasure of
the trauma of World War II in the German author's work has been too
successful a formula. What can descriptions of dilemmas achieve when
the causes are remote, and the descriptions remain unpublished? Grass
perpetrates a book, and then complains of the 'routine corruption' of
the Writers' Building where 'dusty bundled papers, piles of them, high
as wardrobes, never disturbed, unless by the draft of the fans' are simply
'filed away among other filed-away files' (Grass 1989: 94).

THE IMPERATIVE TO WRITE ABOUT LEPROSY

The power of those who can write, and who are published, is never
more brutally apparent than when it comes to writing about those
who are disenfranchised in Calcutta, especially those about whom the
traveller-volunteers continually write: those who suffer from leprosy. It
is simply a fact that I can hold a pen, that I can type words into a
keyboard. Yet these physical distinctions may be less significant than the
institutional differences which allow me, travellers, scholars, Grass,
Lapierre, and others, to write about leprosy. This is an area where
Bengali writers who are unpublished, or published only in limited circulation, also have some comparative power. This much was recognized
long ago by the late Bengali author Premendra Mitra:

> To be honest, I feel quite hesitant about writing this story. I don't think I
> have the right to write about these two people. Not merely because those
> who read the story will insult them with their pity. But also because I doubt
> I have the kind of empathy required to understand the dark reality of their
> lives. After all, how large are our hearts? We are easily exhausted after we
> distribute our sympathies amongst the few around us; and as for generosity,
> that is a much abused word. Nevertheless, let me try to say what I want to...
> (Mitra 1990: 72)

There is, of course, no question of not writing, despite the frequent
doubts and questionings about why we write. It is the morality of
writing, and of reading, that must be continually questioned. I wonder.
Travellers' texts which explicitly address these problems still do not
solve the dilemma; in February of 1990 a friend from England visiting
me in Calcutta makes a journal entry:

> I've been trying again to get out an article I've been asked to write about the
> body for a journal, at the same time, I've been working a few hours each day,

on a very casual basis, in the street clinic treating leprosy. I wonder if this seems as ironic to others as it does to me – reading in Calcutta certain exemplary texts, and thinking about John's questions of the institutional obligations placed upon us to write (still more absurd was the request to write on the de-centred self and colonialism – I cannot begin that one here), and doing this work, and Günter Grass in Calcutta talking about decomposition and shit, feeling guilty about writing at all, and wondering if all these things might connect up somehow.... Complicit in the production of yet another set of questionable questions – just what is the connection between writing on the body and the bodily decay of leprosy? Obviously we should be a little nervous about attempting theoretical moves in such a space – someone said last night that 'too much discourse can be bad for the body' – it crosses my mind that writing about leprosy is bad for the body too, or at least I can't see how it does much good – especially as I've had the opportunity to 'do something' about it, that is, to treat lepers. Too much discourse is probably bad for writing too. (Craig: Journal)

But this, perhaps, is only the writing anxiety of someone obliged to write; and after all, this is clearly insufficient to help while the international hierarchy, the World Bank–IMF, the Third World debt system, and the World disorder (this refrain) remain. This anxiety about writing is one which generates a considerable amount of text. It is a deceit which both Grass, as well as less well-known visitors often express. Visitors find it hard to write about Calcutta, I have read or heard this so many times that it has become a dominant refrain of my collection of popular representations of the city. Again, this is expressed in another visitor's reflection:

When I first went to Calcutta I visited a home run by the Sisters of Charity (Mother Teresa's order). I was dismayed – I did not think I could work there like the other tourists I met, who seem to tick it off on a list of cultural musts for the visit to India (the Taj, a lion park, work with Mother Teresa, bhang lassis) – and later in that day, setting just that thought down on paper, one of the 'Mother T' volunteers said to me 'it's hard to write it up, eh?' So I was attempting just that – impressions from a few observations. Not very 'charitable' of me at all, and since I never went back I am insufficiently qualified to comment on the goings on there. But just what sort of qualification would satisfy I do not know, and this is the problem that plagues everything I try to write on this. Would Christian zeal help? Can I repeat the gossip I later heard about multiple use of unsterile syringes, of missionary conversions, of cruelty and loneliness? I cannot evaluate this gossip or gauge if these are lies. There is not much I can offer in writing about it (June: Journal)

A letter from this same volunteer who wrote to me after returning from Calcutta included more detailed comments on leprosy which I reproduce for the record, and because this letter, and this passage, make explicit the assistance I received from so many of those mentioned as 'travellers' in this text:

> Leprosy has, as you know, an almost unique place as the mark of the outcaste, although the presence of lepers in the middle of the city requires a more careful consideration of this sign of ostracism. Medically, leprosy is a bacterial disease involving damage to the peripheral nervous system destroying those conduits which carry messages of touch, pain and heat to the brain, and messages from the brain to activate muscles. The loss of sense perception results in repeated injuries which slowly produce deformities, clawed hands and noduled skin, in extreme cases also loss of sight. In India the Lepers Act of 1898 is still legally valid (Jha 1979: 67) and forbids a leprosy patient from washing at a public tap, or travelling in a public vehicle other than a train (I don't know why train travel was allowed). Leprosy has been said to affect 1% of India's total population of 800 millions. And for the last few months I have had this infection on my left hand which doesn't ever totally go away – not to mention a permanent case of giardia which has had me at the microbiology unit of the university for stool tests more often than I care to remember. Just to get a part-time job at the University where I've always worked they now demand an X-ray for tuberculosis. Is this where the pressures of the institution are finally imposed upon me? What seems to most intrigue me about your fieldwork is that it is resistant to description, it doesn't easily enter theory except perhaps as anecdote, and even then it escapes and collapses into self-reference. Here I am looking at what you have been doing and trying to match it up with what you have said and it doesn't seem to fit. The idea that somehow a critique of world system capitalism can come out of the frustrating futility and contradictions of charity work in Calcutta is absurd because, despite the theory, the local does not flow into the global so easily. (June: Letter)·

Experience of Calcutta is carved up with a vivisectionism that follows old rulebooks and travel guides in a duplication of empire in another disguise – after all, tourists come to consume India too. Surely this is all the hunger for travel brings. With a twist our bodies are once again divided and ruled, a grid tattooed on to the flesh through the skin of the world, all by the logics of market forces and the manufacture of destinations.

Calcutta is just 300 years old, so it is strange to hear that it is dead alongside cities like Varanasi (4,000) and Delhi (2,000). But for all the hype of the Calcutta 300 celebrations, with a logo designed by Satyajit Ray himself, it seemed that the main topic for consideration was merely the drains – they overflow during the monsoon and are used as general metaphor. Grass, too, is obsessed with shit. The city built after Charnock arrived, punting up the Hooghly river in 1690, needs a new sewerage system desperately. Artists dedicated proceeds from a Calcutta 300 exhibition to the Cleaner Calcutta Fund. Everybody is talking about how to *re*present the city, but this talk of shit does not mean that Grass is correct, does it? The city is a many-headed monster like the deities of its Hindu goddery – Calcutta has many faces, many truths.

And only now, perhaps, is it time to face up to all these body metaphors. We adorn our commentaries with the visage of anthropo-morphism – everything must eventually front up to this. Looked at between the eyes, dead centre, in a cold stare, we must agree – nodding our heads – that a special privilege has been accorded this space we only ever see as a mirror-image. The narcissus of metaphor is written on the polished surfaces of the commercial shopping mall to teach us to avoid the trauma of exotic reflections – there are not so many mirrors on the streets of Calcutta, and so to see yourself is rare; you would need to look closely into local eyes: something many visitors avoid in order to keep self intact. Still the lepers queue for treatments outside the Modern. What we are looking for, I think, is a metaphor to tell us all about what we are doing when we write about travel.

ON WRITING INDULGENCES

Is writing a 'tool' for making sense (making routine? domesticating?) experience? It seems that the urge to write is deployed for similar reasons by the traveller engaged in some kind of quest of 'self-discovery' and by the academic engaged in 'research'. The academic writer encodes experience and thought in a next... next... next... narrative of expla-nation. The authority words and phrases which enable this narrative include everything from 'thus it can be shown' to the gymnastics of 'discursive and structural displacement' – all these codifications are re-inforced by exemplary texts (the canonical studies) and offer, in too many cases, little more than a higher-order journalism. Writing about Calcutta easily falls prey to an unproblematised 'research' project which confronts untruth with the hammer of knowledge. If, as Derrida says, things were so simple, then word would have got around. Reading Grass and wanting to write about India as it has been understood by the discipline of anthropology led me to these questions, but main-stream Western scholarship about India is not concerned with writing. Anthropological approaches to the subcontinent seem caught in a kind of nostalgia for their very own Raj, a Raj of Bailey, Berreman, Srinivas and Dumont.[6] Much of South Asian ethnography cannot move until it has declared allegiance to the governing council of hierarchy, caste, village and Rama. This is not even to begin to consider what the scholars of religion are doing deep inside their Puranas, Vedas and Upanishads. Important as their efforts may be, the anthropologists at work where the dust and cobwebs of the Queen Victoria Memorial or India Museum reading-rooms have never been churned faster than the same slow pace of the ceiling fans (to borrow from Grass) all seem out of date. These arcane scholars are unlikely to be concerned with the postmodernisms and post-Marxisms that preoccupy the students of Calcutta's universities, nor with the Modernisms and Marxisms that remain strong there too.

How is it that institutional affiliations contrived to make me feel that I was expected to write about others? Those 'destitute' people who visited the clinic, whose existence as personalities would then become secondary to their status as patients, as sufferers from a disease (which medicine will cure, which is 'constructed' and should be linked to capitalism, and so on). Immediately this raised problems: the problems of all writing, the problem of discourse, the problems of action, responsibility, morality; the problem of writing here, now, for such and such an audience, for you, perhaps – I don't know – for 'them'?

I tried to list my questions: What are the scatological co-ordinates of writing? Of writing about culture, especially other bodies, other cultures – is it always a matter of perspective? Or is it the way you hold the pen? What perspective could I have taken towards writing about leprosy? Calcutta? The dubious association made between poverty and this city under the sign of charity? For all the effort and sore wrists that the recent flurry of commentary on representations has produced, what has been learnt about all this?

I thought of all the visitors to the city who, just like me, struggle with letters home, photographs, diaries, impressions, first, second and revised expectations, disappointment and confusion, thrills, joys, and the reassuring normality of sometimes being bored to tears. Mapping Calcutta in a variety of ways, I wanted to unravel the conventions of representation of the city in the films of Ray, Sen and Hauff, as well as in the books of Mitra, Devi, Gangopadhay, all these people – but not that I think there are an isolable number of versions I could lay before a reader. I fell into the same traps as other Western visitors: the place is too big, it defies description, it cannot be fitted into the pages of a book, or we'd all be able to live inside the glossy covers – could we accommodate ten million?

The pains and pleasures of writing are cut out of texts. Not represented, they are set adrift in a realm outside of writing on culture – isn't this very strange? (And is it so unusual, to mention this one example, to be eating when you write or read? The guilt I should maybe feel at writing–eating–reading about those who often do without. To consume the flesh of some beast while consuming the readable thoughts of some other beastly writer? Are these carnivorous systems really so separate? Since when, moreover, were carnivores able to write? Is this the process where Grass gets his interest in garbage and excrement? In Salman Rushdie's *Midnight's Children* Padma, the dung goddess, asks 'what is so special to need all this writing-shitting?' Calcutta had the first sewerage system in India – 1859 (Banerjee 1990: 94)). Georges Bataille names the other, the heterogeneous, the incommensurate, as:

> the waste products of the human body and certain analogous matter (trash, vermin, etc); the parts of the body; persons, words, or acts having suggestive or erotic value; the various unconscious processes such as dreams or neurosis; the numerous elements or social forms that homogeneous society is power-less to assimilate; mobs, the warrior, aristocratic and impoverished classes, different types of violent individuals or at least those who refuse rule (mad-men, leaders, poets, etc.). (Bataille 1976/1991: 142)

Writing becomes indulgent. Cut off from this lifeline as if with a knife, a stream of ink separates from me as I push my pad away, push my chair back from the table. This disconnection from a page of my work – if I am reading or writing – severs myself from my self. I have written these words like refuse dumped pile on pile amid coffee cups and dirty plates, and I don't know how to clean up. (The meal of yesterday decays inside me and comes out as waste matter – 'Delhi belly' in Calcutta – the oscillation of life and some shit which stinks of death: decomposition is decrepit as this becomes a necrophiliac kind of reading. A book is a dead body, a piece of stale flesh, cooked or rot-ting, neither lives. Yet there is something nourishing in connection with this rumination, a kind of sustenance in fermentation.)

Not to mention... a certain two-faced silence allows a rhetorical signalling of something, without claiming to touch it. There is always someone trying to point without the stigmata of the voyeur. Untoucha-bles and unmentionables abound and proliferate everywhere, an entire corpus of explicitly silent exposed parts.

METAPHORS OF WASTE

I think there is something significant in the propensity of visitors like Grass to describe the city in the metaphorical register of waste. Such associations accord closely with much of the Western academic and media stereotyping of the city; as a 'model of urban hell', as described by visiting scholar Leonard Gordon at another of the Calcutta 300 seminars. In a lecture at Jadavpur University, Gordon portrayed Western visitors' experiences of Calcutta over the last three hundred years as a mixture of horror and fascination. He suggested three main images that belonged to the model of urban hell in Calcutta: refugees, the Black Hole, and the Kali temple. His litany of other people's insults to Calcutta demonstrated the general North American fear of the place, but whether these 'hellish' representations are, indeed, representative of Calcutta was not discussed in detail at the seminar. Many in the audience thought that Gordon's paper only repeated various platitudes without further comment. The suggestion was made from the floor, in a manner that evoked the tense reception of Grass at his seminar, that articulation of stereotypes does not do enough to dislodge them unless it is placed in an analytical context which transforms understanding.

The model of 'urban hell' is also a pervasive one among travellers; it informs many comparisons with other cities, most often New York: 'this is what New York will look like in twenty years – shitty' (Rachel). Urban chaos is cause for distress for many travellers, and almost invariably manifests some form of 'culture shock' featured in tales of first impressions and arrival scenes. When Fiona first came to Calcutta she hated it. She said she'd had to get drunk and talked for six hours with her Irish partner before she was able to deal with the view out of her window: 'I had to keep getting up to see that it really was India out there – I just couldn't believe what I saw, such crowds, and the toilets'.

There is, of course, no one version of the city. Everyone has their own, and not all are views from a bathroom window. Indeed, some travellers express very different ideas of the city over the time of their stay. This was evident most clearly when, after more than two years, I formally sat down with long-term volunteer doctor Peter to discuss Calcutta for a newspaper article. Peter thought that the process of defining and coming to understand a little of what happened to longer-term visitors to Calcutta was important. They come to change their minds about some things, and then change them again, over and over:

> 'Calcutta is an international city in the first instance, although this point is generally missed because those outside Calcutta have antiquated views of the city. I believe there is no final version of Calcutta, only many, and they are scattered all over the world, hence it's an international city.... This, I think, means not only that every tourist that has been here has a different version of the city, but that everyone has many versions, many impressions, even you and I, each of the Bengalis, everyone will have a number of different Calcuttas.

And the healthy thing about this sick city is that just when you begin to feel comfortable and understand something it turns around and throws you. The longer I stay the less I know.' (Peter)

Peter's view was that Calcutta was written differently in each person. He repeats the 'Calcutta aphorism': 'When the bottom falls out of your world, come to Calcutta and watch the world fall out through your bottom.' With so many possible Calcuttas, is it any wonder that contradiction and confusion, repetition and reversal are dominant themes? If everything you ever heard about the city is as dialectical as this, is it any wonder that the city has such exemplary status?

Among all the images which are invoked for the city, for many the most grim is that of death. Rajiv Gandhi, as well as visitors like Patrick Swayze and Günter Grass, have all linked the city to death. In a rather angry dismissal of the city, one traveller exclaimed: 'Calcutta is a dead city. Full of shit. Sure, you can see the life of the people here, or go to some concerts, but it was born a long time ago and has now died. Can't you smell it?' (Gian). Certainly the city smells in parts; a consequence of limited public conveniences, steadily improving. This is a major shock for a good number of visitors, and a source of great frustration for many residents and for the municipal authorities. Yet obituaries written by tourists are a little premature. In a comment that at least indicates the beginnings of auto-critique, another traveller pointed out: 'At first you only see the people in rags, later on you notice the middle classes, but even the poor have more dignity and more "life" in their poverty than many other people' (Joe).

BOOKS IN CIRCULATION

To return to the previous chapter and the rooftop of the Modern Lodge: among the volunteers who come to work in the Preger clinic there is a kind of 'canon' of classical travellers' texts that are often read. These are texts like *The City of Joy* and *Show Your Tongue*, which form and reinforce perceptions of the character of the city, but there is also a more general travellers' canon. This includes the travel writings produced and promoted, and distributed, by the formal 'industry' of travel writing and bookstores, but also circulating informally, passed from backpack to backpack – a series of dog-eared 'standards' which form and reform traveller identity and have significant resonance for budget travellers on a global hunt for the banana pancake.

Deleuze and Guattari comment, as a fold within a certain capitalism at a transitional moment, on the literature of those backpacker-traveller icons Ginsberg and Kerouac: 'men who know how to leave, to scramble the codes, to cause flows to circulate' (Deleuze and Guattari 1972/1983: 132–3). A writing that corresponds with a burgeoning capitalist project transgressing older boundaries is required to shatter the barriers of the limit, and yet cannot – 'They overcome a limit, they shatter a wall, the capitalist barrier. And of course they fail to complete the process' (Deleuze and Guattari 1972/1983: 133). The writer is complicit in the dialectical expansion of the global apparatus extending across boundaries, including grammar:

> a stream of words that do not let themselves be coded, a libido that is too fluid, too viscous: a violence against syntax, a concerted destruction of the signifier, non-sense erected as a flow, polyvocality ... an author is great because they cannot prevent themselves from tracing flows and causing them to circulate. (Deleuze and Guattari 1972/1983: 133)

But into this flow of words, this transgressive circulation, Deleuze and Guattari provide a very sane insertion when they comment that the problem of literature is poorly understood when it begins from the question of an ideology *in* literature, or 'from the co-option of it by a social order' (Deleuze and Guattari 1972/1983: 133). They note that it is people, not works, that are co-opted, and deride 'Ideology' as a confused notion: 'because it keeps us from seizing the relationship of the literary machine with a field of production' (Deleuze and Guattari 1972/1983: 133). In an exemplary passage which suggests again that writing offers a metaphor of great importance, the style, or even the absence of style, is: 'the moment when language is no longer defined by what it says, even less by what makes it a signifying thing, but by what causes it to move, to flow, to explode' (Deleuze and Guattari 1972/1983: 133). And if style can be read as an index of a certain moment in the history of capitalist production, by way of the kinds of flows, movements and explosions it may cause, then the inscriptions of any moment must be read for such markers. This can be a guide to what is said of Calcutta.

Yet there is also exemplary writing, surely. Not all literature (and not all of Kerouac and Ginsberg, Lapierre or Grass) can be dismissed as just 'style'. There is always authority in style, but there are some writings that I prefer to others for reasons not solely to do with form. Some Calcuttas, too, are better written. The point is that there are more ways to read works than are ever immediately obvious. It is not the case that versions of written Calcutta are simply wrong, or that a certain photographic image of some scene in the city is not a representation of that scene — there are, however, other approaches. Close attention to what might be called the metaphorics of description alerts us to other possible ways of reading an image. For example, the themes of travel, of flow and of movement, evoke transnational production at the same time as suggesting the lyrical possibilities of style, of the flourish of the pen. Among many ways of following the itineraries of style in the texts of tourists in Calcutta at a particular juncture in capitalist history, the marker of writing allows many possibilities. As an inscribing apparatus, a machine traversing the world, writing signifies global production, and so it is already co-opted. And if it is co-opted, it also contains within it the trace of something else, a trace of other possibilities, markers waiting for incorporation. In this always volatile situation, Deleuze and Guattari were keen to find the moments of friction amid the stylized morass:

> Artaud puts it well: all writing is so much pig shit — that is to say, any literature that takes itself as an end or sets ends for itself, instead of being a process that 'ploughs the crap of being and its language,' transports the weak, the aphasics, the illiterate. At least spare us sublimation. Every writer is a sell-out. The only literature is that which places an explosive device in its package, fabricating a counterfeit currency, causing the superego and its form of expression to explode, as well as the market value of its form of content. (Deleuze and Guattari 1972/1983: 134)

All our themes are here in this passage which lauds Artaud, by a kind association with his own venomous critique, as the locus of an explosive counterfeiting style — yet Artaud, too, causes flows to circulate, breaks the wall, and still cannot succeed. The critiques only confirm the form of the machine, as if the words themselves were in circulation without meaning — as in the form of currency. This challenges our notion of the import of exchange, theories of the gift and of distribution:

> society is not first of all a milieu for exchange where the essential would be to circulate or to cause to circulate, but rather a socius of inscription where the essential thing is to mark and be marked. There is circulation only if inscription requires or permits it. (Deleuze and Guattari 1972/1983: 142)

So it may well be necessary to posit a theory of meaning where the theory of production and of labour is to be linked to the protocols of planetary distribution. This would be confirmed within the widest definitions of writing, which perhaps Deleuze and Guattari anthropomorphise too much, but which none the less seem to offer up the structure of all production as a mode of inscription:

circulating – exchanging – is a secondary activity in comparison with the task that sums up all the others: marking bodies, which are the earth's products. The essence of the recording, inscribing socius, insofar as it lays claim to the productive forces and distributes the agents of production, resides in these operations: tattooing, excising, carving, scarifying, mutilating, encircling and initiating. (Deleuze and Guattari 1972/1983: 144)

But what experience is marked, or encoded, through these productive forces and distributive agencies if not exactly an experience of marking – of marking one's self upon the text of the world, or specifically here, in Calcutta. Just as Lévi-Strauss writes of a Calcutta he can see only through his experience, his experience is seen through the exercise of writing, and perhaps of a certain anguish of being faced with the abject impoverishment of a crippled beggar. Similarly, the sensation of Lapierre's novel might be understood as a consequence of the form of seeing Calcutta as a site for such historical fantasy. The project of Grass's writing also 'confirms' Calcutta in a particular way, excluding other possibilities, etching one city in place of a (now im)possible other(s).

THE RETURN OF LEIRIS

In the promotional insert of his epic work *L'Afrique fantôme*, Michel Leiris is described as an author 'sick of his life in Paris' and in search of escape, adventure and self-realization. He views 'travel as poetic adventure, a method of concrete knowledge' (Leiris 1934, quoted in Clifford 1988: 165). But Leiris's escape does not offer many adventures, since 'capitalism … [has the] increasing tendency to render all true human contacts impossible'. Despite his distaste for metropolitan cities, 'by the end of his journey, he yearns for return' (Leiris in Clifford 1988: 166). Leiris asks if he is obliged to record everything, every experience, every thought or feeling, while he is among the Dogon (Leiris was a part of the famous Dakar–Djibouti expedition led by Maurice Griaule in 1930). He records such events as a satisfying bowel movement (Koepping writes: 'maybe Leiris actually has the guts not to glorify the experience of field-work as he eliminates the romantic from the morning shit' [Koepping 1989: 41]), and complains that he is working against the poison of publication. And what does he achieve in the end? In his autobiography, *Rules of the Game*, he reports: 'ethnography only succeeded in turning me into a bureaucrat' and:

travelling, as I conceived of it (a solitary distancing), far from being a way of making oneself other than what one is by changing one's setting, is only the pure and simple displacement of a person who is always identical to themselves, a nomad only in the spatial sense ... a desire not to go away anymore came over me. (Leiris 1948/1991: 197)

This fantastic comment offers a symmetrical counterpoint to the arrival of Lévi-Strauss in India with which this chapter began. In *L'Afrique fantôme* Leiris writes that he is 'cured of the "exotic mirage" – surely a step in the direction of a more realistic view of things' (Leiris 1934: 532). This 'more realistic view', at the end of a huge book more akin to the African novel of Raymond Roussel than to any contemporary ethnography or travel writing, leads Leiris to forsake travelling. And specifically, he is cured of wanting to travel to the very place Lévi-Strauss was destined soon to visit: 'the exotic mirage is over. Gone is the desire for Calcutta' (Leiris 1934: 509).

In this chapter I have examined writing technique and style in the formation of Western views of Calcutta. The contested representations of the city – which were at stake in the debates, for example, around Lapierre's novel *City of Joy* – will reappear in Chapter 6. Such debates and their effects indicate the scope of the global circulation of representations of Calcutta, the systems of distribution which enable books on these matters to proliferate, and the ways in which the particular experiences of particular writers come to be formed, and can form solid evidence for the need to attend more closely to the hegemonic privilege accorded to such works. The stench of shit in writing about Calcutta, and the attendance to garbage and squalor that is the motif of so many visitor writings on the city, have to be understood as snapshots taken within a particular representational frame. The technologies of book production, and the circumstances of those who visit to write, produce Calcutta according to these themes as a cipher which travels all around the world. These, in turn, interrelate with all that is discussed by budget travellers on the rooftop of Modern Lodge. It is the structure of technologies of representation which give focus to the imagery of decay – it is not simply there, but is discursively produced – which further evokes the developmental and 'charitable works' interventionism of those who would demand that something must be done to 'clean it all up'. Grass bemoans the intellectual scene which is irrelevant amid squalor in a way which implies that local 'intellectuals' don't care enough. The invisibility of the communist organizations working to improve Calcutta is another effect of his orientation. Once again this is the framework which attributes blame locally, and it is Grass, not local intellectuals, who is unable to acknowledge complicity in his own excremental production.

NOTES

1. This would also include how I came to 'read' and 'write' Calcutta; the subtext of every page of this work.

2. It is worth remembering that Lévi-Strauss is visiting India only five years after Europeans had been killing each other in millions for the second time in twenty-five years, and that Calcutta had not yet begun to recover from both famine and partition, for which Europeans could also be held responsible.

3. For detailed discussion of the Naxalite revolutionary movement in Bengal from the late 1960s, see Banerjee (1980, 1984); Dumas (1991).

4. This 'familiarity' now extends through the film version. See Chapter 6 below.

5. The recent collections edited by Susie Tharu and K. Lalita, *Women Writing in India*, released by HarperCollins Publishers might change this. The two 600-plus-page volumes in paperback are accessible translations and widely available in bookstores in India and throughout the world. No other collection in English has been so impressive, and an assessment of its varied receptions would be worthy of a separate commentary (Tharu and Lalita 1991, 1993).

6. Ronald Inden's *Imagining India* is a useful rebuttal of the excesses of this anthropology (Inden 1990). An assessment of the impact of his critique of South Asian scholarship as imperialism would extend to another study, but there is no question that his writing is more lively and committed than that of those he lampoons.

CARTOGRAPHIC CALCUTTA:

AMAZEMENT

'Nobody really understands the city; we are groping about for phrases and images with the dexterity of a suburban zonal planning committee.' (Emma, an architect: Letter)

Among the myriad cultural productions that make up the representations of Calcutta available to visitors – films, books, photographs – by far the most explicit representational modes are those produced for the immediate consumption of tourists. Maps, guidebooks and postcards present the city in handy, portable, two-dimensionally convenient ways. This is a 'reconnoitre' of what can be called cartographic Calcutta: its representation on the map. I elaborate upon the way a seemingly abstract guide or representation of the city is more closely aligned to the production of subjective experience than many would imagine. Just as I have argued that Grass's imagery provides a literary-metaphorical map of sorts which guides visitor experience in the city, explicit maps also carry a hegemonic and ideological load. Finding a way through Calcutta is a major project for all visitors. 'New' cities are easy to get lost in, so guidebooks and maps are necessary, and monuments become landmarks orientated more towards the city than the histories they memorialize. Such markers offer a key to the ways a city can be made and experienced. Residents and visitors alike would often be lost without reference points; but tourists need maps and guidebooks which calibrate with expectations and evocations formed before their arrival (often of the city as a place of immanent exotic adventure) and often throughout their stay. Ferguson[1] notes that 'the guide sets up an expectation of ... the city via its landmarks' (Ferguson 1993: 17), and suggests that 'maps establish routes on a ground level from monument to monument which enable the tourist to move freely through the unfamiliar city' (Ferguson

1993: 17–18). Maps are an adjunct to the monumental vision which orientates the traveller in a foreign place. For some, however, a kind of traveller protocol requires a renunciation of the convenience of the guide in favour of a more individualistic and 'authentic' exploration. It is also possible that the physical representational 'souvenirs' of maps, images of monuments and postcards can be presented as an exigent, if often kitsch, mode of inscribing presence in, or of, a place.[2]

In an important metaphorical construct which entwines travel with writing on the city in a way that orientates both experience and reading, Mitchell says that a map is like a preface (Mitchell 1988: 148). Deleuze and Guattari take this text metaphor further: 'The map is open and connectable in all its dimensions; it is detachable, reversible, susceptible to constant modification. It can be torn, reversed, adapted to any kind of mounting, reworked by an individual, group or social formation. It can be drawn on the wall, conceived of as a work of art, constructed as a political action or a mediation' (Deleuze and Guattari 1987: 12). So it should be no surprise that much traveller writing tends to seek out and reference the metaphors and images of transport to map the city, and continually to seek co-ordinates of coherence and orientation. It is just this which guides Scott through his daily write-up of Calcutta:

> The city becomes a thoroughfare for a rush of images which trundle along one after another like cabs, rickshaws and pedestrians jostling their ways along the road. The paths of these images intersect and cross, sometimes following predetermined routes, at other times searching out shortcuts. Some journeys cross the whole of the city, winding forwards and back and touching every corner, some remain on just one street corner, small and barely noticed, but just as significant as any major motorcade rushing by with official escort. (Scott: Diary entry)

MAPS AND GOVERNMENT

In 1989 a Central Government edict declared that any map of India which did not comply with topographical Survey of India maps would be considered illegal.[3] Maps of Calcutta readily available to tourists varied considerably, with none of them – not the Lonely Planet Guide, or that of the Indian Tourism Development Corporation, or the offering of the TTK Mapping Company – providing more than approximate, 'not-to-scale' versions of the city. There were some travellers who were alert to conditions which affected their choice of destination: 'It's the Government which determines where we go, where the international air routes take us. That's why Calcutta isn't really on the map for us' (Emma). This 'routing' determination has international and local effects, and political considerations impact upon all aspects of travel. Although new arrivals to a city might be taken by taxi along circuitous and expensive routes, the most effective way for travellers to find any particular place is to ask taxi-drivers for directions and, with specific addresses such as street numbers, to rely upon dhobi-wallahs (clothes-washers) who, interestingly, usually have the most comprehensive knowledge of local streets (this is significant because local skills are hereby co-opted into wider, even global, needs and inscriptions). Local knowledge is important, since Calcutta maps seem particularly inaccurate in both scale and content, although there are good strategic and historical reasons for this: street names changed from old British Raj appellations, for example, or the brilliant irony of changing the name of the street on which the American Consulate stands as a protest against the US aggression in Vietnam, so that a search for an American visa leads the traveller to No. 1, Ho Chi Minh Sarani. A fine thing.

It is important at least to outline the intersections between Calcutta's political history and the seemingly more innocuous trappings of tourism like the paraphernalia of maps, guidebooks and the itineraries of taxis. The shape of a city is never accidental, and urban planning strategies, as much as what is disclosed on maps, are consequent upon military and defence agendas, communications, and transportation requirements – of goods and for deployment of troops – and upon the intricacies of political symbolism. For example, the 'vast expanse' of parkland that occupies the centre of Calcutta, the 'lung' that is the Maidan, is a product, at least initially, of the defence requirements of the British military, who cleared the surrounds of their citadel Fort William of all dwellings after their defeat at the hands of Suraj-ud-daula in 1756, so as to provide clear firing ground for their cannon (a different kind of black hole). This Maidan park has become a boon for the city as an open recreational space (able to host, simultaneously, dozens of cricket matches and political meetings, as one local wit observed), a site of massive political rallies, and a focal point for much of Calcutta's public life. Open space contrasts with the busy blocks of the built-up city, although there are lines of escape and marks of political history within density too. It would not be too far fetched to suggest that the housing of the current Bengali government in the Writers' Building, which was the head office of the East India Company and later of the British administration, is more than a convenience of accommodation, as it provides a commentary on the shift of power in the state after Independence. New elites replace the older administration under so-called postcolonialism. Other examples could be found.

The organization and representation of a city is rarely straightforward. Maps are not a representation of material realities so much as historically and socially conditioned representations of the lived, and contested, world (Stratton 1990: 68). Maps 'map' power – a point made by Pratt in more general terms when she notes the curious iconic drawings of elephants and the like that filled the blank spaces of early European maps of India. She argues: 'like the rise of interior exploration, the systematic surface mapping of the globe correlates with an expanding search for commercially exploitable resources, markets, and lands to colonise, just as navigational mapping is linked with the search for trade routes' (Pratt 1992: 30). Tourism, and its study, can also be understood within a range of causal and affective registers, of which the least insignificant of all would be the economic considerations that could attend studies of international travel, and/or (over against) the cultural imperialism that may accompany an academic mapping of Third World backpacker activity.

How the city is mapped presumes more than the one-to-one correspondence of city as habitat, at least to the point of presuming differing habitats according to the kind of use assumed for the map. Tourist maps constitute the city as a place to be explored, as a site for the geographical unfolding of experiences, as topos of visiting. Such maps work differently from, say, those of use to local residents, the mental maps of taxi-drivers (which overlap somewhat with the tourist trade), or public-transport routes (the same maps may also be read in different ways). The unfolding of experience via the tourist map, or in a different way via the guidebook, continues to posit Calcutta as an accumulation of images experienced – walkthrough images – a tableau laid out across time in a packeted geography.

Henri Lefebvre raises questions about the relation between mapping and travel when he suggests that if 'the maps and guides are to be believed a veritable feast of authenticity awaits the tourist' (Lefebvre 1974/1991: 84). In his classic work *The Production of Space*, Lefebvre argues that it is capitalism which has produced 'space' in such a way that, with the aid of the tourist map, a 'ravenous consumption' raids the landscape. He argues that 'Capitalism and neo-capitalism have produced abstract space, which includes the "world of commodities", its "logic" and its worldwide strategies, as well as the power of money and that of the political state' (Lefebvre 1974/1991: 53). A vast network links the power of the state through a complex of financial institutions, major production centres, motorways, airports and 'information lattices' which lead to the 'disintegration' of the town as anything other than a space to be consumed (Lefebvre 1974/1991: 53). One of Lefebvre's key points is that representations of space 'have a substantial role and a specific influence in the production of space' (Lefebvre 1974/1991: 42), such that maps of Calcutta can be understood as both a product to be used, but also – and perhaps more importantly – as a means of production. Speaking of space in general, immediately after his contemplation of the space produced by maps, Lefebvre argues for an understanding of space that attends to its political location: 'this means of production, produced as such, cannot be separated either from the productive forces, including technology and knowledge, or from the social division of labour which shapes it, or from the state and the superstructures of society' (Lefebvre 1974/1991: 85).

In terms of the production of space, it might have been relevant to look to Heidegger, but Lefebvre seems somewhat hostile. He notes that despite Heidegger's interest in the 'dwelling' place of being, 'there can be no doubt about the main thrust of his thinking here: time counts for more than space' (Lefebvre 1974/1991: 121). Yet he is able to agree that 'space – the woods, the track – is nothing more and nothing other than "being-there", than beings, than Dasein' (Lefebvre 1974/1991: 121). Heidegger's interest in time is not *explored* here, but interestingly, Lefebvre's discussion of Heidegger is followed in quick succession by a reference to anthropology, and specifically to the work of Lévi-Strauss, and immediately afterwards to the destructive effects of the 'tourist hordes' (Lefebvre 1974/1991: 121–2). This progression in Lefebvre's thinking is surely not without some significance[4] . What would this work look like if he had taken up these influences (remembering that he had approved of a 'materialist' Heidegger)? It is also worth noting that for a time Lefebvre was close to the Situationist International and its prominent spokesperson Guy Debord, who wrote, in *The Society of the Spectacle*:

> Tourism, human circulation considered as consumption, a by-product of the circulation of commodities, is fundamentally nothing more than the leisure of going to see what has become banal. The economic organisation of visits to different places is already in itself the guarantee of their equivalence. The same modernisation that removed time from the voyage also removed it from the reality of space. (Debord 1970/1983: para. 168)[5]

SCIENTIFIC ORDERING

Sociological and scientific researches have multiple, and sometimes covert, motivations beyond their most obvious justifications. No one can now deny that the social sciences have been implicated in militarily motivated research, just as the 'hard' sciences, with calculations of trajectory, speed and weight – Galileo playing with cannonballs, the arc of archery, Leonardo's war machines – have been 'motivated' by the demands of the military since Antiquity. Today the military–industrial complex of the new world disorder and its geopolitical divisions leaves aside no effort to extend its interests, as ever, through researching techniques of surveillance, photography, representation, corporate espionage – even, perhaps, in the pursuit of the tourist dollar – in ways that are sometimes frighteningly explicit. (Other examples: consider Geertz's thinking on Evans-Pritchard and Ruth Benedict in *Works and Lives*; the controversies around the University of Sydney Anthropology Department involvement in Chiang Mai; US Army participation in LSD research, known as the Electric Cool-Aid Acid Test, semiotica and the Gulf War, and so on. In these and other examples the complicity of academic production with the planetary work machine is clear.[6])

Among the potential, often unintended, consequences of the various representations and cultural understandings generated in social science research as well as in urban planning and tourist promotion, are a series of studies which amount to experiments in social control. In *Imagining India*, Inden questions the 'purpose' of social scientific observations of 'others', and claims that 'more often than not' this 'has been to constitute those others as agents who can be managed' (Inden 1990: 22). This involves notions of behaviour that can be predicted and controlled. He suggests that the attempt to create a science of society 'was and still is imperialising because it claims that a privileged, unitary knowledge can displace the disputable knowledges of the agents about which it knows' (Inden 1990: 22). Such a science then opens the door to an administrative expertise which may use this 'superior knowledge … on behalf of market forces' (Inden 1990: 22). Maps share this orientation, and so the politics of knowledge in a study of urban representation in the context of international imperialism requires that we read them as more than just handy ways to visit a city.

METAPHORS OF TRAVEL

Tourism studies seem to ignore the charged global circumstances of the contemporary situation – new modes of transport, capital and information flows prevail. An initial entry into this debate might begin by pushing the metaphorics of travel itself.

We should be charitable towards travel. As it is the 'topic' of this analysis a reader might – not unreasonably – presume that a certain engagement with travel – even participation, fascination – could be supposed on my part throughout. As with a traveller, the point of providing a critique of travel cannot be to stop travelling, however much a moralism for better travel might prevail. More than this, however, my own engagement with travel must extend across many zones, traversing various tropics, down numerous avenues and along all corridors. At times I want to argue that there is, now, nothing outside travel. Travel in the context of everything studied here – a study tour – co-ordinates our experience and understanding of the world. Travel, close to travail, works as a metaphor of all exchange. Keenan says: 'exchange ... is a system that *traffics* in abstractions' (Keenan 1993: 175; emphasis mine). Marx writes: 'In the value-relation of one commodity to another its value character emerges or *steps forth* through its own relation to the other commodity' (Marx 1867/1967: 141–2), and Heidegger could well be carried along this path too. Travel is a metaphor of movement and meaning; from transport, which carries across, to tourism, the ideology of travel, made available to everyone. Van Den Abbeele reports Rousseau's democratization of the philosopher's tour 'by implicitly allowing anyone who stumbles while out for a walk to claim great thoughts' (Van Den Abbeele 1992: 130). The entire horizon of thought, theory and representation is circumscribed. *Theoria* requires travel – 'the etymological sense of the word theory ... is that of a vision or a spectacle' (Van Den Abbeele 1992: 65). Theory becomes sightseeing, even if a 'line' of thought does not 'develop along well-marked paths' (Papastergiadis 1993a: 25). Travel is re-present-ation, through a metaphoric displacement, interwoven and intricately cross-referenced in order to travel everywhere with no final destination, no undestined place.

A stumbling block for conventional thinking about travel, as it might be applied to the experiences of visitors to Calcutta, is that the trope of the journey has often assumed the straight (linear narrative) line as its guide. The difficulties that linearity, and narrative, can have with the convoluted trajectories of experience have become a favoured topic for contemporary cultural analysis. This is complicated all the more with visitors who never escape the map of packaged tourism, since 'for all of their claims, they never really left home' (MacCannell 1992: 2), and their journey remains the same.

Maps are explicitly reductions of a complex multiplicity into a two-dimensional code. The process of mapping presumes a 'prefigured' form that can be transposed, so that – subject to the possibilities of condensation and reproduction, and to conventions of cartographic representation – aspects of public convenience and touristic import can be codified and transcribed on to a paper grid. In a way that might evoke Lévi-Strauss again, looking down from on high at his subject matter, or conversely equating the patterns of South American myth systems with astronomical maps of the heavens to a degree, these reductions privilege the person *standing* over and above the two-dimensional representation (Lévi-Strauss 1966/1983). According a certain power to the map of the world, they are thereby separated from the world as represented, and are thus of a 'frame' of mind to be able to manipulate it (they may also get lost); harking back to Heidegger's 'enframing', the map-reader is able to treat the world as an object, as something which stands ready to be understood...

This 'objectification' of the world is reported by Greenblatt in a way that describes some of the main themes of this work. Greenblatt sets out his own project as wanting 'to emphasise the multiple sites of representation and the crowd's movement among them', in a way that gets at the problem 'of the assimilation of the other' as linked to what he calls 'adapting Marx, the reproduction and circulation of mimetic capital' (Greenblatt 1991: 6). Whether this adaption is valid or not, for Greenblatt, 'in the modern world-order it is with capitalism that the proliferation and circulation of representations (and devices for the generation and transmission of representations) achieved a spectacular and virtually inescapable global magnitude' (Greenblatt 1991: 6). This magnitude is then characterized as the ability to travel across vast distances, usually in search of profit 'to encounter and represent radically unfamiliar human and natural *objects*' (Greenblatt 1991: 6; emphasis added).

Recognition of the reductive necessity of representation may lead us to see that the 'blinkers' are on the map, not on the eyes – or rather, in the printing process. Enframing: Heidegger suggests that 'every seeking gets guided beforehand by what is sought' (Heidegger 1926/ 1962: 24). Any other recognition fosters the illusion of a pure experience. This has been sold as an adjunct to tourist maps for a long while – the 'cultural baggage' which comes with the visitor is built into the production of the map as much as it is a characteristic of those who use maps. To think that any mode of textuality can 'fix' Calcutta is a real madness, as mad as that in an anecdote from Borges: where a map-maker made a map so precisely detailed and correct that the citizens chose to live in the map instead of their city, which was becoming rather tattered, while the map was resplendent with nicely ruled lines and neat angles. In the widest sense, the mapping of Calcutta is something like this, where inscription at work at all kinds of levels, extending from scholarship and literature to travel diaries, letters and home videos, amounts to a never-ending cartography where residents and visitors are only ever somewhere inside their map, squabbling over the draft.

While there are some visitors who struggle against the 'official' map-makers – say, against the Lonely Planet Guide or the West Bengal Tourism Authority – there are more who accept the convenience and comfort of having their experience of Calcutta drafted for them in advance. (And why not? Maps do help.) It is still worth considering how visitors' predispositions predetermine the deployment of differing kinds of maps, and how differing degrees of energy are exerted upon maps in order to generate their meanings. Deleuze has offered the idea that 'Maps are maps of intensities', and that 'geography is no less mental and corporeal than physical in movement' (Deleuze and Parnet 1977/ 1987: 38). This suggests that the ideological work of representing Calcutta is 'intensely' at 'work' in the touristic reading of any map of the city.

Any map? It is a good metaphor which opens the possibility of saying that guidebooks, films, and all the various crisscrossed referencings of texts – in the broadest sense – on Calcutta tend towards a unifying documentation of the city which constructs it as a comprehensible entity. In an immense overlay of representations, a vast series of like images find, and communicate with, each other to make it possible to imagine an orderliness under the name 'Calcutta' which can be visited, known, and (perhaps) controlled.

In this sense, cartography is a mode of enclosure, and the con-structed boundaries are a kind of stagnation – this could be said of national boundaries and of graveyards, as well as of academic disciplines. For example, with regard to the politics of nation-states, some may say we would do better not to name a 'nation', as this encircles a heter-ogeneity and conscripts it to nationalism and the fictions of national culture. People live in far more pliable and fluid ways than the inscrip-tions and demarcations of these representations convey – life changes, adapts, duplicates, inverts, and so on, according to the stylistic and strategic choices of the commentators who say so. Attempts to de-lineate definitional boundaries is work aligned to that of undertakers and morticians who deal with the dead. Provocatively, Spivak says in

an interview about (among other things) the identity boundaries of
Indian nationalism:

> Indian-ness is not a thing that exists. Reading Sanskrit scriptures, for example
> – I can't call that Indian, because after all, India is not just Hindu. That 'Indic'
> stuff is not India. The name India was given by Alexander the Great by
> mistake. The name Hindustan was given by the Islamic conquerors. The name
> Bharat, which is on the passport, is in fact a name that hardly anyone uses,
> which commemorates a mythic king. (Spivak 1990a: 39)

The adept of strategic essentialism will shift the boundaries of her map
to her own advantage: 'For example, when I'm constructing myself as
an Indian in reaction to racism, I am very strongly taking a distance
from myself. If an Indian asks me what I am, I'm a Bengali, which is
very different' (Spivak 1990a: 39).[7] Alexander's great mistake was to
take this map as a code for identity.

THE MAPPING RHIZOME

Edward Said's work would keep us alert. His attention to the global
geography of Empire in *Culture and Imperialism* (1993) goes beyond the
focus of *Orientalism* (1978) and suggests scope for more work needed
to unravel the map of contemporary cultural geopolitics. It is necessary
to begin such work because:

> to ignore or otherwise discount the overlapping experience of Westerners
> and Orientals, the interdependence of cultural terrains in which the coloniser
> and colonised co-existed and battled each other through projections as well
> as rival geographies, narratives, and histories, is to miss what is essential about
> the world in the past century. (Said 1993: xxii–iii)

and:

> Once we accept the actual configuration of literary experiences overlapping
> with one another and interdependent, despite national boundaries and
> coercively legislated national autonomies, history and geography are transfig-
> ured *in new maps*, in new and far less stable entities, in new types of connec-
> tions. Exile, far from being the fate of nearly forgotten unfortunates who are
> dispossessed and expatriated, becomes something closer to a norm, an expe-
> rience of crossing boundaries and *charting* new territories in defiance of the
> classic canonic enclosures. (Said 1993: 384; emphasis added)

Said attempts, like some (nascent) explorer, to map a new intellectual
landscape and rethink national and international identities. The point,
however, would be to take this *further*. In these densely packed passages
which frame *Culture and Imperialism* and summarize some of the main

points of all of his work, Said's optimism for defiant boundary-crossing merges with his celebration of hybridity in a way which, I think, is in danger of collapsing differences that are important. Despite hybridity, some peoples are subjected to forms of exile and dispossession that are not so easily rendered literary or acceptable. Although to compare the relative exile of a Salman Rushdie with those subjected to the consequences of partition-enhanced communal strife between Muslims and Hindus, or between Pakistan and India, is to compare unlikes, the difficulty is instructive. Hybridity as a concept, like comparison, and simple notions of representation on a map, far too often achieves only a more refined homogeneity which, further, is highly suited to map the 'new types of connections' which characterize contemporary imperial and capitalist relations. Increasingly capital is hybrid, flowing, border-crossing – and there is something to be said for those who argue that this may be the 'cultural logic of late capitalism', and that it is articulated in 'postmodernism' (Jameson 1991). Guattari repeatedly argues that under capitalism 'deterritorialization' is the new cultural co-ordinate which locates us all (Guattari 1992: 122). In this deterritorialization, capital incorporates all manner of bits of culture into its ever-hungry commodity machine. Like a map that can represent everything, this machine appeals and absorbs, appropriates and consumes, enframes and reframes, every which way.

Guattari sees this as a global danger which is first found in the city: 'on the international level ... cities constitute the connective tissue of ... a network which tends to control the whole of human activities' (Guattari 1992: 124). This is dangerous, because the map extends to a boundary which absorbs even the most multiple and hybrid entities into its matrix, and offers no escape routes:

> connected by telematic means and a great diversity of communications media ... the world city of contemporary capitalism has been deterritorialised ... its various components have been scattered over the surface of a multipolar urban rhizome weaving across and growing tightly into the planet. (Guattari 1992: 124)

This mapping rhizome could include the rich media centres and intelligentsia, as well as sites of the poorest urban conglomerations. All this is orchestrated by the skilled analytics of academic studies, which need to be extended rather than constrained. The map must explode (before we do):

> Hence the pivotal importance of a collaboration, of a transdisciplinarity between the urbanists, the architects and all the other disciplines of the social sciences, the humanities, ecology etc.... The urbanistic drama that is outlined

on the horizon in this end of the millennium is only one aspect of a more fundamental crisis which puts into question the very future of the human race on this planet. (Guattari 1992: 125)

One visitor to Calcutta, with a somewhat morbid outlook, suggested that cities were designed as monuments to death, with the cemetery or the cremation site located in the centre of the calculations of town planners. Planning on any grand organizing level came very late to Calcutta, but it is true that the burning ghat at Nimtollah, the Park Street European cemetery and the (Muslim) graveyard at Tollygunge, are placed in a way that would allow a historical map of death in the city to trace both the river, the British presence, and by extension the history of Bengal and, again, its terrible famines: what is the geographical residue of events, for example, such as that of 1943, when 'maldistribution' of food in India under the British during the war (some would argue that this is a euphemism for a starvation policy) meant that thousands of Bengalis met their death on the streets of the city? Such maps would evoke meanings that cannot be easily contained within safe and conventional readings.

There are maps that resist two-dimensional conventions, and it is important to recognize the extensions of cartography beyond the page into the *realms* of the 'mental map', and so forth. The city is not just a physical space but also a conceptual arena which plays out across a non-geographical zone of meanings; and while it seems most convenient to *chart* this non-spatial *terrain* with the metaphors of geography – *arena*, *across*, *zone* – it is possible and important to *point towards* another *dimension* of the cartography of Calcutta. Travel writing might usefully be considered under this cavalcade of metaphors, since transportation tropes and travel writing attract each other as writers get carried away with certain convenient modes of representation. Ways in which the language of transport conveys other meanings of the city are extensive.

A visitor to Calcutta maps the city in a way that offers a very different approach to some of the main tropes of map-making:

> It is nothing but an intersection. A place of migration where paths cross and too many overlaps lead to confusion – not just the simplistic East meets West crap, which is too idealistic even when presented with irony. Here East meets East in a thousand ways, and the West meets the West and is shocked. Everything intersects (John: Travel diary).

This map reduces aspects of a global view of cultural differences, with a localized observation of the multiplicity of events in the city. The intersection of this hybridity is a powerful reminder that the reductions of representation appear in many places, and this has much to teach us about the ways in which we think: so that here it is not so much that East meets West, but that the West again finds its representations of otherness to be another opportunity for self reflection – 'West meets West' – so that the maps of visitors have still less reference to Calcutta than is supposed, and that many journeys never depart from self-reference, or perhaps never arrive at the other shore.

It should be no surprise, then, that some confusions seem more prominent in this world of travel, and that the metaphor of the maze comes to have a privileged 'place' (which place, where?) in the cultural productions of 'the West'. To follow this notion down a more philo-sophical path, we might consider how the composer Pierre Boulez raises a new cartography as a way of mapping Western thought:

> It must be our concern to follow the examples of Joyce and Mallarmé and to jettison the concept of a work as a simple journey starting with a departure and ending with an arrival ... the modern conception of the maze in a work of art is certainly one of the most considerable advances in Western thought, and one upon which it is impossible to go back. (Boulez in Michelson 1989: 64)

If we were to *follow* Boulez following Joyce and Mallarmé on a journey which included a visit to Calcutta, we would first of all have to invert the formula of a departure leading to an arrival, since to visit a city one instead usually begins with an arrival and ends with a departure. In the above quotation, Boulez seems to remain on a journey more concerned with advances and with the impossibility of turning back in Western thought, such that this maze seems still to be directed by a conventional way of journeying. Nevertheless, the maze metaphor is very prominent in descriptions of the city by other visitors. (In a com-mentary following Boulez, Michael Healy follows the circuits of the maze in another journey, and has written, after the experience of a short visit to India, that Western thought is becoming more diffuse, 'empty of unities and centres and frameworks', so that we are left 'going round and round in circles ... that spiral back on ourselves'; as evidence he referrs to the abundance of video shops in Indian cities which suggests to him that: 'the ghost in the machine is *Indian*' [Healy 1985: 53]. I do not really know how to co-ordinate the itinerary of this particular departure).

There are aspects of travel that cannot be conveniently mapped, even with reference to the still-two-dimensional complexity of the maze. Within 'Western thought', in a way that perhaps Boulez has not yet anticipated, *travel* divides up into a multiplicity: departure, arrival, strangeness, otherness, estrangement, alienation, exile, crisis, redemption, reconciliation, trust, return, death, end, and more. The two-dimensional is not the outer constraint of the epistemology of the map, but there are reasons to search beyond its limits. Going *further* (?) than Boulez along the geography of this question, Deleuze suggests that:

> You only escape dualisms effectively by shifting them like a load [a backpacker metaphor], and when you find between the terms, whether there are two or more, a narrow gorge like a border or a frontier which will turn the set into a multiplicity. (Deleuze and Parnet 1977/1987: 132)

Perhaps, reconnoitring the terrain of these metaphors, Calcutta guide maps should be understood as reference to a flight corridor or frontier for visitors and travellers which marks an intellectual point of departure most often described as chaos, frequently subjected and organized by 'official' cartographic reduction and transcription, and very occasionally explored as a potential 'line of escape' (Deleuze) from the tyranny of regulation.

So metaphors of travel provide a way of making sense of the maze of Calcutta, allowing travellers to express problems of orientation, of finding a way through the labyrinthine city. These kinds of metaphors are especially appropriate vehicles for travellers trying to find their way in a strange city which is *visited* but not *known* in the way a home town might be. The modes of concentration required by the visitor are different: 'Walking through the streets can be tough, and sometimes you forget to look at what is going on, concentrating too much on your destination'. (Cecilia – this criticism of tourists is also made by Nietzsche [1887/1969], who likened them to stupid and sweating animals climbing a mountain who forget to stop on the way and admire the views. Harsh.) Attempting to solve the maze, to orient oneself, or simply wandering in a kind of random pattern, are commonly presented as the 'project' of being in Calcutta, as well as being claimed by some (Adrienne) as a metaphor of self-discovery. Vincent Crapanzano says as much when he discusses travellers: 'Spanning worlds, translating without really translating, explaining without really explaining, describing without really describing,' they are 'doomed less tragically than comically to failure' (Crapanzano 1992: 93). Yet these travels provide 'at least the illusion of a transcendental vantage point for self reflection' (Crapanzano 1992: 93).

An important aspect of the labyrinth metaphor is the idea of exploration. Calcutta as a site for endless discovery is often discussed, to the extent that sometimes 'the longer you stay here the more you realize you hardly know the place at all' (Peter). Just what it takes to 'discover' Calcutta, as the travel brochures and guidebooks would have you do, is a matter of quite different opinions. One volunteer expressed her view with some frustration: 'You need to stay here fifteen years before you understand anything. How long do you need to stay in Calcutta? How long could you stay?' (Fiona).

Another volunteer, who had heard Fiona's comment, wrote:

> Calcutta is my example as I sit in its stomach. How could one begin to describe this city – it's audacious to try – an English girl, ignorant of language, culture, politics, here for a pitiful few months; with my bias, prejudices and all the preconceptions of a 'Western' upbringing, I'm exposed to the most miniature part, without the facilities to make sense of it. And yet images crowd in, impress themselves, force thought, and I have to find its expression in myself. Calcutta speaks, but so much of it is noise and I hesitate to separate out individual voices, as something suggests I can never understand them. (Tammy: Letter)

Another visitor observed that the tourist-volunteers seemed to be put, or put themselves, into a situation where everything they ever believed could be questioned. Where nothing was certain any more, and nothing secure (Suzie), it was difficult to find your way, but you had a responsibility to do so, however different 'reality' might be to the ways it had previously appeared. Unfamiliarity is an enabling condition for some travellers. Adrienne tramps the streets, almost lost, and says: 'I see more when I'm feeling lost, not frightened, but just a little unsure of the way; I look more closely'. This theme of loss appears often in the more 'counter-cultural' kinds of expression: 'You come here not so much to find yourself as to lose yourself' (Helen), and: 'To disappear into the confusion of differences which is Calcutta, and India, where you have to reinvent your identity because all your reference points – from toilets to language – are misplaced' (Roland). When confused and 'average' middle-class youth travel to a place where they can only lose their way – for all the learning experiences and 'character-building' aspects of this kind of travel – the political and ideological consequences and context of international budget tourism become more troublesome. Representations become cluttered, chaotic. Home, order and predictable familiarity are privileged in contrast to the 'disorder' of difference. Another traveller repeated the Lettriste International experiment of trying to navigate the city, in this case Calcutta, with a map of another city, that of London. Spectacularly unsuccessful. Walter Benjamin, commenting on Baudelaire, writes: 'the revealing presentations of the big city ... are the work of those who have traversed the city absently, as it were, lost in thought or in worry' (Benjamin quoted in Home 1991: 21).

When the metaphorical register expands into unexpected realms, such as another variant of the labyrinth offered by Catherine, diverse effects need to be analysed:

> 'Calcutta is crazy like an ants' nest upon which someone has poured boiling water. Everyone is trying to get from one place to another at the same time with no rules, except maybe the social version of the random particle theory – people moving about at varied speeds and no possibility of prediction of the inevitable occasional collisions.'

Lévi-Strauss also sometimes described social life in similar ant-metaphor terms (1966/1983), and the separation of the observer and context which operates in such descriptions is a recurrent one in sociology. At the same time, the scientific gesture claims some affinity with the natural sciences, and attempts to predict the workings of the world. Understandings expressed through these kinds of metaphors – be they those of the social scientist or of the speculating traveller – are suspect not least of all in their importation of images from strange categories to make sense of human lifestyles: people are not ants, nor are they particles in an atom, however much they may drive themselves towards destruction. 'This is a more natural city; everyone does whatever they want. Look at how they drive all over the road' (Rachel).

Accidents do happen, and the traffic situation does generate a number of interesting comparisons:

> 'Calcutta is vastly different to Delhi, which is for tourists just a vast arrival station of cultural differences. It's a simple opposition; the culture you left against a new and fascinating-confusing one. People don't stay in Delhi long, whereas in Calcutta tourists have more time and are forced to negotiate their differences – to navigate the traffic, not always managing to avoid a few bumps and scrapes. The taxis in Calcutta have lots of dents – in Delhi you're either fine or smashed by a bus.' (Birgid)

ALTERNATIVE MAPS

Looking for maps that do not enclose the city, or at least to find modes of map-making that leave spaces (of escape) for counter-hegemonic inscriptions of experience, might be a good description of the attitude of those who would renounce the Lonely Planet Guide pre-figured versions of Calcutta. In Modern Lodge travellers expressed a need for, and began to make, maps of the city which could be placed somewhere between the mainstream cartography and the expectations of existing maps, and the chaos and loss of not having a map at all.

Against the predictable 'monument' tourism of the travel guides, which took in the Victoria Memorial, the Indian Museum and Kali Temple, since 1992 an 'alternative tour' has become popular among the backpackers of Sudder Street. This 'tour' includes, in a haphazard and eclectic way, a visit to the College Street bookshops near Calcutta University, possible participation in a Communist rally, coffee in the Indian Coffee House, lunch at a small Bengali food co-op, curiosity shops, various film houses, dance halls and cultural venues, Nahoum's cake stall in New Market, views of the statues of Lenin, Marx and Engels, M.K. Gandhi and Netaji Subhas Chandra Bose, and so on. It is symbolic of these alternative tours that the statues offered more than bronzed histories as they provided opportunities to gain access to important aspects of contemporary Calcutta's political life. The statue of Lenin overlooks one of the busiest intersections of the city, Gandhi was 'festooned' with lights for the fiftieth anniversary of the Quit India movement, and Netaji Bose, adversary of the Mahatma and cultural hero in communist Calcutta, sits astride a horse at Five Points Crossing (also mentioned in Grass's writing on the city, and site for birth-centenary celebrations – and Netaji's possible return? – in 1996–7). It was from such 'tours' of the political aspect of the city that calls for counter-maps of Calcutta emerged.

For all the 'received' images of Calcutta that circulate in the travel brochures, academic and literary texts, and in the guidebooks, the 'production' of the city is also very much a 'productive' activity of every traveller. To differing degrees visitors not only internalize the tropes of representation of the city but continue, elaborate, embellish and evaluate them. The majority of visitors participate in the dissemi-nation of the stereotypes of Calcutta to be found in the most popular literature and in the most readily available guidebook, or marked on the most accessible map. The experience of making an alternative map of Calcutta offers, with all its contradictions, a useful lesson in the tyranny of representation. Alternative versions of Calcutta, outside the stereotypes, are difficult to maintain, hard to find, and continually silenced, overlooked or forgotten, through lack of the same sort of infrastructural supports offered by accepted maps and the convenience of the Lonely Planet guide. Nevertheless, the city *is* mapped in ways

Lonely Planet cannot imagine, and the notion of the map, and the ways in which people come to understand and inscribe space, should not always be reduced to the same flat and boring routines.

The alternative maps, however, were little more than an attempt by some travellers who had stayed a reasonably long time in Calcutta (longer than those who were simply 'passing through') to make available some of the things in the city which made their visits memorable. On the principle that things not described in the guidebooks will be only 'accidentally' found by travellers, there was an attempt to pass these 'accidents' along to newly arrived backpackers and volunteers. The sharing of experience, hints, clues, and so on, is an important part of backpacker culture and arrogance – these often-lost, reinvented, and lost-again maps became a sort of codified version of the Modern Lodge rooftop discussions. Perhaps even the alternative and counter-Lonely Planet aspect of these tours and maps made them more credible or fashionable under the aegis of the unusual or the exclusive, so that those 'in the know' could think themselves more privileged than the 'average' visitor.

This, of course, is not as much an 'alternative' as the word might suggest. These maps are still machineries of perception. ('What is it that tells us that, on a line of flight, we will not rediscover everything that we are fleeing': Deleuze and Parnet 1977/1987: 38). While travellers who stop 'long-term' in Calcutta disconnect from the conventional circuits of tourism to some degree, the non-glossy aspects of the city can be 'marketed' as well. When the 'everyday' becomes more interesting than the monumental, difficulties and incongruities become routines of pleasure. Large hotels and swimming-pools are ignored in favour of the rough romance of the banana-pancake trail and cheap 'local' colour. New conventions emerge to cater for market differentiations, so that recently one large travel publisher released a City Guide to capitalize on a very suburban experience of the city. The map promoted an 'informed' experience of Calcutta, including sites of various charity organizations selling handicrafts, emporiums, missions, and cultural markers for a kind of 'alternative' or 'intelligent tourism' that does not seem too far removed from any other mode of consumerism. The danger here is that everything can be fitted into the mould of consumption (in this case through a kind of alternative policing of space).

Different kinds of map might still be made. Following another observation by James, a traveller in Calcutta who said: 'Calcutta is nothing but corners of streets, everyone crossing the road in any which way, and the government saying the chaos of unrepaired and crowded roads keeps down the traffic speed, and therefore there are less accidents', an experimental map might track actual use of a street on any particular day. The street where most travellers stay, Sudder Street, is uneven, the footpath is more often rubble than flat, the holes in the road are large, and dangerous during monsoon flooding, and yet 'the chaos seems uniform' (James again). Everyone seems to find an appropriate path or position, there is a 'code', there are protocols to learn, and patterns into which visitors 'fit' – in spaces, or corridors, designated for them (no doubt Gunter Grass's cow would pass by sometime). Some hawkers attract tourists to one side of the street, others avoid a particular corner, street children occupy a disused sidestall, the heads of passers-by turn at the more popular café to see who is there, a newspaper-wallah stops customers in the middle of the road – a tracing of the patterns of these trajectories would reveal the 'code' of use of the street in economic as well as cultural and political terms. Another visitor, with unintended aural irony, called the chaos of everyone wandering all over the road the 'staggering urban clutter of Calcutta' (Vanessa).

'Walking in the city is a zigzag, serpentine, stop-and-start, crab affair' (Vanessa again). Even the dignified promenade under the splendour of the colonial verandas of the Oberoi Grand Hotel along Jawaharlal Nehru Road can be a series of collisions punctuated only by occasional moments of co-ordination and symmetry when the entire crowd pushes the same way at the same time.

> 'Slouching and side-stepping on uneven pavement, taking a detour to avoid a burst pipe, roadworks, the underground, or some heap of rubbish. The continuous noise [a constant 60–80 decibels in many streets] becomes a barely noticed background hum to an urban dance. Bicycle bells ring from nowhere, Ambassador cabs lurch like demons down the street, walking in this city is an adventure.' (Jennifer)

De Certeau comments: 'The motions of walking are spatial creations. They link sites one to the other' (De Certeau 1985: 129). Among what might at first appear to be chaos, there are techniques of pedestrian locomotion which are developed quickly by visitors to the city – excluding the chauffeur-driven guests of the Oberoi – which amount to a certain jaunty, jostling step and a preference for abandoning the bustle of the pavements in favour of the edge of the road. To walk in danger of being clipped by a bus or car, giving the pavements up to the commerce of hawkers and the all-too-basic dwellings of displaced families, is an option which makes the roads still more congested. There seems to be no respite from this. Amazingly, Calcutta appears as a pedestrian's city.

Perhaps this amazement, which is also the recognition of the partiality of all representation, is something like that wonder with which Borges approached the city of Aleph which could not be mapped:

> what I want to do is impossible, for any listing of an endless series is doomed to be infinitesimal. In that single gigantic instant I saw millions of acts both delightful and awful; not one of them amazed me more than the fact that all of them occupied the same point in space, without overlapping or transparency ... what I shall now write down will be successive, because language is successive. Nonetheless, I shall try to recollect what I can. (Borges 1971: 13)

The maze or labyrinth model of the city converges with one of the favourite mystery-fantasies of intellectuals since, at least, medieval times, conjured with by Bataille, Borges, Eco, Kafka. It may remain undecided as to whether or not the ultimate 'fix' of the scholar is the paranoid realism of Kafka's *The Trial*, where the frustrations of bureaucracy always threaten to drive on to a screaming hysteria, but within which the citizen is obliged to behave with good humour, as if all were routine. Or perhaps it is Eco's *The Name of the Rose*, where a lost text by Aristotle on the importance of laughter is rediscovered, only to be consumed in a fire that destroys an irreplaceable maze-like library (remembering Alexandria and the destruction of its library) lit by a defiantly anti-Dionysian guardian (a death shrieking in the flames, stuffing poisoned pages into a ravenous and frenzied mouth). It would be difficult to find a more manoeuvrable metaphor of the unending desire and ultimate undecidability of knowledge. No other register could present itself with such facility for representing so much in such tantalizing complexity, yet finally provide so little. (There is something here for a critique of Said's flat hybridity.) That the maze seems more and more drawn towards the city should not be a surprising consequence of our experience of wandering, perhaps with less and less comprehension, the streets of Calcutta.

The city-as-a-maze is one which forces the traveller to ask directions, to articulate what is otherwise drawn on paper with the – perhaps forlorn – hope of explication. Hollier's reading of Bataille's labyrinthine texts leads him to suggest that the labyrinth:

> does not hold still, but because of its unbounded nature breaks open lexical prisons, prevents any word from finding a resting place ever ... multiplying meanings by inverting or splitting them: it makes words drunk. (Hollier 1974/ 1989: 60)

Amid all these maps, which must sometimes overlap with contrary codifications, it should not be surprising that I am often lost. When I ask the way I become more confused, or I am drawn into some other exchange, another direction, which demands a change of plan. Sometimes the plethora of images fragments into incomprehensible differences; at other times it seems all too much the same. Lost in differences and lost in similarities. My own desire to make maps of Calcutta can also be charted alongside these themes; the irreducibility of the city to any mapped representation; the two-dimensionality, and linearity, of 'Western thought'; the convergence of travel and terrain metaphors in the way these projects are described; the stops and starts of attempts to escape the maze, spiral, labyrinth; and the convolutions of counter-hegemonic efforts continually (interminably) to sidestep the dead ends of representation.

Along the way I have found my inadequate mapping skills a recurrent obstacle to ever completing even a half-finished version of this project. I often wondered if I had the stamina to continue, whether I had the discipline to connect all these scattered bits and pieces together, to 'write it up'. The technology is not so easy to manipulate; pre-folded along creased lines. All the time there has been a plan, or plans, and never any illusion that this catalogue of fragments would not require work on the part of the reader, but still I wondered if it would all come together with the haphazard coherence I thought was there, but feared was invisible. The months of editing my notebooks loomed ahead like a terrible weight; I kept postponing the task, finding excuses for diversions, excursions, delays. I kept on going back to Calcutta, filling my passport with stamps, my notebooks with more notes. All the roads I followed led to others and never to a main thoroughfare, and all the roads were clogged. I became more and more doubtful of the readability of the entire enterprise. While it is something that will always be re-written over and over, and while I would like to avoid the reductions and fixations this inevitably entails, I think I would have liked the security of having taken notes on the notes (yet another delay/relay), and of providing a map to this map, a guide (to this) book.

CARTOGRAPHY IN ITS PLACE

In *Hosts and Guests: The Anthropology of Tourism*, Greenwood asserts that 'tourism is the largest scale movement of goods, services and people that humanity has perhaps ever seen' (Greenwood 1989: 172). In the same volume Lett qualifies this perhaps with an exclusion of military

travel: 'Modern tourism accounts for the single largest peaceful movement of people across cultural boundaries in the history of the world'
(Lett 1989: 275-6). These discussions within the growing anthropology
of tourism represent significant changes in the map of the world, yet
somehow the tone of such comments seems terribly mundane. While
they are able to rehearse the themes of conventional travel studies
literature, an overly optimistic evaluation of tourism as a 'profound,
widely shared human desire to know "others", with the reciprocal
possibility that we may come to know ourselves' (McKean 1989: 133)
seems prevalent. One traveller at the Modern Lodge wryly noted that
what mass tourism was about was 'coming miles and miles away to
look at people you'd ignore at home' (Emma). A critique of 'otherness'
as something to be packaged and marketed through tourism (Greenwood 1989: 179) is inadequate if it remains only the subject of anecdotal
accounts, as Greenwood complains. Summarizing the work of other
analysts, Lafant and Graburn write in *Tourism Alternatives: Potentials and
Problems in the Development of Tourism*:

> The tourist industry's system of production is now considered one of the
> world's most powerful driving forces. Through mergers and concentrations,
> these companies have become agents of an interconnected network penetrating
> many sectors. The transnationals of tourism are the avant-garde for strategies
> of capital internationalisation. The system of tourist production has evolved
> into network-companies, models for transnational companies in the world
> economy. (Lafant and Graburn 1992: 97)

The need for detailed studies to chart the particularities of tourism as
articulated by Nash (1989: 52), is not filled by the majority of travel
writers; or travellers who write, and who remain within the Lonely
Planet grid of these conventions; the stay-at-homes.

> Let's go, let's go, all aboard your armchairs! ... you must get an idea of these
> journeys and of the people who think travelling is really something. Today
> the world is cut up into little paved squares and served up on a platter, yet
> there are still some doughheads out there who talk about their 'travels' with
> papal seriousness, as if they were the first ones ever to have gone anywhere
> ... [they] have been to the suburbs and back! As long ago as I can remember,
> I have dreaded people who talk about their vacations. (Aragon 1928/1991:
> 41–2)

Aragon's contempt is for those 'adventurers' who expect great revelations
from people they have just met in strange foreign cafés – 'avoid them
like the plague' (Aragon 1928/1991: 42). This is as good an approxima-

tion of any of the general boredom with travel conversations that still prevails in academic literature.

Where more than ten years ago Crick could lament the dearth of detailed anthropological writings on travel (Crick 1985), it is now the case that anthropologists, and sundry other writers, seem plagued by far too much literature. Tourism studies is becoming a boom industry. Yet perhaps the particularity of Crick's lament – that despite a few good general texts, we still have too few ethnographic studies of traveller behaviour in specific places – remains valid. The boom has been in the area of a kind of 'booster' philosophy of tourism which is only mildly critical of the industry. Courses in universities on the development of leisure and tourism abound, travelogues occupy more and more space in the bookstores, and the debates which flared over Crick's alleged conflation of the persona of the tourist and of the anthropologist has now mellowed into a polite, even insipid, negotiation of distinctions. It seems that tourism is the most conventional aspect of the global economy.

Academic studies, including this one, contribute to this situation. It may seem valuable to be able both to satisfy the demand for a localized study of touristic activity – an ethnographic study of a 'tribe' of tourists – and to map out formal distinctions between the work of anthropologists and the play of tourists in the context of global politics – some sort of literature survey of recent debates about the negotiation of cultural difference – but I fear that neither of these projects is ultimately very useful. This is because I think there is still some point to the taunt that anthropologists are a species of tourist – they just have more up-market tools – and as such they participate in a global economy of cultural differences which can be seen in all locales, but cannot be understood without reference to much wider matters. While it is important to remember that a travel brochure is not a monograph on culture, slippage between the forms deserves close attention (Garcia 1988: 93).

Pico Iyer has called tourists the 'terrorists of cultural expansion … anyone with a credit card could become a colonialist' (Iyer 1989: 13). In her thought-provoking volume, Rana Kabbani has noted the close links between Empire and travel writing: 'To write a literature of travel cannot but imply a colonial relationship' (Kabbani 1986: 10). This colonialism is founded on an imperial power that includes the authority of academic institutions to articulate the 'real' space of exotic sites. Along the way Kabbani has a dig at the derivative writing of travellers: 'It is as if the imagination of the traveller, in order to function, has to be sustained by a long tradition of Western scholarship, by other Western texts' (Kabbani 1986: 10). There are conventions of description and conventional clichés which are renewed over and over, so that the continuities of travel literature may be traced across long periods of time. Kabbani's work is to follow the echoes of Burton and Lawrence in contemporary writings about Arabia. A similar project could find much older sources than I have presented for this representational cartography of Calcutta.

However, the classic Orientalist narrative of the splendidly rich and exotic East is curiously less readily associated with Calcutta than with almost any other part of India. While Calcutta was the port through which wealth flowed into England, it is the Black Hole that is always remembered, while the rest of Indian Orientalist history abounds with tales of 'exotic travels' which require the reader to wade through sagas of fabulous and ostentatious wealth, Nizams, palaces, banquets, tiger hunts and feasting. At best Calcutta gets Kipling, who wrote powerful words on the city: 'built on silt, I am Asia. Death in my hands, but gold!' Exotica versions of the 'Orient' rarely entail scenes of poverty or exploitation, preferring instead a spicy history of riches, which then flows into fantasy films like *Octopussy* (discussed below in Chapter 6), *Indiana Jones and the Temple of Doom*, and so on. This contrast, which makes Calcutta only the Kipling-routine of 'city of dreadful night', and glosses the rest of India as mysterious and mystical, is like a prophecy imparted to the visitor before arrival, and all too often confirmed. The front cover of the Lonely Planet guide now carries a classic postcard portrait of the Palace of the Winds in Jaipur. No surprise there.

Neither academic nor touristic literature − and none of these maps, of course − can be independent of projects of consumption under the social formations of capitalism. This includes the ways in which resistances and creative realignments of previously mapped-out expectations can be renegotiated and drawn into the consumption processes of visiting Calcutta. The flows of life are continually inscribed and re-inscribed by this cartographic mentality. While the city can never be totalized and gridded in full sufficiency − unlike the achievement of Borges's map-maker − and indeed, the purpose of a map is never 'full' representation but, rather, adequate and convenient reduction, there is still a slippage which conflates reduction with representation with illus-tration with manifestation. To some extent this applies with the logic of: 'if there is nothing marked on the map, then there is nothing there', but it also operates in other modes of representation, just as reductive as maps.

Debates in geography offer a relevant coda for this chapter. Marxist scholars brought to geography the recognition that 'mental maps' of social domains were produced in specific socioeconomic formations. Of course geographers are produced under similar conditions, so that it is possible to read the programmatic statements of urban scholars like Dear and Scott in ways that are also relevant to tourism studies and the place of maps in cultural production. In a suggestion that also applies to cartography, Dear and Scott posit that:

> urbanisation is decipherable only as a mediated outcome of the social dynamics and imperatives of the capitalist mode of production in specific conjunctural circumstances ... urbanisation and planning [and maps] can never be effectively treated as objects of theoretical study divorced from some wider theory of society. (Dear and Scott 1973: 4)

This comment can also remind us that the project of this specific study of tourism is one where some attention to a variety of contexts is crucial – in the social sciences the contexts of study are diverse: practical problems and theoretical interests; the priorities of military-orientated urban planning; political histories and socioeconomic hierarchies; the global orders of tourism; epistemologies of 'Western thinking' and the New World Order; the covert agendas and unforeseen (?) applications of social research; consumerist orientations; the dark exposures of photography; the language and metaphors or protocols of representational forms; the demarcation of boundaries and differences; desire for alternatives and counter-hegemonic productions; and so much more. All this might also be explored as a context for making sense of maps, in this chapter, as it is for the discussion of the camera in the next two chapters (5 and 6). Enframed as they are, maps bring Calcutta into focus: the *way* one approaches them is, of course, a guide to the Orient(ation).

This chapter has explored metaphors of travel and the city, drawing attention to the use of the notion of the maze or the labyrinth as a guide to an otherwise disordered experience. The map, as a mechanism which can order a city, overlaps with a traveller's expectations, guides a traveller through strange streets towards expected monuments and sites (sights). What is sought on the map is, more often than not, found – as Heidegger would have us believe. The production of space is intricately co-ordinated with the metaphorics of travel, especially in so far as these appear in official representational forms, and industry adjuncts. The means of production of mapped space is also the map – a landscape that is both 'imaginary' and with significant effects in a global economy reaching in to describe also local space. Even in its labyrinthine forms – and indeed, in attempts by some travellers to indulge in, and/or escape, this cartography with alternatives – the map remains a tool of power. Tourism alternatives reinscribe the city in ways which are quite closely derived from the established protocols, and from within the consumptive logic of inscription and globalized commodity exchange.

NOTES

1. Ferguson's study (1993) of maps and travel guides of Venice from Jacopo de Barbari's 1500 woodcut to Baedeker, the famous cultural guide published from 1829, offers a useful attempt to unpack travel ontology.

2. As kitsch I have in mind here the series of twelve or so ghastly colour reproductions of the Queen Victoria Memorial available as postcards on Sudder Street. These postcards are printed just slightly out of focus, or with the colour registration a millimetre out, or with garish foregrounded foliage from the memorial gardens. They are so bad that they are truly great.

3. This chapter was a maze itself before a guiding hand plotted a better course. I am indebted to Michael Dutton for much-needed and valuable support during important stages of this project.

4. Thanks to Jonah Tennick for pointing out these connections.

5. At one stage in the 1960s Debord was Lefebvre's research assistant; some complaints have been made against Lefebvre for citing Debord only twice in *The Production of Space* – such complaints are ironic coming from the champions of plagiarism. Interestingly, the arrival of the UK punk group the Sex Pistols allowed these points to be coded in the slogan-anthem 'Holidays in other people's misery' (Pistols, 1978: *Never Mind the Bollocks*).

6. I reviewed Geertz's book in an essay for the journal *Social Analysis* (Hutnyk 1990). Heated debates over the activities of University of Sydney researchers in Thailand began in the mid-1970s and still continued into 1992, with a seminar in the Department of Anthropology which was notable for the polarization of two strictly demarcated 'sides' of the argument. The question of researchers in the direct employ of the US army is one which could completely undermine scholarship's right to claim any legitimacy whatsoever. See Cohen (1993) for a stimulating discussion of the politics of academia under capitalism.

7. At this point I should thank Nikos Papastergiadis and Scott McQuire for making it possible to link up with Spivak here, travelling all night up a mad highway in Australia, back in what seems like less than ten-plus years ago.

5

PHOTOGENIC CALCUTTA

This chapter and the next consider the most popular of technologies of representation available to tourists: the camera. Tourists are characterized, and caricatured, everywhere as camera-wielding beings who take photos of everything. The technological production of a kind of photogenic Calcutta as a series of appropriated images (which need not necessarily be *of* Calcutta) can be explored through the ways in which the camera is handled by visitors.

Fascination with representation in recent times seems to correspond with the emergence of computer graphics, heightened levels of information exchange, and the proliferation, internationally, of an economy of the image. Cameras have been widely available for some time,[1] and while it is not necessary to agree with Crary that it is so significant that 'most of the historically important functions of the human eye are being supplanted by practices in which visual images no longer have any reference to the position of the observer in the "real", optically perceived world' (Crary 1990: 2), the interrelations of vision and technology do become problematic.

> Emergent technologies of image production are becoming the dominant models of visualisation according to which primary social processes and institutions function. And, of course, they are intertwined with the needs of global information industries and with the expanding requirements of medical, military, and police hierarchies. (Crary 1990: 2)

Representation has long been of concern, and it is perhaps only recently (see Foucault 1966/1970) that the 'real-time' observing subject has come under scrutiny. While worrying about representation and its histories, I want to employ Heidegger's notion of enframing and

Marx's discussion of commodity fetishism as a means to tighten the focus on discussions of 'the gaze'. Crary's pursuit of the ways in which 'techniques of the observer' calibrate with global 'events and forces' and 'forms of institutional and discursive power' (Crary 1990: 3) provides the backdrop. The presentation of Calcutta to travellers, as explored in the chapters above on travel literature and in Modern Lodge, can now be placed alongside those items most closely associated with the returning traveller: the holiday snapshot and the souvenir. These are what the traveller brings back from Calcutta; they are the material link with the 'outside' world, or home. Just as the traveller who arrives with loaded baggage carries much besides rolls of empty film, the returning traveller carries away more than exposed rolls and a backpack bulging with memorabilia. I want to take the souvenir and the photograph together to show that the conditions in which they are taken by travellers are quite similar, and must be understood within the circulating and technological contexts I outlined with reference to Marx and Heidegger in Chapter 1.

INSTAMATIC ANTHROPOLOGY

There is a photograph of a nun, one of the Missionaries of Charity doing the work of Mother Teresa in Calcutta, and this nun is skipping with a rope among a group of children. I'm not sure why this photo catches me so much – she is facing away from the camera, back to us, yet it is as if she were looking; the sari covering her head could equally cover her face. The upturned sole of her bare foot confirms that she is facing away; as I look closer it is revealed that there are two skippers, one almost fully hidden behind the nun, probably a schoolchild. Among the group of watching children a third of them look past the nun into the lens – this photo has more than bounce; what springs to mind is not the serenity or austerity which might easily be expected to cover the countenance of such a nun, but instead something far more lively, and I want this photo to stand for what has so often been 'skipped over' in popular conceptions of Calcutta: there is more life bound up here than a brief glance might entertain.

Discussions of photography and the image in tourism studies seem to me always to be framed with nostalgia. The image that one retains is somehow deployed as a mirror for experience, a kind of mimetic souvenir, a token which enables a return down the path of reminiscence, reflection and understanding. At the same time a critique of the image, and of the gaze (Urry 1990), seems also to have the structure of nostalgia – a nostalgia for a more authentic vision, for a photography which does not 'steal' the image away, which reflects without the transgression of power that is often (not always) easily recognized in the photographic moment. Among contemporary social theorists it is Baudrillard who articulates this nostalgia most eloquently. What is also interesting is the photographic or cinematic code in which it is framed:

> We used to live in the imaginary world of the mirror, of the divided self and of the stage, of otherness and alienation. Today we live in the imaginary world of the screen, of the interface and the reduplication of contiguity and networks. All our machines are screens. We too have become screens, and our interactivity has become the interactivity of screens. Nothing that appears on the screen is meant to be deciphered in depth, but actually to be explored instantaneously, in an abreaction immediate to meaning – or an immediate convolution of the poles of representation. (Baudrillard 1988: 7)

During my study of foreign tourism in Calcutta, over and over again, through what Amitav Ghosh called the 'endless flow of Indo-babble' in discourse about travel, I heard the same kinds of metaphors guiding the ways in which India was to be understood by the travellers I met. Of course I myself often utilized the same themes; and so very frequently they were those of the media world, of film, screen, photo, image. Yet at the same time it was as if we all knew already that this was just a scene of illusions – the image threatened to 'slide off the screen' at any moment. All the talk of *Maya* within Indian philosophies had somehow found its way into the technological frameworks of what might be called Western understanding. This repetition of screen-like images in the ways travellers, especially backpackers, talk about their experiences indicates, at least, a particularly specific construction of those experiences through a mechanism of othering learnt, I suppose, in front of the television, at the cinema, and from the family photo album. However unsure I remain about this, it is still plausible to argue that the construction of experience through the medium of preservable two-dimensional (moving or still) representation is one of the most important contemporary phenomena of international travel, and consideration of this in the context of the disparate economic and social privileges of tourists and others could indicate the path towards more sophisticated responses to the problems of cultural difference, at least in so far as tourism, and perhaps anthropology and photography, are concerned.

The camera is *the* international signifier of tourism. With the mass explosion of leisure travel in the latter part of this century, many photos have been taken, an amazing compendium of images – sunsets, mountains, beaches, etc. – now piled up and in boxes under beds and above cupboards in every home, everywhere. Holiday photography is the record which shows, no matter how rushed the visit, that what was seen was what was there; and it is always realist, things as they appear to the mechanism. That photography has a place within the economy of tourism will be readily recognized. The extent to which it is one of the major framing devices of all 'tours' is perhaps less clear, but to consider just the superficial appearances, in only the preparations for travel, there would be abundant occasions to refer to photography. The travel brochure, the passport, the visa application, the duty-free film, the 'camera-safe' luggage X-ray, and so on. Travel is overexposed to photography.

At the same time a more complex involvement of photography in the experience of travel can be signalled with reference to philosophies of perception. Photography has changed the way the world can be viewed, yet following the shortcomings of art history, the history of photography has paid too little attention to the sociopolitical ramifications of this. More generally it might be argued that cultural representation under contemporary capitalism goes on through technologies which have until recently largely escaped detailed serious and sustained analysis in terms of techniques of representing culture – the frame of the visual, the tropes of narration, the authenticity of images, and so on. The ethnocentrism of European modes of representation of the visual grows out of the frame of painting, which promoted certain ways of knowing the world, the body, and so on, and has continued today into the frames of Kodak, Fuji, Agfa and the thoroughly pictorial orientation of documentary and realistic photography. At the same time this ethnocentric perception is not confined to the visual, but participates in a wide matrix of technologies which co-ordinate a very specific mode of cultural awareness and a constraint of possibility that hardly seems visible from within the consumer world of cameras, videos and tape-recorders, yet is utterly and overwhelmingly 'framed':

Memories you can keep. (Kodak advertising slogan 1987)

Would you trust your memories to anyone else? (Kodak 1993)

In the hands of travellers from so many nations, cameras whirr and shutters click at an alarming rate, a global industry. Culture, meaning, experience – the circulation of these forms is the work (labour) of 'enframing', and today this work operates through technologies of reproduction which ever more rapidly bring a world of endless repetition/duplication of images and meanings (and experience) which can be grasped, had, owned, bought and sold, in a convenient form. This is true for an ever-increasing segment of the population of the planet, including many of the workforce of the 'Third World' states. Susan Sontag sees the development of camera technology as something which 'carried out the promise inherent in photography from its very beginning: to democratise all experiences by translating them into images'; and, somewhat uncritically, she notes that photography is a way of 'converting experience into an image, a souvenir' (Sontag 1979: 7). Does she mean that my passport is a souvenir of democracy? Almost everybody now carries at least one familiar (family) photograph, or at least a pass card, but I don't see much democracy in that. Thus the mechanisms of the camera spill over into tourism, cultural difference, imperialism, politics, and so on, in so many scenes – the interrelated technological appropriations of capital through which everything is understood as if it were snapped-shot in the frame. Cameras point at culture everywhere, poking into the darkest flashlit nooks and crannies, capturing anything and everything in a million rolls, a massive campaign. At 35mm a second (I am intentionally confusing formats here). The co-ordinates of cultural identity and comparison are fixed in small, easy-to-carry squares. It is as if a great reduction machine were at work turning life into a billion miniatures.

PICTURE THIS

A story I heard in India – perhaps on the rooftop of Modern Lodge – described the scene of the young Picasso, beginning to gain some international fame, being asked by a North American journalist if it was true that he was such a good painter he could paint anything. And as a kind of test, the journalist presented a photograph of a woman which he carried in his wallet (this is the way journalists sometimes behave) and said: 'Could you paint my wife?' Picasso studied the photograph for a few seconds and replied, 'No, she is too small,' and then, after a pause, continued, 'and besides, she is too flat.' Questions of fidelity to the real can be inserted here. In *The Tourist Gaze*, John Urry writes that the 'power of [a] photograph ... stems from its ability to pass itself off as a miniaturisation of the real, without revealing its constructed nature or its ideological content intimately bound up with the tourist gaze' (Urry 1990: 139). It is clearly not only the captions attached to photographs – 'my wife', 'the tourist' – which direct ideologically motivated interpretations. The point of the Picasso anecdote, however, is also that any critical perspective on such interpretation cannot claim power to dispel the 'ideological effects of the gaze'. Interpretation still colours his response; he could probably recognize the wife.

Anecdotes themselves can function like snapshots to give the idea of a scene, just as – cliché – 'a picture paints its thousand words'. One of the more significant consequences of backpacker travel to Calcutta is the retrieval of a host of stories (some of which escape the conventions of 'the rumour of Calcutta'), a treasure trove. An entire archive of traveller tales has largely been ignored in urban studies and tourism economics and consigned instead to guidebooks and 'literature'. The imagery of the traveller, however, plays a crucial role in the formation of opinion about the city. Calcutta as the font of storytelling would not be anathema to its intelligentsia, but the snaps the travellers take home are perhaps less developed than might be hoped. The traveller comes and goes quickly; Virilio sees Calcutta, like any other major metropolis, as an 'image-site' at the end of a speeding airliner (Virilio 1984/1989: 7) and in his text the city flickers at the end of a media transmission while its corporeality begins to disintegrate. Now every city is to be seen through a filter, through an electronic haze in a wider economy; and by pointing the device at some corner of Calcutta, the photographer is immediately – snap – ready to escape with a 'souvenired' version of it for the 'outside'.

What is it that is taken 'outside' in all those rolls of film shot by the travellers, volunteers, visitors? What kind of Calcutta do they represent? There are a number of set conventional images which collate some rather narrow stereotypes for the city – the rickshaw-wallah pulling his cart, the destitutes queuing at the street clinic, the overcrowded double-decker buses; but over and over, the poor. Every photo is seen from some perspective; there is always an angle. And while all photographs can be said to be 'constructed', this, of course, does not mean they are without political effects (for good and bad?). Nothing is ever seen just as it is; all angles, especially camera angles, are positioned and determined by factors of context and contingency. Even pointing the camera without thinking invokes a complex set of figuring preconditions.

Photostop. I woke one morning and went for breakfast at the Fairlawn Hotel (when breakfast there was cheaper than it is today, before it became a set for *City of Joy*). I arrived just before an effervescent North American tourist, with an enormous zoom-lens camera, who had been photographing lepers and other street-dwellers as they woke up. 'The culture of the streets', he announced to all. Bruner has written of the camera as a 'wonderful device for closet voyeurs, in that they can look, even stare, without embarrassment' (Bruner 1989: 441). A visit to Fairlawn to meet the well-off North American tourist was an already loaded invitation to be provoked by the vast contrasts of wealth and values that are displayed – but even being prepared for this, and attempting some sort of balance and reserve, I found it impossible to understand how anyone could enter into such a voyeuristic enterprise with no sense of embarrassment or hesitation at all. Provoked, I asked as politely as I could whether he felt at all guilty intruding on people's lives in this way. A blank expression for two seconds was followed by the rationalization that he'd paid his guide five rupees to wake the sleepers up in the first place. It is no surprise that I found this obscene. (Part of my outrage here is fear that this book is not all that different. Anthropologists have long since traded tobacco, blankets, beads, money and solidarity for stories. Who should I be paying?) The ease with which Calcuttan street-dwellers are exposed to such transparently imperialist appropriations is a product of the 'open' nature of the streets-as-abode. Exposure itself is one of the problems the people face even beyond the occasional annoyances, and still more occasionally the revenues, of tourist-voyeurs.

Calcutta is opened up, then, for those from the outside, in pre-ordained ways. The ways in which the city is imagined by the visitor are vivisectionist and have little relation to the life of residents, treating the city instead as a corpse for observation. The vision of this vivisection cuts through the living areas of the city to extract the central organs, the heart – the monumental scenes of Howrah Bridge, perhaps – in hard and awesome focus: the 'poor' living beneath the flyover. This scene is not so much panoramic as epic in its representation of poverty in Calcutta. And the aesthetic orchestration of poverty for the camera is a consequence of an audience which will consume this poverty with compassion, as 'news from the front', or from the urban hell 'end of the world'. Calcutta has achieved this special reputation outside its precincts. The camera provides more and more actors for this melo-drama which unfolds as much in the Western press as on the streets themselves.

In certain ways tourists and travellers are without identity, a mobile army of camera-clicking suction cups sweeping into cities and villages as subtly as a cyclone, a 'frenzy of photo-mania' (Crick 1990) – of course this cannot apply to all travellers, but there is an alarming degree of purist consumerism to be observed on the tourist trail. Rather than give anything at the places visited – and tourists now visit almost every place – it is more or less all take. Click. An anonymous consuming cultural machine, buying, eating, looking, writing, filming (at the more organized levels not even their foreign exchange remains within the tourist sites for the most part, for it is spent on prepaid foreign-owned packages in the country of origin [Crick 1994]); the paradigm of faceless consumerism, a sucking vortex of dollars. And so, without a cultural identity – and by this, of course, I mean that tourist identity is mostly one of money, the equivalence of everything, so many differences among the cultures of the West which are reduced to the common denominator of wealth – tourists hardly ever need to reflect seriously on a predicament as voyeurs; or, when there is a chance to do so, there is always the safety net of cynicism and apathy which is even part of the fashionable post-tourism pose. No need to act – except, perhaps, to point out how I, like every other individual, do not act like all the other tourists and travellers. Just how is it that almost every tourist seems to claim to be different in such similar ways?

WHAT IS PHOTOGRAPHY? SOUVENIRS

Photographs amount to a material manifestation of the imaginary work of producing understandings and opinion about Calcutta, which can make sense only within the wider processes of commercialization and consumption of India. The city is inscribed in a variety of ways within a variety of contexts, a plenitude of imaginary sites, each with certain political loadings and each according to sets of specific preconceptions and expectations, overt or covert, many of which impinge upon the images produced by tourists in determining ways. As with discussions on the rooftop of the Modern, in travel guides and in literature, the common tropes for representing Calcutta as the poor city, the over-crowded city, the teeming city, the deformed city, also appear prominently in the photographs of travellers. These tropes appear as consequences of choices no more complex than simply the 'what'-to-photograph, 'when'-to-photograph decisions of clicking the shutter. All this amounts to the subjugation of Calcutta within the economy of an ethnocentrism that continually elaborates dominant modes of perception and understanding. Much more than a critique of photographic representation is needed here. To challenge the clichéd imagery of Calcutta, it will be necessary to challenge the choices that are made in the consuming and appropriative zone within which shots can be taken; and, further, to challenge the realist sanction of photography, which, outside of the art-studio photography of New York, Paris, and so on, has rarely been disrupted from its mirror-function, its projection of the city as it supposedly *is*. Beyond the viewfinder there may be other possibilities not so easily subjugated to the ideological co-ordinates of divisions such as First World–Third World, developed–underdeveloped, exposed–overexposed, and so on:

'I just froze as I was taking a photo and it hit me – I put myself in their place and could realize how I'd feel if they were taking photos of me while I was hanging out washing in my backyard.' (Mitch)

'My view of India is filtered through train windows and camera lenses.' (Paul)

'I caught myself taking photographs of fishermen but ignoring the middle-class as if being middle-class wasn't also part of India. No one wants a photo of a sadhu standing in front of an electricity pylon, or sitting inside a black-and-yellow Calcutta taxi. People back home expect the sadhu to be covered in ash and looking devout.' (Mary)

The peculiar character of the material productions of the visitors to Calcutta, their letters, diaries, photos, films, all carry the halo of documentary, memory and preservation, even as they also inscribe ambiguities. Among traveller photography, besides my own amateur shots, I have seen untold number of photographs of authentic-looking Indian scenes (in which few travellers appear), alongside occasional shots of other tourists, especially five-star-packaged ones, looking lost, and casually posed scenes of 'my' Indian guide, friend, adopted family, and so on, all of which amount to so many exemplary and imaginary sites in which the consumption of culture masquerades as comprehension, and which have an uncanny resemblance to the otherwise anathematic advertisements in the travel brochures. Some travellers are at pains, however, to point out that the sky is not always blue, as it is in the travel guides, although 'good' photograph days have blue skies. If it means anything to say that photographing an event or a site, is a simulacrum of that event or site it is necessary to examine the structure of the 'authenticity' and nostalgia that is deployed here. It is possible that writers who stress the voyeurism of 'the gaze' without such an analysis do little more than produce text (keeping academic book production in business). Authenticity-striving is a version of the traveller's quest, and that of the analyst. Walter Benjamin suggested something like this, and perhaps an alternative, when he wrote, in the late 1930s: 'Culture appears reified. Its history then becomes nothing but the residue of memorabilia that have been unearthed without ever entering into human consciousness through any authentic, that is political, experience' (in Buck-Morss 1989: 289).

It might be suggested that the photograph, as memorabilia, is here 'taken' in a political context, but reified. Photographs as memorabilia are akin to souvenirs. Despite appearances, the souvenir is hardly just a thing. Its object status is little compared to its significance as a marker of cultural experience, of difference, of travel to the frontier, of status itself. The object of the souvenir is almost immaterial. Olalquiaga says: 'souvenirs are instant ruins: they freeze a moment in time' (Olalquiaga 1992: 35). The souvenir must be understood in the context of a history of plunder, but also alongside the varied forms of the commodity, the gift, give-and-take, and charity. Who shall attend to the charitable intentions of those organizations, so often international NGOs, who have set up factories for the fund-raising manufacture of trinkets and crafts? Catalogues of politically correct gift ideas for Christmas arrive by post to homes in Europe, America, Australia, to raise funds for Western NGOs, but there is little more than tokenistic mention of the people who produce those 'traditional' artifacts for Western consumption. Fair trade would be well and good, if it really could be fair – but under capitalism it is not, despite best intentions. Isn't it a fine thing to buy souvenirs for charitable ends? Who gives what? In so far as souvenirs are bound up with power, with unequal cultural relations – in colonialism as well as tourism – there are also spectral stages of authenticity, theft and exchange, which need to be addressed. Economics, then:

> leisure is one way among others of squandering – of destroying – the surplus energy.... Pure leisure (and of course labour strikes) is merely added to the outlets that the available energy has beyond what is required for basic necessities ... eroticism ... luxury products (whose energy value is calculated in labour time) and amusements, which are the small change of the holiday; then there is work, which in some way increases the amount of production ... and lastly wars. (Bataille 1976/1991: 187)

In his second volume of *The Accursed Share* Bataille points to the imperative that we must consume – even waste, squander – excess energy. Are photographs like this? Linking holidays to wars, eroticism to work – Bataille's thought disturbs. The links relevant to this book would stress the representational privilege that accrues to those who can take holidays, cross-matched with the economics of the international division of labour and the exoticism of those (holiday) representations, linked again to the destructive war and exploitation that privileges First World over Third. The consequence of Bataille's thoughts linking eroticism (exoticism), consumption, appropriation, excess and decay in this way is not often enough the obscene but stark realization that the consuming machine which is capital is like a hungry ghost, eating its own excrement wallowing in the cesspools (Lafleur 1989: 281) and that we are its agents, we ourselves are the ghosts. Abstracted and alienated from the values, meanings, artifacts – lifestyles – that we ourselves produce and consume, this phantasmagoria of surplus is decay itself: the decay of good intentions, of experience and of meaning. There are echoes of Lévi-Strauss and Günter Grass here, and of charity, but the photograph cannot so easily be placed in their – or in Bataille's – care. In the journal *Lusitania,* Gregory Ulmer suggests that travel can be understood as a sacrifice which 'is part of the order of unproductive expenditure' (Ulmer 1993: 10). Alongside war, cults, spectacles and monuments, travel can be seen as a necessary expenditure in an economy which demands 'considerable losses' (Ulmer 1993: 10), though not as much a useless squander as the redemptive sacrifice of the Mother Teresa charity workers doing it for God. In the same place, Gayatri Spivak is at pains to point out that the consumption of surplus in potlatch 'is not the same as surplus value or profit' in Marx (Spivak 1993a: 56). She says she does not want to 'take the road' of potlatch within a Marxist understanding of surplus value as that which is objectified labour consummated as profit. (A brief note on surplus should be included here: surplus value is not profit, but that value which is more than what is required for the reproduction of the worker, and which is then made to deny 'its value nature' in producing more capital or in being 'spent in consumption' [Spivak 1993a: 56]. Surplus value must be 'recouped' as profit through circulation.) Photographic expenditure is certainly a cost of travel, photographs are readily consumed, and conspicuously, for varied uses. Giorgio Agamben has argued that ethnography has discredited the 'prejudice that no object can be invested with value if it is not something useful' (Agamben 1993: 48), so even the most useless of photographs – out of focus, perhaps, or repetitive postcardy scenes – might be inserted into this nostalgic economy.

Budget travellers, for all their renunciation of the high-cost extravagances of tourism, would be holders of an accursed share under Bataille's eye. So-called *budget* tourists are very much oriented by cost. The market or the bazaar, the price of accommodation and food, and in general the price of consumer items and services, are the figures that guide the budget traveller. How much is the entrance fee? Who pays for dinner? Postal charges to ship purchased items home? Five rupees for a photo. From the visa charge before the journey to the departure tax at the end, budget travel is a business of accounts, receipts, and exchange rates. Expenditure without reward. Only more generous interpretations romance travel as the accumulation of experiences.

Just as photography may render suffering photogenic, souvenirs reduce the entire world to a flea market, and everything can be collected. Global culture is not a homogeneity but, rather, the reduction within the same framing device of all differences, endless differences commuted into the sameness of 'things' that can be purchased and brought home from the enormous jumble sale. There are conventions about going home, many of them directed towards friends' and relatives' expectations of presents and exotic tidings – the last days of a stay in Calcutta are spent shopping and taking photographs. Some travellers – as can be seen from a visit to craft markets in Western cities – are able to subsidize their travels from the sale of 'trinkets' they have brought home from the exotic 'Third World'. Tourism does its part in the wholesale extraction of handicrafts and other locally produced goods from the subcontinent. The contribution to a kind of cottage version of international trade which is represented by those hundreds and thousands of backpacks filled with souvenir items is not without significance. The point at which foreign exchange enters the marketplace is important here.

Every purchase tells a story: the umbrella from New Market, the book from College Street, the chocolate from Nahoums (best chocolates, good chocolates, fine chocolate). People buy shirts, trousers, cloth, saris, shawls, wall-hangings, mobiles, brass figurines, brass utensils, plates, drums, books (I am especially susceptible here), toys (and here), bicycle horns, bags, jewellery, and more. This list catalogues some of the most interesting items: 'The best thing I ever bought in Calcutta was my black umbrella from Burra Bazaar, it is so beautifully made, with a decorated bamboo handle and a fantastic lotus flower frame' (Bronwyn). The black-cloth lotus-framed bamboo Calcutta umbrella was always destined to become a souvenir cult item among longer-term visitors. With the cheapest 'special best quality' versions available for less than 50 rupees, and better-quality ones not much more expensive, the black-cloth umbrella scorned by many Bengalis in favour of more convenient nylon fold-up models was a must. These black brollies satisfied some backpackers' eccentric desire to appear properly, and dapperly, British: especially useful during the monsoon months. One or two extra to take back home for friends were easy last-minute items, rolled up in a blanket, or carried on board as hand luggage.

Do travellers consider those who produce these souvenirs? To the extent that a few organizations like the Bengali Women's Trade Union Auxilliary or Community Aid Abroad advertise 'non-exploitative' and 'fair trade' (CAA pamphlet) working conditions at the site of production of the goods which appear in their glossy brochures, perhaps there is cause for some approval. Certainly some volunteers working in Calcutta were alert to such issues, and made efforts to shop from emporiums set up by the organized charities near the Sudder Street area; despite greater (relative) expense, better-quality goods were sometimes available as compared to the New Market shops (Consumer Price Watch Committee, Modern Lodge Branch, 1994). However, a rhetoric of non-exploitative production gleaned from glossy brochures does not immediately confirm that those who work in the production homes which supply Oxfam and CAA are adequately compensated for their difficult and often boringly repetitive labour. Responses to questions about this elicited various justifications ranging from 'but they wouldn't have jobs otherwise' (Heidi) to 'at least the profits go to a good cause' (Jason). Issues of small-scale commodity production are more complex than tourist evaluations of cottage capitalism allow.

What should be understood is that the souvenir or photograph is a form of commodity which can be analysed in terms which bring out Marx's insight that the commodity expresses a social relationship – that in the market (which is now everywhere for tourism): 'persons exist for one another merely as representations of, and, therefore, as owners of, commodities' (Marx 1867/1967: 85). Souvenirs are social before they are objects; they are things made of power; encrypted relations of power; ciphers; signs. The souvenir or photograph of Calcutta taken by the Western visitor may evoke a mood, a nostalgia for the context of its origin in an emporium, on a hot crowded pavement, or in a cluttered market stall – but may be read more revealingly as a marker of a social relation. More than a status symbol or an ornamental display (souvenirs are kept, stored up on the mantelpiece, here more like potlatch than gifts), also a sign of power, a trace of imperialism. What remains of heat, smoke, bustle, when the image of travel is carried home? Little perhaps, but the social relation which allows the transportation and the nostalgia is exactly this. The image remembered is also a marker of an economic and social privilege.

Other comments from travellers indicate a little of the scope of India as a market. One can find almost anything in the chaotic rummage that is the consumer's Calcutta:

'I've done out my house with bits and pieces I've picked up on my travels – it's like a warehouse of Eastern artifacts.' (Joseph)

'I did a course on Indian art which was presented as a kind of up-market Indian travel guide.' (Lucy)

'I collect dolls or figurines from every place I visit – I want to have a miniature world full of different people. Not really to relive my trip, but to show visitors something interesting from where I've been.' (Jacinta)

'This shirt I had made up in the Punjabi style, but in this blue colour – it is good that I will have something Indian that I will wear at home. Though it was difficult; I had to wait two days, and then I came to the shop at five minutes before lunch, so I could not leave the shop for over an hour because I was locked inside.' (Antoine)

Souvenirs come to represent experience; often in a way that has a meaning that is specifically relevant to the visitor. Such souvenirs can be without obvious value for others – for example, a metro ticket from Calcutta's underground rail service, a Campa Cola bottle, a tongue cleaner, a video copy of a Mrinal Sen film. Experience is also collected like a souvenir.[2] Wanting to know through the authenticity of experience, through the notion of 'having travelled', is another mode of consumption, and of appropriation – however genuine and sincere the intentions. The concept of experience is an enabling constitutive one for travellers as well as other visitors; anthropological 'participant observation' is dependent upon the same conception. Travellers must 'experience' Calcutta as different. The point about travel is that it is experience away from home, with itineraries mapped through the lens of a global consuming apparatus. This may be understood to range across extremes: from what may be serious scholarly interest and investigation, or – and I am not too cynical here – a more empathetic affinity with the spiritual allure of 'India' (very much in a *fascinans et tremendum*, hocus-pocus, mystic John-and-Yoko, out-of-body Hare Karma way). The souvenir and the photo, as a reminder of a place visited or an experience gained, also asserts the idea of a face-to-face authenticity which is now past – and this, too, is a mystical nostalgia.

There might also be reason to consider the relative economy of souvenirs bought in 'weaker currencies'. The phrase 'monopoly money' is not uncommon among travellers referring to rupees (or Thai baht, or Malaysian dollars). Derrida's essay on gifts and counterfeit money calls attention to the power of money to make equivalences out of differences (a basic Marxist point), and he uses this to enter into a long discussion of the status of a variety of exchanges in a way that is applicable to the study of the politics of souvenirs. (Although Derrida's theory of the gift 'souvenirs' colonial examples too – his Eurocentrism is a given.)

Of what value are these souvenirs? As icons which represent the experience of travel, they come to stand in place – as do photographs – of things which rely more on memory. At a simple level they are substitutes, but these material reminders, if they are triggers of memory (violent shots), also serve to show something more. They claim a certain status, or at least a claim which would authenticate – as evidence brought back from afar – a narrative of experience which is to be told, shown or written, to others: 'I have been away, and I have the proof here with me.' It is no accident that some photographic prints are called proofs – although these have an intermediary status, and must still be printed in full. Somewhat similarly to proofs, souvenirs require a narrative of acquisition to become operative.

COUNTERFEIT STUDIES

Sometimes it will be claimed that travel broadens one's horizons, improves the mind and soothes the restless soul – and I do not want to fail to take this seriously. But it would be ludicrous to think that tourism can save the world through the widened horizons of the children of the middle class, and it would be a parody to suggest that all the ills of tourism can be healed by some kind of scholarly critique. Yet there is some cause for a more serious social-scientific analysis of what is at stake in this domain. While not all scholars have demeaned themselves by uncritically taking up the soft ideology of 'tourism for cultural under-standing' – perhaps following long-established anthropological concern with what the people involved think about what they are doing – there is scope for closer attention. In this context the work of Malcolm Crick has opened up many interesting questions, most provocatively when he queries the status of:

> researchers who reckon themselves superior to tourists because of their efforts to learn about other cultures, [and so] are, of course, not like the naive fools so often caught by the local touts. Are they not simply 'sophisticated' tourists who deservedly get caught by 'sophisticated' con artists? (Crick 1994: Manu-script: 206)

The relationship between what tourists think of their activity and the commentaries and explanations of 'disciplined' researchers might be refocused with regard to the fact that many social scientists, while in 'the field', take photographs and collect souvenirs. Their efforts may be uneven, their images not always good ones, but somehow their 'social-scientific' status of their shots always accords more authenticity than holiday snaps. (Their kitsch souvenir collections appear in this text less often.) I have heard travellers complain that the anthropology lectures they attended at university before they came travelling were little more than collections of holiday snaps; the intrepid anthropologist with his or her 'tribe'. (I have shown photographs of travellers to a political science class; is there to be no end to cyclical duplicity?) It is a matter of the frame in which these events are presented; the framing of the scholarly photograph is already quite different before the researcher arrives, focuses and shoots, because the disciplinary support systems of texts, research visas and universities, and the 'pursuit of knowledge', carry so much greater weight. The holiday snap is comparatively adrift as opposed to the scholar's representation which is pasted as a plate in a monograph served to a specific readership, even where there is little difference between the snaps. It does matter very much who takes the photo, and where they stand is not simply a matter of finding the best light. Still, the fantasist with a camera is a sort of utopian anthropologist, able to go anywhere and get the best shots with the best equipment. And let us not forget that most of these cameras are produced by the cheap labour of those in the very Third World sites – or rather, in factories just adjacent to those sites – which are photographed by tourists. The irony that it is the 'exotic' peoples who now provide the labour to provide the mechanisms of their own representations, by others, is particularly sharp since it is rarely recognized as exposing the imperial bargain. It is this link between photography and tourism that Fussell seems to find so frustrating:

> Cant as the tourist may of the Taj Mahal and Mt Everest at sunset, the real target today is the immense Ocean Terminal at Hong Kong, with its miles of identical horrible camera and tape recorder shops. The fact that a tourist is best defined as a fantasist equipped temporarily with unaccustomed power is better known to the tourist industry than to anthropology. (Fussel 1980: 42)

It is not necessary to conflate the project of 'knowledge' with the soft ideology of tourism as cultural understanding to recognize that what is at stake in both projects entails a similar economy. Even allowing differences of degree, the desire to produce 'understanding' and to comprehend experience is common. There are other constraints which condition differences – social science presents itself as more sophisticated, as scholarly. There is no doubt that the ready-made formats of the travel guide and the stock postcard image are insufficient for the purposes of 'research'. Similarly, commercial considerations and weight of numbers conspire to 'produce' a great many more tourists than anthropologists. Is it such a surprise that commercial centres like Hong Kong devote the front line of their stores to camera supplies rather than ethnographers' notebooks? Off the plane on the run, load up with film, and shoot, shoot, shoot – the Kodak, Fuji, Agfa campaigns have the urgency of combat, F-stop shock troops (is this a case of tourist self-loathing?).

This is not even to raise the question of the authenticity of the representations themselves,[3] although if we are all aware that photographs are sometimes inauthentic, that they sometimes 'lie', we so very often forget this and accept the mechanical fact of representation as authenticity. Holiday snaps, even when they are treated with utmost disdain by all who are shown them, are still accorded more credibility than any of the hundreds of photographs of UFOs, Yetis, or Loch Ness Monsters. The point is that all these photographs are thoroughly foregrounded by complex expectations and ways of seeing – a key argument of this book. Kabbani captures exactly this when she points out that the productions of travellers 'do not depend so much upon the traveller's individual gaze' (1986: 122) as upon their education, the myths they have reason to cherish and the political and social structures they belong to and function within. The location of the photograph as a tourist memento has a very different circulation from the published shot, so that the sanction of publication attracts a greater general responsibility in comparison to the experiential and specific character of the memento. When these aspects converge, and the memento snap is published somewhere, as may sometimes happen, the sanction shifts, experience acquires a different narrative and authoritative credence as part of public discourse. The sanction moves from 'my experience' to 'generalized event' as the photograph moves away from the private narrative into depersonalized locations and its authority expands – stripped of its reference to 'my experience', it comes to stand for Calcutta itself.

Curiously, the realist sanction of photography seems to be reversed when it comes to the souvenir; often kitsch. Souvenirs pose a problem in terms of authenticity as they can, in so many ways, be fakes, and can be intentional fakes (enabling the authenticity of the false, which might be best represented with traveller fascination for a 'kitsch' balsa-wood model of the Taj Mahal, which for certain others would carry a more profound meaning). A skilled (crafty) tout can sell all sorts of goods as 'authentic' to different audiences in different ways, just as news reports, photojournalism, and eyewitness accounts address authenticity to a range of possible consumers; another tout might sell what to all but certain tourists would be absolute local junk; and individual travellers – as did the Modern Lodge guests – might seek junk, using their own 'found objects' as souvenirs (is a Mahatma Gandhi bottle-opener an *authentic* souvenir?). Souvenirs can also be 'faked' by location – as not being from where they are purported to be from. Elaborate explanations may be fabricated to sanctify otherwise meaningless knick-knacks; whole myth-ologies, anecdotal and circumstantial evidence, elaborate conjectures, may become attached to objects. Are these inauthentic? Even if they are 'made up', can such elaborations be denounced as false representations? In the same way in which all evidence can be forged, there is no doubt that such exchanges apply to tourist souvenirs also.

This is not news. The structure of the sign, the essence of represen-tation, already teaches this. Derrida says as much when he shows how complicated 'truly fictive' narrative is with regard to the gift (Derrida 1991/1992: 94). A writer, already a fiction, can invent a fictive narrator who will tell, as if true, a fiction about a forgery. A false truth about a true falsity – all of this Derrida attaches to the structure of the money form with regard to his essay on Baudelaire's story of the counterfeit coin given to a beggar:

> in order for there to be counterfeit money, the counterfeit money must not give itself with certainty to be counterfeit money; and this perhaps is also the intentional dimension, that is, the credit, the act of faith that structures all money, all experience or all consciousness of money, be it true or false. (Derrida 1991/1992: 95)

From this we might wonder if Derrida means to say that credit is the structure of all experience, or of all experience of money – both interpretations are plausible. Certainly the credit-ability of the souvenir, as well as the souvenir's narrative, is what is at stake in terms of accountability. Need authenticity be accounted? (At what cost might we take account of this wealth of metaphor? Can we afford to remain bereft, not to invest the necessary in order to take stock and evaluate the purchase of such metaphoric currency? Marx on the money form, as discussed above in Chapter 1, is the context here.)

Derrida says: 'Authority is constituted by accreditation', but he means this in the double sense of both credulity and 'capitalised interest' (Derrida 1991/1992: 97). The souvenir carries a certain value, which must be invested to constitute itself as souvenir, and this must be under-stood within a cultural economy which is, after all, capitalism. But furthermore, credit is gained by giving the souvenir – as story and shown object (proof) or as gift from afar – and so it is worth considering the status of the gift in this scene: the retrieved or plundered object made into an offering of value to another is always more than a mere accessory to authority claims. In Baudelaire's story a counterfeit coin is given to a beggar. The one who gives – as so much anthropology describes – is the one who claims power. This would have to be measured in the context of charity, also – which is often a righteous kind of giving which claims 'heaven' as its own reward and so, in exchange, claims all. Derrida links this to representation:

> As an identifiable, bordered, posed subject, the one who writes and his or her writing never gives anything without calculating, consciously or unconsciously, its reappropriation, its exchange or its circular return – and by definition this means reappropriation of its surplus value. (Derrida 1991/1992: 101)

Charity, then, is yet another way of making a mark for capital.

The authority or credulity of the souvenir and its narrative is based upon what can easily, and without remainder, be fictive. The souvenir and narrative can be false, yet still be invested. Indeed, the most successfully reinvested images of Calcutta are patently forged from dubious sources (I have in mind *The City of Joy*). Among the many ways in which this might occur are those souvenirs peddled by the crafty touts; the fabricated village handicrafts of charity organizations; and the many and various objects that are actually 'from' somewhere else but are claimed, credited, with Calcutta origin. Alongside these, the elaborations of authentic 'souvenirs', which are truly found on site and are then embellished with a fictive narrative, are little different from the 'false' souvenir, since this remains a souvenir, while the place it represents becomes less stable. Perhaps it does not matter where the souvenir comes from, nor if the narrative which authorizes it has the ring of truth or merely a structure – a narrative structure – which lends authenticity. The Calcutta that is souvenired among all these knick-knacks and narratives has more to do with an economy of storytelling, status and media than of geopolitical lived-in space. The distance between Calcutta and the world of souvenirs, as with any representative structure, is one of flux. What is important is that the souvenir circulates, allowing a recoupment of its (surplus-) value.

If the image of Calcutta were considered in terms of Marx's analysis of the commodity fetish, we might see this as an immanent critique of 'representational' relations. Marx says:

> The mysterious character of the commodity form consists therefore simply in the fact that the commodity reflects the social characteristics of human labour as objective characteristics of the products of labour themselves.... Through this substitution, the products of labour become commodities, sensuous things which are at the same time suprasensual or social. In the same way the impression made by a thing on the optic nerve is perceived not as a subjective excitation of that nerve but as the objective form of a thing outside the eye ... [Marx then finds a better analogy in religion where the 'products of the human brain appear as autonomous figures endowed with a life of their own'] ... I call this fetishism. (Marx 1867/1967: 164–5)

How uncanny this analogy would be had Marx referred to the camera obscura here. The image of the excited eye very much recalls the mechanism of the camera invented thirty years earlier. Nevertheless, this passage is mysterious enough; he goes on to say that the commodity form 'is nothing but the determined social relation between humans themselves which assumes here, for them, the phantasmagoric form of a relation between things' (Marx 1867/1967: 165). Marx's use of the term phantasmagoric is, according to Agamben, traceable back to his enchantment with the planned phantasmagoria of the first Universal Exposition in Hyde Park in 1851. Soon after, at the Paris Exposition of 1867 – the year Marx published the first volume of *Capital* – the organizers declared their method: 'The public needs a grandiose concept that will strike its imagination; its spirit must halt, astonished, before the marvels of industry. It wishes to contemplate an enchanted scene, not similar products, uniformly grouped' (in Agamben 1993: 38). This enchantment could also be that which provoked Marx to describe the commodity form of a simple table as an idea which escapes that which made the table – labour – and enters an abstract world where, out of control, 'it stands on its head' [as in Hegel?]; the table has 'evolved out of its wooden head whims more wonderful even than when of its own accord it begins to dance' (Marx 1867/1967: 164). Marx was mad – a footnote to this passage adds that Chinese tables do dance.[4] Dance as a metaphor for circulation, perhaps? Movement? Travel? The warning sounded here is important, however; the dark magic of this enchantment is 'the transfiguration of the commodity into the enchanted object' (Agamben 1993: 38), where the products of labour enter into an ever more global market, and exchange value begins to eclipse use value. It is not unlikely, also, that substantial 'commodities' from Calcutta graced the pavilions of the grand Expositions of Europe from 1851 onwards. And it is not without significance that protests against the construction of the Eiffel Tower for the Paris Exposition of 1899 were, Agamben declares, based upon arguments that 'the tower (in addition to giving the coup de grâce to the labyrinthine character of old Paris by offering a reference point visible everywhere) transformed the whole city into a commodity that could be consumed [and photographed] in a single glance' (Agamben 1993: fn40).

As I have suggested above, the mimetic effects of the camera and the nostalgia of the souvenir can be understood as examples of this commodification of an (unequal) social relationship between produced-subjects and tourists. Lukács summarizes the 'essence of the commodity structure', and characterizes relations between people as taking the form of a thing which has 'an autonomy that seems so strictly rational and all-embracing' that it conceals 'every trace of its fundamental nature: the relation between people' (Lukács 1968/1971: 83). The importance of this for the role of the camera and the souvenir as technologically produced 'things' is one of showing that the 'rumour of Calcutta' encrypted in their production is an expression of the relations between different classes of people under capitalism and imperialism. The dual nature of the commodity is, rather, a dual nature of labour − as an activity and as a commodity (used, appropriated, etc.). It should be remembered, then, that the fetish of Capital is the fetishism of capitalists who attribute value-forming power to capital, when all it 'really' has the power to do is to command labour. Class-conscious workers will recognize this, and see capital as a power which they will resist.

THE GIFT OF PHOTOGRAPHY

Calcutta is a city which has been built by labour which can be specified − actual labourers engaged in actual toil. But the rumour of Calcutta, the imagery by which the city is known, is the production of a somewhat different order. There is a dilemma here to do with representation which causes headaches for the Bengali government, which would like to have some say in the kinds of inscriptions that are produced about Calcutta. Recent controversies over the film *City of Joy* could be a case in point[5] − but more generally, it seems, a debate over censorship is responding to a complicated double need with regard to technologies of representation. There is a felt need to regulate the haphazard and ad hoc inscription of Calcutta which is going on through the proliferation of cameras in the hands of so many visitors to the city. Representation is somehow out of control, yet at the same time it is possible to discern quite specific patterns and continuities in this representation (stock images of poverty, etc.). To regulate this haphazard inscription by

demanding certain standards and, in the case of the film, a problem-
atically defined 'ideological balance' is at the same time shown alongside the need to challenge the proliferation of representations with
disturbing continuities which suggest that the inscribing of Calcutta as
the site of poverty is not haphazard at all.

Is it in the nature of the technology that this dual dilemma occurs?
It is not possible to regulate the flood of cameras snapping freely in a
constant frenzy in almost every corner of the city. Sontag noted that
the photographer was 'an armed version of the solitary walker reconnoitring, stalking, cruising the urban inferno, the voyeuristic stroller
who discovers the city as a landscape of voluptuous extremes [an] adept
of the joys of watching, connoisseur of empathy' (Sontag 1979: 55).
The 'cottage-industry' or informal character of visual inscription (for
those who can afford a camera) can always slip through any attempt at
material censorship or regulation – sneaking photos from afar with a
telephoto lens, ever quieter and faster and more automatic mechanisms.
Urry paraphrases Sontag (quoted above) when he says that photography
'involves the democratisation of all forms of human experience, both
by turning everything into photographic images and by enabling anyone to photograph them' (Urry 1990: 139). This intentionally invokes
the money/commodity form. But not everyone has a camera, although
perhaps the camera-effect extends into all hands? (What does this
argument have in common with debates about guns?) Ulmer suggests
that 'the camera is an effect, not the cause, of the "depth of field"
point of view that dominates Western thought from the Greeks through
Freud' (Ulmer 1989: 8). It seems to be not just simply a matter of load
and shoot. Since the development of the daguerreotype, Europe's
cultural others have been incessantly photographed, mostly with a
greater realism than the medium promised in Europe itself (as opposed
to painting) but also with an exotic loading (see Crary 1990, McQuire
1995). I would like to argue that the 'viewfinder' of photography
remains well within the 'frame' of a very conventional – and human –
concept of technology which serves, largely, to present subjects in a
way that is wholly modernist in its fidelity to presence. The structure
of realist photography is already structured by the presentation of the
scene – a gift of being-there which seems to return and return.

So is it the ideological production of the meaning of Calcutta that
entails this dilemma? The forces which encourage a certain depiction of
the city are so great as to seem to be beyond disruption. The vast
literature and popular imagery of poverty sustained by an internationally
and economically reinforced reputation which continually resists attempts

to portray any other side of the city predisposes visitors – in varied ways – to slot experiences of Calcutta into the received frame. The dilemma is a challenge to the dictum that the camera never lies, but although we know that the camera shows only one perspective, gives just one side of a multifaceted object, takes a dim and unfocused view of context, is suspended in the snapshot of time, isn't it the case that we still hold out the hope of a full and adequate representation? As if a multiplication of lenses would bring us closer to truth, to that fidelity to the real. The 'gift' of photography is that it promises an originary return; the world made photogenic can be saved – this remains a kind of impossible charity work. The old fallen story. It should be clear that the multiple exposures of mass media do not wipe away the channelling and conditioning and determining effects of established patterns of representation, even though some might like to hold out for some kind of dysfunction of the technological and of the censors in order to see opened new spaces, new lines of flight, the possibility of new scenes.

Virilio has called the media forms of inscription – video, photo and writing – a translation machine which entails a 'geometrification of looking' (1984/1989: 2). Everything is ordered into a *quattrocento* kind of spatiality, a cartography of perception which would accord with Virilio's camera rigidity. In contrast, a less structured kind of looking would evoke the traveller, tourist or anthropologist, just wandering the streets, talking to people, glancing left and right, up and down, looking haphazardly at whatever catches their (our?) attention in the winding crowded Calcutta streets. But this would be nothing more than a ripple in Virilio's regime, as even the least intentional modes of looking are heavily conditioned by a geometric ordering of otherwise cluttered perception. An anthropologist might claim that 'participant-observation', the casual interview, and other less structured and 'dialogic' aspects of ethnography might offer an alternative to these technocratic cartographies, but this is also an illusion which forgets that anthropologists look, listen and participate with books in mind – they are always on the verge of perpetrating some sort of literature, they carry the university and its attendant constraints with them always. There is no perspective that will not be constrained in some way. The camera itself brings this out clearly – much more, but also sufficiently – by imposing its frame.

What Michael Taussig finds significant about the camera is the 'curious and striking recharging of the mimetic faculty caused by the invention of [such] mimetically capacious machines' (Taussig 1993: xiv). What is more striking is that this mimetic charge comes to be understood as a kind of mechanization of perception – this gives us the curiosity of a technological enframing which produces and is produced by capacious camera effects at a time when interpretative skill and computer capacity seem to converge. Yet Taussig remains concerned with the 'construction' of social life, and asks: 'how come it seems so immutable? How come culture appears so natural? ... construction deserves more respect; it cannot be name-called out of (or into) existence' (Taussig 1993: xvi).

PHOTOGRAPHIC IDENTITY

'I'm amazed at the winding streets which never match up with the views I have from the windows of my room. Even if I took photographs from the windows of the various buildings I look out from I could never quite square them up with a map of the streets.' (Suzie)

'I am not a camera.' (Gary)

'I slip into a photographic mode after sitting about an hour in a chai stall; it is easier, the camera has become a little less visible.' (Suzie)

'I like to go alone into the streets and wander, I get lost among the maze, no other tourists have seen just what I have seen, even while it's just one more lot of everyday events. No, I don't have a camera.' (Adrienne)

It is ironic to find Moorhouse's patchy book on Calcutta published in the Penguin 'Travel Library' series, as if the massive city were somehow on the move. The travel library is always-already an outsiders' library, written from a visitor's perspective. And it is also ironic to find Moorhouse recognizing that perhaps there are problems with the project of representing Calcutta. While he does not see the importance of his own words for what he has done in his own book, he nevertheless explains:

you return from Calcutta, unless you are very tough or a professional, with a camera which may be full of exposed film but which contains hardly any record of people. Quite apart from the risk of violence when a camera is raised, which is considerable, you are also deterred by the indecency of the act. (Moorhouse 1971: 128)

For some, the act of photographing is impossible in Calcutta; having become acutely aware of the voyeuristic nature of its projection, or simply feeling some sense of discomfort, many travellers seem to leave their cameras in the Modern Lodge safe. Kodak and Canon may sell their equipment with the promise of memory on film (note the curious character of this idea: if it were a memory, it would not need to be preserved on paper), but maybe the best moments of travel experience cannot be captured through the visual. Certainly the pictographic dominates the narrativization of travel after the return, and for some it conditions a day's, or even every day's, travel programme ('Gotta get a shot of the bridge', a shot of Queen Victoria, etc., etc.), and often scenes may evoke the idea of a photograph – 'What a nice shot that would make' – but there are tastes and smells and sounds and even scenes which cannot be accommodated within the fields of vision appropriate to photography. The camera always sets up a certain distance.

As in a passport photograph, souvenirs produce identity, and this is complicated, and bound up with other areas of this work discussed in Chapters 2 and 4. One prominent example is fashion: traveller 'identities' proliferate on the stalls of the travel market, in a way which suggests that an analysis in terms of the production and consumption of personal images would not be misplaced. Brian Massumi noted that 'it used to be that assuming or redefining an identity took a lifetime. Now it can be done in as long as it takes to/shop for an image' (Massumi 1992: 134). Where images have become a commodity, and traveller identities and ways 'to be' in India have become codified – with varying degrees of formality and reference to the marketplace – it is important to look at what is produced. This would include not only the material trappings of these purchased identities, such as fashions and paraphernalia, but also conceptual purchases – everything from literature read to the price of cinema tickets and the complexities of identity and memory. It should be no surprise that travel literature 'produces' more than just text in this zone – the fetish of the photograph or souvenir as nostalgia for travel is, like all fetishism, something which presents what Agamben calls the fetish-paradox: 'the fetish confronts us with the paradox of an unattainable object that satisfies a human need precisely through its being unattainable' (Agamben 1993: 33). The souvenir reminds us of the trip we are no longer on, or the life we cannot lead, the person we are, but can no longer (or not just now) be.[6] Identities are commodities, too, and we trade them now on the market of world travel – whole (fragmented) personalities are pieced together out of bits of glossy brochures, bits of cloth gathered together under the logic of fashion, old texts and textures orchestrated through an image-laden marketplace that saturates all aspects of our lives (not only is all simulacrum [Baudrillard 1983], but all simulacrum is the market). In this way colonization reaches the furthest zones of the body, thought, world, idea, and more, and reclaims all values through its ever-flashing exchange. It is a metaphor of distance.

In a stimulating point-form passage on travel photography, Urry sets out a few, somewhat generalized, ideas on the construction of travel with the camera:

> Photography gives shape to travel. It is the reason for stopping, to take (snap) a photograph, and then to move on. Photography involves obligations. People feel that they must not miss seeing particular scenes since otherwise photo-opportunities will be missed. Tourist agencies spend much time indicating where photographs should be taken (so-called viewing points). Indeed much tourism becomes in effect a search for the photogenic, travel is a strategy for the accumulation of photographs. (Urry 1990: 139)

For some it is the escape of travelling that is destroyed by the techno-logical record – somehow the permanent material representation changes the quality of an experience. The desire here is possibly an attempt to escape the regimentation of surveillance, to hope that it is still possible to live outside the routines, to live in the spaces between the grids imposed by habits, laws, governments and technocracy. Like bustees and pavement dwellings, perhaps, at the edges of state surveillance there are opportunities to escape; although the bustees are very well ordered in specific ways, too: there are many forms of hierarchization.

[It is important not to overlook the ordering of bustee life. The informal sector of work in Calcutta, largely organized from those who live in the bustees, must be considered a more or less long-term factor for the Indian metropolis (Sethuraman 1978: 15; Sivaramakrishnan 1978: 136). Those who travel to work in Calcutta from other Indian states do often slip between the interstices of both sociological and state surveil-lance. Indeed, most of the staff of the Modern Lodge were, before the establishment was sold, from outside Bengal. Lubell has noted that there is a distinction to be made between these people who migrated into Calcutta from East Pakistan – on the whole entire families – and those who migrated from rural Bengal or from nearby states – who are often males leaving families in villages to earn income in the city (Lubell 1974; Lubell 1978: 112). Many visitors would be unaware of any such distinction as they point their cameras at families encamped by the side of the road.]

It remains an open question whether the multiplicity of forms of inscription (personal notebooks, photos, memories are all inscribed) can indeed escape from the bureaucracies of surveillance – do we dream of an illusory cultural production exempt from the tax of administration, and always running ahead or around the next corner rather than following behind? Official documentations have become so sophisticated – are our amateur, independent and personal efforts the repository of popular cultural life or, rather, a shallow remnant, a fading image, of a long-gone creative autonomy? Certainly the military, multinational and technological agencies have been the ones to offer innovations; and, more importantly, this has enabled the marketing, on a grand scale, of so many cameras and books and other such tools of surveillance and proof that these are available everywhere, and never before to such a degree. But does this mean that institutional agencies retain control over publications? To a great extent the conventions of academic work have determined the shape of this commentary, but is the situation so tight that there are no avenues down which we can go to avoid the impositions of received forms? What kinds of camera effects can disrupt the conventions of the camera now? What shots of Calcutta will offer another city in its place? Is it possible to swap Calcuttas? Are there so many that we can choose? What are the constraints upon our choices?

CIRCULATION OF COMMODITIES

What has been called 'the commodification of everything' (Wallerstein 1983) is also a major component of budget travel. Pietz has underlined the importance of the first chapter of Marx's *Capital*, which analyses the 'process of the historical production of universal forms' (Pietz 1993: 147), among which the possibility of exchange is arranged. Keenan calls this an 'axis of similarity [which] enables a comparison, makes the different uses of things commensurable' (Keenan 1993: 162). This possibility is achieved by an abstraction which is, first, an erasure of difference. The money form as universal exemplar of this under capitalism allows everything to find a price. Everything can be measured and, cynically, everything can be bought. Keenan, remembering that the commodity expresses a social relation, reminds us that 'exchange is possible because abstraction reveals the common humanity [labour] surviving in the thing exchanged' (Keenan 1993: 171). This commodification, however, is not an abstract conceptual event, but takes its form in a myriad of local contexts. The market is manifest, there are buyers and sellers, products, producers and purchases. This complexity introduces some interesting problems. Tourist travel seems to collapse the distinction between extant forces of production and historically or situationally contingent relations of production, since the technical aspects of travel already presuppose relations between those who serve as travellers and those who are visited. What does this mean for an analysis of the development of the mode of production in this zone? Where travellers consume services 'on the spot' there is, possibly, some reason to consider them – along with the service providers – as agents in the production of that which is consumed. This question of the relations between consumption and production must be taken up again. The point here is that the relations between visitors and visited are ones which we must also understand in (but not only in) economic terms.

At a global level these relations have been transformed; new technologies for the circulation of goods, and for the circulation of those who would consume goods or services, as well as new forms of production and new opportunities for exchange, all produce new subject positions which encompass the whole of the travel industry, from ticket seller and travel agent to the Kodak snapshot-processing technician and those who pose for the photos – tourists and locals. Everyone is drawn into these relations and forms of production, and whole nations – witness Thailand, with five million-plus visitors every year – have been made over into a huge cultural marketplace: 'Culture is being packaged, priced, and sold like building lots, rights-of-way, fast-food and room service, as the tourism industry inexorably extends its grasp' (Greenwood 1989: 179). This 'commodification of everything' is not to be thought of as some sort of conspiracy by a cabal which knows what we want better than we do but is, rather, a 'logical' extension of the consumer culture that now finds ways to traverse the world, normalizing – by its logic – all relations according to the needs of the market.

> There is nothing to regret, the world moves in every which way, men and women cross the planet every which way, through interposed images and sounds, or directly through the displacement of their own person. But let us immediately pick up the paradox. Everything circulates: the types of music, the advertising slogans, the tourists, the computer viruses, the industrial subsidiaries and, at the same time, everything seems to freeze, to be stationary, as the differences fade between things … everything has become interchangeable, equivalent within standardised spaces. The tourists, for example, travel virtually motionless, herded in the same types of airline cabins, pullmans, hotel rooms, and seeing ride before their eyes landscapes they have already encountered a hundred times on their television screens or on touristic brochures. (Guattari 1992: 123)

What is at stake in this place where everything circulates but nothing moves? Human self-constitution, it is now well known, occurs through the *labour* of producing *meaning*. Against the Habermaniacal critique that Marx reduces communicative action to *mere* instrumental activity while social labour *produces* humanity (Habermas 1983), might we not suggest that the development of the means of production has moved very much into the information or communicative sphere, and hence the relations of production are driven all the more by meaning? This might be to accuse Habermas unjustly of reformism, a lack of reflection upon the conditions of his own production, and failure to see what Marx had meant when he referred to 'social production'. But so?

If social production is taken to imply a complex social context, it is meaningless to consider the technical abstracted from any such context. What was intended when the distinction between the forces and the relations of production were set out on paper? While it is important to acknowledge that technical abilities of a certain level are historically given – meaning scientific techniques and human skills, for example – and it is important to recognize these as organized by a certain historical level of social formation, it is perhaps more important to recognize both forces and relations of production as subject to the production of values, or meanings. Heidegger's comments on technology are again relevant, allowing us to see that the forms of technology bring certain versions of the world into focus, or existence, and occlude others (in whose interests?).

In what must be a response to Habermas, Derrida takes up the issue of the status of technology in a way which, despite an 'apocalyptic tone', might lead us back to Marx's intentions: 'Is it not necessary to have a new critique of the new effects of capital (within unprecedented techno-social structures)?' (Derrida 1992: 57). He goes on to consider Habermas's notion of communicative competence as a possible 'new' critique, and finds some disturbing trends:

> Claiming to speak in the name of intelligibility, good sense, common sense, or the democratic ethic, this discourse tends, by means of these very things, and as if naturally, to discredit anything that complicates this model. It tends to suspect or repress anything that bends, overdetermines, or even questions, in theory or in practice, this idea of language. (Derrida 1992: 55)

If Habermas has simplified the notion of social production, it is possible that the charges brought here by Derrida would be consistent. In the context of 'unprecedented techno-social structures' in late-twentieth-century society – which Marx could not have clearly imagined – the multiplication of modes of communication suggests that what some might call the development of the mode of information capitalism requires interrogation. One danger here is that all this talk of the democracy of the image, of dialogue, dialogic anthropology, 'communicative action', authenticity, the gaze, and so on, all of which proposes a 'model' of language transparency, is perhaps, rather, a pernicious new form of bourgeois culturalist makeover which we ought to resist.

Academics working in their various disciplines, filmmakers and documentary photo-journalists, as well as writers of fiction, and of travel fiction or guidebooks, handicraft merchants, and also the advocates of development, self-determination and/or cultural difference, all channel, through a global touristic vortex, culture into a deterritorialized marketplace. In this market, which has only the geographical limit of the entire world, a normalization and standardization process operates by means of media codes and criteria – accessibility, translatability, ease of consumption – to shape all cultures and all differences into forms appropriate to and authorized by the 'capacity' of the market. 'What the market will carry' determines the degree of sophistication of normalized, standardized cultural products – taking into account the level of development of the means of consumption, which means the mode of touristic consumption, or how much 'work/leisure' can be expected to be necessary to 'consume' (make circulate) the codified information. There will be various market niches, and class privileges will specify the elaboration of codes – more 'sophisticated' cultural meanings will be consumed by the managerialist classes – but in general the point holds that these structural variations will be subject to the ubiquity of media under conditions of 'information capitalism'.

Tourism is astonishingly capable of these deterritorializations which both commodify and (seem to) democratize all locations through a global, mobile, media-frenzied, omnipresent, transnational, hegemonic, dematerialized normalization process. With the traveller-volunteers of Calcutta this process has the added consequence of fitting into a wider aid-orientated (restricted development) NGO/World Bank mode of neocolonialism, also using all manner of tele-technological mechanisms to achieve its aims (the glossy photographs of the Oxfam catalogue are a case in point). The reterritorializations of media mean that the question of exchange must be taken up from a different angle by considering the various *technologies* of perception as discussed in the earlier parts of this work. With writing, certainly with photography and film – perhaps less obviously so with the localized dialogues of the Modern – it is the machineries of the production of Calcutta which cannot be separated from what is said about the place. As Heidegger points out with his concept of 'enframing', and as Deleuze and Guattari follow after him (Deleuze and Guattari 1972/1983: 17), there is little difference between what is said and how it is said. It is worth taking up the metaphoric surplus of these earlier themes in order to think through the ways exchange must now be understood as a part of an ever more unequal global production.

If production can be considered as an image machine, as a way of inscribing meaning and value within a global economy – as transnational commentary – then there are forms and styles which might be said to correspond to the variously distinguished and defined demarcations which circulate in the history of production. All that can be done here is to indicate, perhaps, the possibility of such demarcations, and elaborate on some of them. Part of my purpose is to explore the metaphorics of international travel and representation as frames for the contemporary particularities of this economy. Another study might take up other moments of historical importance. To keep this moving, to avoid getting stuck, a theory or strategy of manoeuvre, its economy and related metaphors might offer an heuristic device, a machine, an inscribing apparatus, to enable a second look, a replay, a review – possibly to enter into circulation against capital (if we enter the circle with Heidegger and Marx, perhaps) with this machinery of the image. This is not just the simple project of seeing if it is at all possible to think things differently; it is also to recognize that the way we think and the way we see, and the ways we collect images, the ways we photograph and write, are very much the consequences of manoeuvres, and the politics of this entails moving again. Circulation. Travel.

But this encircles us too. Lyotard shows how our choices (and probably this form of critique) are determined by an almost redemptive or religious photo-iconic frame:

> the important thing is the final return, what we can get out of it, which as we know is the attitude adopted nowadays on their holidays by all wage-earners, as well as by the rich, their bosses and masters: the desire to bring back images, photos, film, prestige, the tourism of the return, retourism, a succession of explorations that always follow the same outline. (Lyotard 1989: 4)

To return with so many rolls of film, to return as the bearer of the ashes (Lévi-Strauss?) of so many events, to return with the eternal representations is the eternal return.[7]

ANOTHER TOWER

My decision to study the production of stories and representations of Calcutta was the consequence of many things, but none more 'representative' of the links between authority and perspective than the comment of the West Bengal Chief of Police, whom I visited in his office at Lal Bazaar in order to obtain permission to climb Saheed Minar (formerly Ochterlony monument) when I first arrived in Calcutta. After meeting what seemed like a dozen functionaries in as many separate parts of the headquarters, I was finally ushered into his office and welcomed with an expansive gesture and the greeting 'So, you want a panoramic view of my city?' The next day I was able to climb the 165 feet of the tower in order to observe the police chief's city. And with a 360-degree panorama, his city is very impressive indeed. The cricketers on the Maidan looked so small, and I thought that every perspective offered something both utterly different and yet somehow the same; perspective and perception are like the co-ordinates of a prism sucking many influences into each momentary glance, and yet among all the myriad flashes of Calcutta – from the veiled perspective of the Missionaries of Charity to the gaze of street children staring into an North American's camera – it is this one choice phrase, 'So, you want a panoramic view' (Chiefs of Police sometimes talk like this), that is set apart (never perfectly, since there is no single authoritative perspective) to represent it all.

In this chapter I have considered the photograph and the souvenir productively together: as an image taken, as a mimetic aid, and as icons conditioned by a structured touristic world-view of Calcutta which fits the city into the necessary flows of global capitalist production. A fetish of travel frames the traveller's identity and experience in Calcutta as something to be collected, recouped and stored. Experience of the city is framed at a distance which enables a separation quite amenable to the ideologies of development and charity which are encrypted in the Baudelaire scene of the coin given to the beggar. (This is taken up again in the next chapter.) The shots taken by travellers and their collection of souvenirs can be understood as a part of wider processes of the circulation of values. It is this which enables the 'charitable' orientations of the travellers working at the clinic and living in Modern Lodge, as well as the urgent call of those writers who want 'something to be done'. Again it is interesting to note an invisibility here, in that what is being done, especially by the municipal authorities and the communist parties, is less easily made the subject of travel photography and souveniring. The next chapter continues this examination with regard to film, especially the Hollywood epic *City of Joy*.

NOTES

1. Invented in 1839, and its growing popularity coinciding with a greater expansion of European imperialist power, the daguerreotype soon gave way to the brand-name cameras we are familiar with today, and became closely associated with tourism during this century. The work in this chapter owes much to discussions with Scott McQuire, whose PhD (1995) addresses the history of photography, forthcoming in a book to be published by Sage.

2. The traveller's body, too, even as it wastes away, is shaped by 'fashion' in a way that is akin to the 'souvenir'. 'Today I heard people telling their friend, who seemed pleased when they told him, he looked frail, thin and sick. He had been in Calcutta for a long time and was wasting and enjoying it as he disappeared' (Gayle). Similarly, Adrienne once remarked that she would rather be poor in Calcutta than in any Western city. While there is something to be said for her empathetic identification here, the pleasure of martyrdom attends her comment. As a stance that can be taken by a relatively wealthy visitor with an air ticket home, this identification with poverty is also just a fashionable pose.

3. See comments in the Introduction on Fredric Jameson's suggestion of a shift in emphasis in discussions of authenticity in post-structuralist work from political critique to celebration (Jameson 1991: 198). I remain unsure about the usefulness of his point. Certainly *some* so-called post-structuralists could be criticized for their evocation of the 'authenticity' (or not) of everything – and I suspect that Baudrillard's notion of simulation is singled out here – but post-structuralist work cannot be made an 'authentically' whole and singular body so easily.

4. Heidegger also manages a mad discussion of tables in his *Nietzsche* book (Heidegger 1961/1979: 173–87), in which, again similarly to Marx, he considers what it is to produce a table and what the idea of a table might be. It would be worthwhile looking to the metaphors and examples both Marx and Heidegger use – Marx especially seems concerned with the cold, since he goes on and on about the cost of a coat (Marx 1867/1967). A useful model, though in some ways disappointing and politically abstract (and anti-party), is Derrida's book on Marx and Hamlet, in which there is also mention of Marx's tables, tables with brains, dancing Chinese tables, and so on (Derrida 1995b: 153). For Heidegger and Hamlet, see Ronell (1994: 217).

5. This is one of the subjects of the next chapter.

6. I could include something here about how tourists wish themselves enframed sometimes as 'proof' of presence. The protocol of staged *in situ* shots.

7. Here, on returns, I would like to include the scenes of Suzie photographing the photographer who ends up providing a photograph for the front page of *The Age*, my daily paper in Melbourne. The photograph shows this photographer taking the photograph which was used in *The Age* as an advertisement for a travelling exhibition to raise money for Calcutta Rescue. A photograph a few seconds later shows the journalist taking down the name of the volunteer while the 'patient' is left to do her own dressing. For a time I thought of using these images on the front cover of this book. Correspondences like these probably haunt everyone's research project, but this also shows the reach of the globally circulating images of Calcutta that I have in mind in this chapter. In the end the cover image I chose was Ashis Auddy's tribute to Cartier-Bresson, which offers something like a metaphor for the backpacker view of Calcutta. Look in the reflection for the umbrella.

CINEMATIC CALCUTTA:

CAMERA ANGLES ON THE CITY

This chapter considers cinematic Calcuttas, focusing primarily upon Roland Joffe's *City of Joy*, but also on films by the French director Louis Malle, Germany's Reinhardt Hauff, and others. The Joffe film *City of Joy* is the primary focus because this film was made in co-operation with volunteers from the Preger clinic living in Modern Lodge. It presents a highly worked, advanced media technology, scripted and choreographed version of the rumour of Calcutta, so that the experience of travellers and visitors as portrayed in the film version of *City of Joy*, and to a lesser extent by Malle and Hauff, offers a rehearsal of the themes raised in earlier chapters. Now constituted as a scenic backdrop to the work of the volunteers, the images of these visiting filmmakers, their differences, their evocation and extension of the 'myths' of Calcutta, and the importance of film as a contemporary guiding metaphor of cultural understanding, can lead us through a reflection on the process and technologies of film in a way that unpacks touristic viewpoints. Here I canvass issues of charity work, the motives of travellers, and the frames of perception deployed to make sense of a cinematic Calcutta.

The city is an image, seen through a screen – or rather, *on* one. More and more, international public perception of India is framed by the movie camera. The cultural role of the old literature of Empire has been usurped by film. Once it was the likes of Rudyard Kipling who represented the exemplary Indian city to the world – with much contempt, arrogance and superiority, and while Somerset Maugham sweated beneath an overhead fan in the tropical heat. Now the mainstream film industry, with multi-million-dollar budgets, famous directors like Roland Joffe and superstars like Patrick Swayze, produces the scenes.

Released in 1992, *City of Joy*, directed by Joffe and starring Swayze alongside Om Puri and Shabana Azmi, offers an opportunity to evaluate the role of the movie camera in the presentation of India, and Calcutta (to the world beyond its shores). The distribution circuits of the film are all the more relevant here, since *City of Joy* takes as its subject a 'volunteer' visitor who works in a street clinic very similar to that in which the travellers I met worked. Indeed, 'the same'. With this film showing throughout the Western world (it has also been screened via satellite in India, but has not seen commercial release in Calcutta), potential 'volunteers' are provided with a set of images before they arrive of what Calcutta might be like. Or are they?

Given a large and healthy Indian cinema, especially the cinema of Calcutta's great directors Satyajit Ray, Ritwik Ghatak and Mrinal Sen, it is disappointing that Joffe's film has been able to dominate world attention on the basis that it is 'one of the few feature films to be made in Calcutta by a foreign director' (film notes 1992). Joffe's version of Calcutta has travelled so much further than the Calcutta films of Satyajit Ray or those of Ghatak or Sen, despite their 'art-house' acclaim. The ideological investments of the world system of film distribution demands critical attention. The publicity-machine-induced visibility that a director like Joffe is able to marshal and the peculiarities of international cinema are such that one film by a 'world-renowned' mainstream director can monopolize space in 'mainstream' cinemas, while Bengali representations of Calcutta languish in the obscure corners of various film festivals and specialist video collections. While it is difficult to redress the imbalances of this situation, it is important to direct attention to the ways Joffe's camera contributes to an ongoing ethnocentric orientation that needs to be understood as integral to the structure of imperialist representation[1]. If there were not reason enough to examine what big-budget foreign cinematographers like Joffe are doing in Calcutta, the justification, which close focus upon the *City of Joy* provides, is that insight into the ongoing politics of representation between Calcutta and beyond is possible in a way that ties the themes of this work together in a cinematic tangle.

CAMERA ANGLES ON THE CITY

'We're going to be in the movies!' (Heidi, on being asked to attend filming by Joffe)

Film is a contemporary guiding metaphor of perception. Some critics would agree that the movie camera initiates a new rupture in conduits of perception in the twentieth century. Walter Benjamin's aphoristic style captures the explosive impact of camera technology best:

> Our taverns and our metropolitan streets ... appeared to have us locked up ... then came the film and burst this prison-world asunder by the dynamite of the tenth of a second, so that now, in the midst of far-flung ruins and debris, we calmly and adventurously go travelling. With the close-up, space expands; with slow motion, movement is extended ... the camera intervenes with the resources of its lowerings and liftings, its interruptions and isolations, its extensions and accelerations, its enlargements and reductions. (Benjamin 1955/1973: 229–30)

The moving camera in Benjamin's hands is a demolition machine. Yet this is what allows film to achieve its effects; the joining together of many pieces of film 'actually does seem to work' (Murch 1992: 12), despite the mysteries of the 'cut' which 'represents a total and instantaneous displacement of one field of vision with another in just a few milliseconds, a displacement that sometimes also entails a jump forward or backward in time as well as space' (Murch 1992: 12). With film in an urban setting, a kaleidoscopic vision of the clutter of city life in a place like Calcutta meshes with the ways we become attuned to multiplicity, or perhaps with the ways we have learned a selective appropriation of the otherwise too complicated sensory world. Our editing of perception most often goes unremarked.

Is the film camera (even video) in the hands of a visitor a rupture in the codes of perception of Calcutta, or a continuation of the same modes of foreign construction? Changes in human perception can be linked to the development and uses of its 'tools'; the camera builds upon the innovations of photography, but is registered differently over time. Film offers the closest mimetic approximation of an 'unmediated' human perception, and yet is significantly altered from the moment of the *quattrocentro* viewpoint that sight shares with the still camera.

Much more than the immobile single images of photography, the movie camera is a travelling eye (see McQuire 1995). A camera can become one of the crowd, it can follow someone walking, it can follow, or board, a vehicle, it tracks, it zooms, it can zero in on some detail and can make some small incident in a crowd the central focus of its view of the 'action' – it has the capacity to create such icons as the centre of action, even as they might have been unavailable to or overlooked by unaided sight. And not only can the camera travel, it can be in many places simultaneously. The movie camera, after the film has been subjected to studio edit, can see from several sides at once. The structure of *quattrocento* perception is disrupted in the editing-room juxtaposition of perspectives. Images colliding and/or moving across the screen offer more in sequence than visual representation ever has before. Collage initiates a new dimensionality to the way we can perceive life, a city, and so on. Time, movement, focus, size – all these now influence our mode of seeing – not only through the representation of the single images from which film is constituted, and which are brought to 'life' through their repetition across the projector lens, but in all the shifting capacities of cinema which amount to much more than simple pictures.

The ways in which the camera sees the world, the relations brought into play by juxtaposition and sequence, and the capacities of film to be edited and re-edited must be included in any understanding of cinema. In addition the tropes of viewing film would need to be considered: the reception of already familiar and determined meanings, differences in these meanings according both to the context in which the film was made and the contexts in which it is viewed, the circuits and convoluted avenues of how a film comes into being over and over again.

The famous early public showing of film of a train arriving at a station, which caused a stampede among the audience of the *Salon Indien* at the Grand Café in Paris 1885, is often given as an example of how modes of perception are subject to rapid change. Marx suggested that the steam engine (the iron horse) would radically transform India – if he had but lived some two more years beyond his death in 1883, he might have discerned just what an impact this train could have. A two-dimensional screen displaying flickering images of such a train transforms perception in Paris at approximately the same time as a further capitalist expansion has turned resolutely from coastal colonies towards the hinterland resources and mineral wealth of Empire. In many ways this moment in the *Salon Indien* could be seen as a rehearsal of the impact of mass tourism today, with planes and trains as the vehicle of further capitalist expansion into the world 'hinterland' of non-European cultural wealth and resources. That the film *City of Joy* begins with a train arriving at the crowded Howrah station, by far the most important point of access to Calcutta, is not without a certain historical irony.

Who knows Calcutta anyway? Who can tell? Who authorizes this film to pronounce judgement upon the condition of even one rickshaw-puller among the millions of people in Calcutta? The film focuses upon the life of one family, one place, one city: but the slippage for international audiences will be that this focus shows only one side of

Calcutta, one-dimensional 'poverty' and righteous 'charity', and viewers will not see all.

While it is possible to recognize 'Calcutta' in *City of Joy*, the duplicity and disarming nature of the film's narrative carries a paternalistic and imperialist edge which cannot be avoided. For all that this is a story about one small part of one very big city, for all that it is about the interwoven polarities of poverty, joy and the generalized human predicament, for all that this film is about suffering and struggle and hope against the odds – as Swayze's character Max says: 'It is the joy of beating the odds that is so great' – this film's particularities and its generalizing homogenizations deceive in the most insidious of ways. This is a 'feel–good' film, directed to those outside Calcutta. It is full of the kind of sentimentalism that serves to tell us that at least a few people in the world are still capable of 'good works' and charity, but also serves to render redundant any more analytical examination of exploitation, poverty and opportunism beyond simplistic good-versus-evil narratives.

Many viewers will be enticed into the *vision* of this film, and will come to 'know' Calcutta, or have their 'knowledge' of Calcutta embellished, through a closely edited two-dimensional frame. The Calcutta presented here, and the charity and 'joy' that are evidently the 'human condition' of even the 'most embattled' people is, unashamedly, a cinematic construction. Joffe does say that 'images of Calcutta are constantly shifting in meaning', and that 'all interpretations are valid ... to select only one at the expense of others, as Western visitors often do, is to miss the point' (film notes 1992). But then, which Calcutta to choose? The shifting image of the city as depicted by the visitor Joffe is, of course, a multifabricated, interpreted and 'edited' city – not only in the script and on the studio table, but also on the set specially built for the film, and in the publicity department and the media rooms. It is perhaps more important to ask him how many versions of Calcutta are *not* put before the audience, which were left on the cutting-room floor, which were not seen by the camera, which were excluded, and for what reasons?

The absence of contextual explanations, the cheap shots against communism which will pass without notice by most but not by those in Bengal, the homogenizations of cultural identities, the appropriations of the director, the protests against the filming and the promotional literature, and more, all swirl about in a space (is it also Calcutta?) which is the neocolonial context of the film. Governed by content directives derived as much from Californian–English (Joffe is an Englishman, but works with US dollars) narrative expectations as from the experience of volunteers, let alone Bengalis, the camera lies in a context which cannot always be so strictly demarcated; the boundaries of this (Joffe's) city expand. In an epic story, there is much to be told *about* the making of *City of Joy* and its version of Calcutta, and there is much that cannot be told *by* this film.

MALLE

Before Roland Joffe, a host of Western visitors have carried their cameras to Calcutta. Most prominent among these is possibly the late French documentary maker Louis Malle, director of *Phantom India*, but there are also many others, and increasingly, many anonymous tourists armed with video cameras and the like. There is some documentary reality in this, and the many versions of Calcutta that appear cannot be simply dismissed as wrong, however ideological. (The point, however, is to...) In the many hours of film that have been 'taken' in Calcutta, the city itself moves across the screen, even when the moments or people shown may be long passed away. The series of still frames which make up these films are detached images which cannot exist on their own (except as photographs), and yet they are also a form of record of 'what was really there', but not quite – the problem lies between two points within which there are so many intervening 'screens' such as those of contexts, perspective, choice, interpretation, that the demarcation between image and Calcutta remains indiscernible. The early film cameras fixed upon their tripods – before the development of multiple perspectives, pan, zoom, tracking – were only the limited version of an always limiting perception no more capable of presenting a 'true' Calcutta overseas than any other technological mode. Now, this indiscernibility applies to all production of meaning, within Calcutta or without, yet it can be shown that it is still possible to make distinctions, to assign preferences even where exact demarcations are unattributable.

That Malle's 1969 film *Calcutta* remains banned in India yet appears regularly in the 'art-house' cinemas of Western cities can be taken as an illustration of the ways preconceptions and expectations are generated 'abstractly' among visitors before they arrive. The Calcutta of Malle's film is an abstract one because it can be argued to have more to do with Malle's specific experience in the late 1960s, and may have fewer reference points for contemporary viewers. On a number of counts the film can be questioned: it was made at a time of major civil unrest around the Naxalite uprising and the lead-up to the war with Pakistan;

it was made by a director whose reaction to the city was one of distaste; it does not engage with residents of the city in any meaningful
way; and it has been rejected by state and central governments. A review of the extensive and hostile literature in India on the film raises
further problems of this kind. To quote the most famous example,
Satyajit Ray wrote at the time:

> The whole Malle affair is deplorable.... Personally I don't think any director
> has the right to go to a foreign country and make a documentary film about
> it unless (a) he is absolutely thorough in his groundwork on all aspects of the
> country − historical, social, religious, etc., and (b) he does it with genuine
> love. Working in a dazed state − whether of admiration or disgust − can
> produce nothing of any value. (Ray in Robinson 1990: 328)

Rather than a debate over censorship and morality, however, it is more
important, I think, to evaluate the film and its structural effects in the
light of its continued appearance in the West as − until *City of Joy* − the
most often-circulated cinematic version of Calcutta available.

Malle's film begins with shots of Brahmin men bathing and praying
at the edge of the Hooghly river; there are no voices, there is no
commentary. Among the first shots the camera picks out three faces:
the first seems to look neutrally into the camera; the second appears
angry; and the third stare turns into a scornful laugh. The next sequence
begins with a long pan across the expanse of Howrah bridge. After
these Brahminical ablutions, the bridge shot is the proper 'arrival
anecdote' to the city in a film which ends with outraged detailed shots
of sewers and shit in full bubbling stagnant close-up − something of a
Louis Dumont typology seems to have affected the structure of Malle's
film, from purification to pollution (Dumont 1970). The bridge as seen
by Malle is impressive: the steel framework underneath the span
occupies the bottom two-thirds of the shot; almost lost crammed up at
the very top of the frame is the road crowded with vehicles and
pedestrians surging across into the city. As the camera pans across this
expanse of steel, no sky can be seen above the bridge; the entire
horizon is dominated by a mesh of structural supports − an awesome
piece of engineering.

This long shot of the bridge cuts to a crowded street scene, and
Malle picks out a series of 'curios' where, although the shot is un-
broken, the capacities of the camera allow a montage of discrete images
to be strung together 'impressionistically' through pan, zoom, tracking,
change of focus from foreground to background, and so on. After the
immobile structure of the bridge, this shift into moving humanity −

which soon turns to images of leprosy, and ends by returning over the bridge to the rubble of Howrah slums – displays a correspondence in its structural drift from rigid steel to decayed flesh with that of the shift from the pure to the impure. Malle's editing choices are clearly intentional in a sequence moving from a coolie carrying a basket on his head, a brass band member in uniform, a rickshaw, another man carrying a huge bundle of straw, a sadhu and an urn carried at waist height, a boy sitting in the middle of the road oblivious to traffic careering around him, naked children, overcorroded buses, overcrowded trains, cars, goats... the cumulative effect of such images is that which is called 'Calcutta'. The implication is that a whole city can be documented through such a list, although it is doubtful that Malle would attempt something similar under the names of First World cities like 'Paris' or 'Chicago'.

After more than ten minutes of film a man holds a piece of cardboard in front of the camera to protect his face from Malle's invasion, a boy stares at the filmmaker as he trains his lens on the crowds at a railway station, and then, shifting to the inside of Mother Teresa's home for the destitute and dying, the first words of the film are spoken. Malle asks one of the inmates: 'Why are you here?' – a strange question, which might also be addressed to Malle himself. Directed at a dying man, rather than one of the wealthier or healthier citizens of Calcutta, the question 'Why are you here?' is one that Malle seems to ask of Calcutta as a whole, and, perhaps like many visitors to the city, he does not understand the answer as the question cannot be detached from the overcrowded context in which it is asked by a famous French filmmaker of an anonymous Indian destitute in a Missionaries of Charity hospice.

The propriety of Malle's power-full question 'Why are you here?' is important in other parts of *Calcutta* too. At the Kali temple the pan across the line of beggars outside is uneven and bumpy, a technical flaw absent from much of the film and one which could possibly be explained by seeing Malle carrying a covertly functioning camera by his side rather than holding it up to his eye, attracting attention as he enters the temple (an authenticity effect born of anxiety and deceit). His decision to focus upon the watch among all the presents given at a wedding he films, his shots of people washing at a public pump, pigs snuffling in the drains while children play, and the way the camera seems to slink around the corners of the bustee he visits, could all be used to raise questions about the moralizing imperatives that have conditioned Malle's choices. His commentary adds little to the film, as he continually wants the camera to show Calcutta, he wants us to see – but the camera is less agile than our eyes, is unable to shake its head to say no, has to be forced to spy around corners and cannot look over its shoulder. The documentary folly of Malle is his failure to let go of the illusion that the camera cannot lie, that the camera cannot lie from the particular (enframing) perspective of a rich (sugar empire heir) Westerner.

Malle's only appearance in the film occurs at the end of his slum tour when he is surrounded by a family of Tamil refugees living in straw huts; straw huts are the structural antithesis of the steel bridge which began the film. Malle's cameo is accompanied by a final monologue in which he refers to the Tamils in Calcutta and says: 'They are astonished to be filmed'. Yet the camera seems always to intrude when the one who wields the camera is from outside.

Surprisingly absent from the film, since on at least one occasion it was Mrinal Sen who acted as Malle's guide in the city, is the voice of the Bengali intellectual. Malle allows an ex-public servant to speak of the ostracism he faced after contracting leprosy, but the very vocal middle classes and workers of Calcutta are silent or presented only as the chanters of political slogans. Malle's behaviourist observation ignores local opinion in a way reminiscent of anthropologist Fred Bailey, who once said that only observed behaviour was important, and people's ideas – 'supposing they have any in the first place' (Bailey 1957) – should be ignored. It is not true that presentation of the 'voice' of the subject necessarily makes a better or more authentic film; as Roberge has noted, a concerned commentator: 'cannot give their voice to the voiceless, they can only give their own voice. The image-maker can only project his or her own view of those who do not have the power to produce "their" own images (Roberge 1991: 5). Roberge may be correct in pointing out the inevitability of Malle's ventriloquy, but given his opportunities, the arrogance of omission cannot be accepted; it is no surprise that the film was banned. In relation to the availability of the film outside India, it is important to see the inclusion of certain scenes in context in a number of ways. A single image, such as the interview with a member of a leper community, appears in the context of that community, in the context of other images in the film, and in the context of other representations of Calcutta which are or are not available for viewing by various audiences – at all of these moments the 'image' may take on different meanings for differently placed viewers. In a discussion about the representation of poverty in films of India, Nargis Dutt (star of the 1957 blockbuster *Mother India*) replied to a question about why films on poverty in India – she refers to Ray's *Pather Panchali* – are so popular in the West, explaining: 'because people there want to see India in an abject condition. That is the image they have of our country and a film that confirms that image seems to them authentic' (in Robinson 1990: 327).[2]

The multiplication of camera angles which descends upon Calcutta in the hands of more and more of its visitors does not mean that the volume of 'adequate' or authentic representation must increase. It is worth noting that I operate a kind of dubious cultural authenticity here again when I do not include Bengali documentaries in this study; there is nothing for it but to continue to focus only on 'outsider' views, since these are the terms of my brief – even as these outsider views include 'experimental' approaches, and sometimes collaborative work. In any case, any creative initiatives that may be possible in this context could be erased by the domination of the established image-language with which Calcutta is recognized. Whatever curiosities or disruptions to this language may appear in any particular visitor's representation of the city, the points of reference for most viewers 'back home' of such images will be familiar stereotype scenes of poverty, crowds, perhaps the Howrah bridge, and so on. This is certainly the case with *City of Joy*, where the markers of 'Calcutta' are highly visible – crowds, rickshaws, Howrah station – although there are few black-and-yellow ambassador cabs, few people from Calcutta's middle class, and next to no communist presence. Should the middle class, the race track, the expensive restaurants of Park Street, the large business establishments, the book fair, the film festival or the cultural programmes of places like Rabindra Sadan ever appear on film – as they do in Malle's documentary – they can be consigned away as categories of lesser importance or as remnants of the Raj, and considered not part of the 'real' problem of Calcutta. At best they will be considered, without analysis, to be the 'cause' of the problem of massively unequal distribution of wealth. There is a form of insistence that 'both' sides of the story be told which amounts to a desire for equality from a power position that hardly ever requires such ideals for itself.

It might be said that Western experience of Calcutta is 'framed' not only by specific films, whether those of Malle, Satyajit Ray or Joffe, but also by the idea of film, the structuring effects of the metaphor itself. In this context it is possible to question whether it is Calcutta at all that is prominent on these screens, the image of the city snapped out of place and featured in the looping media circuits of information capitalism. The 'image' escapes reference, and anything which approaches the screen is absorbed into the black hole/black box vanishing effect of the camera, where everything can appear but nothing is differentiated, all images are reduced to equivalence and stereotype through the prejudice of film. Calcutta projected on the far wall of a suburban auditorium in the same way and in the same place that hosts *Batman*, *Bladerunner*, *Apocalypse Now* and *Mary Poppins*, or on the living-room television screens of a thousand video recorders and their holiday epics, is just the extension of the displaced city which was prefigured in the homogenizing effects of the camera described by Deleuze:

> in the final analysis, the screen, as the frame of frames, gives a common standard of measurement to things which do not have one – long shots of countryside and close-ups of the face, an astronomical system and a single drop of water... the frame ensures a deterritorialisation of the image. (Deleuze 1983/1986: 14–15)

For example, within the snapshot and video collections of tourists are the most incongruent comparisons: between the face of the poorest street-dweller and the wealth of the Queen Victoria Memorial, between the cramped clutter of a small bustee and the expanse of the Maidan; between the slick underground railway and scenes of a street-side medical clinic – Deleuze might call this the 'deterritorialisation' effect of Calcutta. Within the frame of the screen, other shapes single out 'icons' of Calcutta for attention – for example, the way well-known tourist attractions might be used to locate representations of 'poverty', as in shots of the poor in the shadow of the deluxe Oberoi Grand. Frames 'frame' in film in a variety of ways; the most common with reference to travel is the frame of the journey, of arrival and departure – it is not only that so many Western films on Calcutta begin with arrival scenes and end with departures (hardly surprising), but other modes of framing – between events, between sequences, and within shots through shifts of focus or perspective – mean that representations of Calcutta are continually coming and going in film.

In a less well-known documentary made by Dieter Hetleb, entitled *Calcutta, One Day*, the kaleidoscopic effect of the visitor pointing the camera at anything that attracts interest provides a seemingly endless string of curios. The choices of this visitor determine what is interesting, where the gaze lingers, where the gaze moves on. The ordering narrative of a day in Calcutta suggests that nothing is omitted – it is a full day – yet the dawn-to-dusk compendium of traffic, cows and sleeping dogs suggests an even more eclectic and Eurocentric prejudice

than in Malle's case. Images of cats and skulls, of Howrah bridge and
the Queen Victoria Memorial, of a man crying, another pushing an
overloaded cart, trams, street people, and snatches of Bengali speech
edited mid-sentence with no regard for sense – the 'daily life' of
Calcutta presented as *vérité*. There is no ordering other than the phantasmagoria of jumbled impressions – and this is so often the case in
traveller video, for reasons that are more than the effects of turning the
camera on at one point and off at another. There are any number of
scenes a camera can make interesting in Calcutta, such that often the
point of making sense or providing any form of intentional structure is
lost in the kaleidoscope of received framing.

CITY OF JOY: THE MOVIE

There are structured points of arrival. The tracking shot of entry into
the city in documentary is often that of the sweep along the street
from the taxi window travelling from airport to hotel. The first scenes
of *City of Joy* are nothing more than a variation on this theme.

The plot is simple. The film begins with the death of an anonymous
patient on an operating table in a modern American hospital. The
surgeon in charge of the operation suffers anguish and despair over his
failure. Cut to India.

Hasari (Om Puri) and family travel to Calcutta by bullock and cart,
bus then train – the acceleration of this travel trajectory is not accidental.
With warnings from a grandmother to 'stay away from the cinema',
they arrive at the crowded Howrah station amid a Communist rally
(the only scene which indicates any formal political presence in the
city). They spend a first night encamped by the Hooghly river, and are
then deceived into renting someone's apartment by the charlatan Mr
Ganguly. After Ganguly disappears, and Hasari and family begin to
settle in, they are suddenly chased from the apartment, which was not
for rent, and was not Mr Ganguly's in the first place. Having lost all
their savings, they mark out a space of pavement.

Dr Max (Patrick Swayze) arrives at Sudder Street's Fairlawn Hotel
(no bar fridge, offers of a 'lady') and takes a shower, musing over his
absent passport, which he has left at an ashram, and his earnest quest
to find enlightenment/escape from his failed life as a surgeon in
America. In the first of what are many uncommon occurrences for this
'typical' American tourist, the porter from the Fairlawn brings Poomina
(Suneeta Sengupta), an allegedly 20-year-old 'lady', with whom Max
has 'some problem' (a euphemism for sex?), but resolves this by going

out drinking. As must happen with all Americans stranded in a 'foreign'
city, Max ends up in a sleazy nightclub, the drinking bout leads to a
bar fight, as goondas bash him – a very unusual event to befall a
tourist in even the most seedy of Calcutta's bars, more likely in New
York – and he is robbed of all his belongings. Hasari, from his pavement
space nearby, intervenes and brings the near-unconscious Max, with
Poomina's assistance, to Joan's 'City of Joy' street clinic. Joan (Pauline
Collins) patches up his wounds, shows him around the clinic, its small
dispensary and school, and pays his way back to his comfortable hotel.

Max 'doesn't like sick people', and resists Joan's obvious plans to
recruit him as doctor for the clinic. Hasari learns to pull a rickshaw,
bringing Max back to the hotel in a mad zigzag through proverbially
crowded streets. The unlikely entrance of such a rickshaw into the
grounds of the hotel is not the least of the inaccuracies (or rather,
artistic licence) of the film – the street protocols and hierarchy of
business and propriety which operate even in Calcutta's relatively small
tourist trade are glossed over in this *realist* portrayal.

Rickshaw work is controlled by the family of Ghatak, whose son
Ashoka (Art Malik) – the one whose gang beat up on Max – demands
that Hasari 'neigh' like a horse if he wants to pull a rickshaw. The
more pragmatic father examines Hasari's chest (for signs of tuberculosis) and demands 'loyalty', and Hasari becomes a rickshaw wallah.
While in Pilkana, the *real* City of Joy, hand-pulled rickshaws have been
long replaced by bicyclist-driven ones, artistic licence again erases the
contemporary conditions of Calcutta, and no recognition is made of
the Calcutta Municipal Corporation campaign to end the use of hand-
pulled rickshaws. Although the hand-pulled rickshaw is still prevalent
in the inner-city area, this fictive shifting of them to the City of Joy is
another calculated inaccuracy: such omissions of urban planning efforts
in Calcutta are significant devices in presenting the city as the exemplar
of massively abstracted 'grinding poverty'. When Hasari has established
himself as a rickshaw wallah, he and his family move into a room in
the City of Joy. Hasari plans to save for his daughter's dowry (no
criticism of this practice acknowledged, despite signs of a school, and
thus by implication the usual campaigns to prevent the illegal practice
of dowry and the many tragedies to which it leads through extortionate
demands).

The notion that Ashoka and the Ghatak family organization are
somehow, consciously or unconsciously, placed in the metaphoric
location of the Left Front Government and its officials in Joffe's version
of Calcutta may occur to some. With the slippage from specific charac-

terizations to generalized 'how things are in Calcutta', and with the conspicuous absence of the communist parties in most of the film, it seems clear that Ghatak, as embodiment of all evil and corruption, will be associated with formal authority in the city. The message is that the only authority in Calcutta is corrupt. This crypto-anti-communist lesson from Joffe will be acknowledged and internalized to varying degrees of conscious recognition – and all the more so if audiences are aware of any of the wranglings Joffe had with the Government of West Bengal, Bengali intellectuals and the Calcutta press over the propriety of making this film. While it is not possible to show that the characterizations of the Ghatak family must be seen as a Joffe slag against the CPI(M) through 'metonymic' substitution, this does raise questions of the motivations of those involved in this sort of filmmaking, and makes one think that perhaps the film is about Joffe's, and Swayze's, frustrations more than much else. The explorations of Swayze's tortured self, the search for enlightenment and meaning, the works of 'charity', in a psychoanalysis by substitution, can be read as Joffe's own experience. Despite criticism from almost every quarter in Calcutta – from the government, which banned his film, to other filmmakers, including Satyajit Ray, who said he couldn't film on the streets of the city – Joffe belligerently and relentlessly pursued his project. He encountered great difficulties in scenes filmed in the streets, although most of the film was shot in a specially built million-dollar set in suburban Calcutta. Swayze recounted the *excitement* of filming with a certain tension in a promotional interview: 'We were forced to just set up the camera and shoot before anyone noticed what we were up to'. (Less generous critics on the roof of the Modern Lodge called this the clandestine realismo approach to filmmaking).

Max, meanwhile, is trying to buy a hamburger in a street-side 'no beef' café. He spots Ashoka, gives chase, but is detained by the police. Rescued a second time by Joan, he comments upon her work in the street clinic: 'Are you just nuts, or are you doing penance here?' Joan replies with the first of many pro-charity soliloquies that would not seem all that out of place at a Modern Lodge rooftop meeting: 'I came on a whim in the first place, but then I stayed. In the beginning it was really frustrating trying to convince them not to be so bloody passive, and then I realized I was fighting a thousand years of passive acceptance.' The theme of passivity is the recurrent explanation of people's predicament throughout the film.

Max: 'Maybe you should stop doing this.' *Joan*: 'Maybe I should … but I'm not very good at loving just one person, it seems to work out better if I spread it around a little bit.' After this exchange Max re-affirms his faith in the Dallas Cowboys, American cinema and Mickey Mouse. Joan's 'simple-minded, but tidy' three-part explanation of the ways of the world – there are *runaways*, *observers*, and the *committed* – does not seem to impress Max as Hasari invites him to share a meagre dinner. After a planting ceremony of seeds in a pot on behalf of his daughter's dowry, the farmer, who must always watch something grow, asserts the 'simple' joys of life. But very soon afterwards, this tranquil scene is disrupted by an emergency which only Max can deal with, and although there is no morphine, diazepam ... local anaesthetic, he is able to assist in the delivery of a breach birth – an awesome scene in which the doctor asserts the full authority of the medical tradition *contra* indigenous superstition and fear. Amid all this, Hasari's wife Kamla (Shabana Azmi) assists the doctor on the strength of her experience as a mother of three, and earns a position as his nurse when – after the loss of his air ticket home, and a little soul-searching: 'I don't even feel good about what we did down there today, bringing another little mouth to feed into this cesspool' – he 'volunteers' to help in the clinic on a continuing basis. *Max*: 'You call this a clinic!' *Joan*: 'We've got no brain scanner either Max, but we're doing the best we can' (these lines, and a scene involving the sale of donated milk, were offered to Joffe, I suspect, from the chief humorist at the Preger Middleton Row clinic).

In the meantime, Poomina has been ordered to attend school under Max's directive. Max and Joan visit Ghatak (Shyamanand Jalan), who offers Max a lesson in goonda philosophy – 'I have learnt not to trust those who say they do things for the benefit of others' – which Max violently rejects. This is an interesting refusal which encodes much of Joffe's message: unlike the passive and yoked people of the City of Joy, Max will not bow down before the power of the oppressor Ghatak. He calls upon the people of the City of Joy to rise up against the Ghatak family: 'You should get pissed at the people who are really using you.' This is as admirable a message as it is naive. Even the most cursory history lesson about Bengal would have taught Joffe that any suggestion that Calcuttans need American coaching in order to organize a political mobilization is wholly absurd. Passivity here works as Western arrogance and denial displaced by self-importance. Near the beginning of the film Grandmother had warned Hasari's sons Shambu and Manooj to 'stay away from the cinema', but Max, a film-buff's fanatic, had taken them to see an action-hero epic. Max is the agent of (cinematic) change, although a mature assessment of the effects of cinema upon him in his youth, when his adulterous father packed him off to the movies while pursuing his affairs, might lead to other evaluations of the impact of paternal directives. While Joffe does not take up the metaphor of movies and paternalism which could be read into this scene, the self-referentiality of his cinema jokes may have unforeseen dysfunctions which should not be lost on critical audiences who are likely to note that the real 'users' in this film are the Americans, Swayze and Joffe, and the imperialist system which makes possible this sort of cinematic characterization of Calcutta by wealthy celluloid 'bosses'. Fatherly protection and paternalistic charity are the guiding themes. The rest of the film follows the script of classics like *The Wild Bunch* and *The Seven Samurai*, as Max leads the people of the City of Joy to organize and, subsequently, Hasari inspires the rickshaw wallahs to rebel against the oppression of the Ghatak 'family'. There are several almost predictable setbacks: Hasari contracts tuberculosis, a common complaint among rickshaw wallahs; he loses his rickshaw to Ashoka and is forced to sell his blood (a sensational aspect of poverty included in the story, about which the author of the book *City of Joy*, Dominique Lapierre, was severely criticized); an attack upon the leprosy clinic is organized by Ashoka and his goondas; and there is a near-death action-camera experience for Max during the monsoon flood (the 250,000 gallons of water for the flood was specially pumped into the watertight set Joffe had built to enable monsoon filming without regular 'polluted' monsoon water – the entire project overseen by *Star Wars* trilogy special effects wizard Nick Allder).

There is one terrible scene where Ashoka traps Poomina and uses a razor to cut her cheeks to 'accentuate that beautiful smile', although Max's surgical skill is sufficient to restore her beauty. Moving from active woman to silent 'child', Poomina develops in a way that under-scores certain gendered and ethnocentric assumptions about Indian women. From an assertive but *fallen* woman who initiates all inter-action between herself and Max, and brings him to the City of Joy clinic, her increasing passivity contrasts with her initial resourcefulness as she is ordered off to school, is attacked with the razor by Ashok and carried to safety by Max, who sews her slit mouth shut – making her unable to speak in the entire second half of the film. After functioning as the catalyst for Max's arrival in the City of Joy, as well as providing a hint of exotic and erotic intrigue, Poomina is silenced almost as completely as Hasari's daughter, who, without a word, and possibly in Poomina's place, is married at the end of the film with the dowry that Hasari has almost killed himself to earn.

After this, the film's denouement is a scene reminiscent of the manger sequence in Bethlehem in late December two thousand years ago. Amid a grey Calcutta, just one shining light beacons for all Christian souls – the clinic of the City of Joy – as the camera pulls back to a full panorama and the credits roll.

OTHER ANGLES ON THE CITY OF JOY

There is much in *City of Joy* that people could find offensive. The simplicity of the emotive codes in which poverty and the conditions of Calcutta are explained away as problems of passivity, and localized exploitation, avoids any analysis of the global economic factors which depress such sectors in the city. Max, even though the audience recognizes that he is from the wealthy 'West', is still presented as the man with the answers, despite the self-help rhetoric of the clinic. It is never acknowledged that Max's own patronizing attitudes and 'answers' are founded upon the full might of neocolonial exploitation of Calcutta by international capitalism. Nor does the representation of women in the film – as smiling, passive, beautiful and increasingly *silent* beings – provide any degree of analytical sophistication. Such formulaic representations of bodies cannot achieve more. The absence of those who in other (local) narratives of the city *are* seen to be doing things in Calcutta – be it the Corporation, or the militant communists and CPI(M) – simply affirms the film's misrepresentations of Calcuttans as passive (apolitically joyous) and Americans as those-who-have-answers. This is not Calcutta, and although I am not sure what is, or how its diversity could be represented (but see the films of Mrinal Sen), it is possible to argue that despite being 'about' Westerners in Calcutta, Joffe's film does not at any stage address an explanation of the problems of the city in terms of international relations, nor does it consider the dimensions of local conditions – positive and negative – in the context of Calcutta's political history, or provide more than a gloss over the factors of class and caste which should take at least some place in any narrative. That he prefers instead to lay all blame on a local petty bully boy, in an emotional and sentimental heart-throb Wild West adventure in which Patrick Swayze saves the day – Hi ho Silver! – is nothing short of amazing.

Can the camera, in the hands of a Western visitor, see otherwise? If 'images of Calcutta are restless and constantly shifting in meaning', as Joffe says (film notes 1992), is it possible to disrupt the code that he has played out here? There are other films of Calcutta, but I do not think the 'difference' that these films display is a difference that enters or effects the codifications that determine Joffe's images. The reasons for this are prejudices and ethnocentrisms that are not specific to the camera, but are neither disrupted nor displaced by it either. Imperialist business-as-usual seems to be the order of the day – the camera is a fold in perception, and yet nothing much has changed. Similarly, Joffe can present himself as a more sensitive filmmaker, alert to many of the pitfalls and assumptions of cultural difference, able to recognize at least a degree of the indeterminancies of meaning in which he is involved – 'Calcutta taught me to take nothing at face value' (Joffe, film notes 1992) – and yet still make a very conventional film which reiterates Kipling-like arrogances.

There are too many of these bad-news stories in a city which gets a bad press. Its inscription as the exemplary site of photogenic poverty and overcrowding is continually reinforced, the analysis and action which might address Calcutta's problems are not forthcoming, and despite all this, Joffe persisted in forcing his production onto the screen. In Calcutta the filming was bizarre: riots outside, and invasions of, the set, hijacking of the cast's food truck, union bans, huge crowds come to see the Indian film stars, stone-throwing, police lathi (bamboo baton) charges, delays of all kinds: the shooting attracted much – perhaps too much – attention. There were also, it seems, some problems with Patrick Swayze's bowels: in April 1991, Modern Lodge volunteer workers were able to auction off a stool sample bottle with the star's name upon it found among junk donated by the departing film crew. If we were interested in authenticity we might expect to find Dr Max in *City of Joy* spending most of his time in the bathroom attending to his diarrhoea. This, of course, would be unseemly in a popular film, however much it would resonate with the experience of visitors and their ongoing shit-talk. The viscous limit of *City of Joy* is reached by blood, childbirth and a fairly sanitized focus upon the stumps of leprosy. With a fabricated slum, with imitation monsoons from pumped bore water, hand-pulled rickshaws where there are bicycles, joy in destitution, and what the film crew described as 'chaos all around', it is still a wonder that the film appeared at all (a tribute to Joffe's cash reserves). During the period of filming there were numerous reviews, pro and con, and promotional articles in the Calcutta press reporting the sensations of riots and intrigues on the set: a whole gossip and rumour system in itself. Subsequently the whole affair has entered more literary writings as a background event in other stories about Calcutta. For example, a character in Sunetra Gupta's novel *The Glassblower's Breath* announces his successful tender for the contract to build Joffe's set: 'So he would be building a slum, a slum to slum all slums in this city of slum, for no slum had proved slum enough for the *City of Joy*.... Do you feel no shame?' (Gupta 1993: 233).

Wholesome purchase and transportation of slum-dwellers' houses went into the construction of the 'City of Joy' set. One volunteer noted that the bustee-dwellers must have thought Joffe was mad: 'He comes in, sees the broken-down roof of hessian and tin sheets and says, 'I love it, I'll have it', and peels off three or four hundred rupees to give to the owner. Then his henchmen get to work, remove the old wrecked roof as carefully as possible, and replace it with a strong solid new roof!' (Kath). Yes, it is crazy. The old roof is fitted into Hollywood's authentic Calcutta. Some of us prone to clichés might exclaim: 'Only in Calcutta', but we know commercial cinema much better than that. As Deleuze says; 'The cinema does not just present images, it surrounds them with a world' (Deleuze 1985/1989: 68).

Given Joffe's no doubt admirable good intentions to try to do something for the people of Calcutta (having already saved the Cambodians, and as a 'representative' patron of Latin America), perhaps a more useful approach would have been to provide an analysis of the range of informal-sector activities which, along with the rickshaws, have become essential components of the functioning of the city. While the film can note, for example, that only these rickshaws can navigate the flooded streets of monsoon time, analysis of the informal work world of the economically disadvantaged sectors of Calcutta needs to be examined in a context where the formal economic order is unable to provide (food, shelter, transport) within the framework of the law. This analysis is available in Calcutta: for example, in the *Calcutta 1981* volume Jean Racine reproduces comments from the local group Unnayan linking sections of the informal sector together in the functioning of the city: 'Pavement dwellers obstruct the pavements. Hawkers obstruct pavements and streets. Rickshaws obstruct traffic flow. So what to do with them? They are underprivileged people, petty citizens, but they play their role, a decisive role, in city life' (Unnayan in Racine 1990). While local studies do take up these concerns, *City of Joy* glosses over such perspectives in the interests of cinematic sentimentalism. Similarly, debate about the banning of hand-pulled rickshaws has continued for forty years in Bengal, and although there is little evidence in the *City of Joy*, this debate has raised the question in the context of the relation between the informal and formal sectors. Rickshaw wallahs (1,00,000 of them) make up the largest informal-sector grouping and provide the most heavily used mode of transport, for all manner of conveyance – trade, school, personal, and so on. It is estimated that only one in five of the vehicles in this sector are licensed and banning of rickshaws, if effectively enforced, would have the dual effect of increasing real unemployment and overburdening an already inadequate formal transport network to the point of paralysis. These are serious problems to contend with, but not in Joffe's helpful film.

City of Joy begins as a story of one – Hasari – who learns to sell his labour, as a rickshaw wallah in the big city, and of another – Dr Max – who learns, I take it, to 'give' his labour for free in the strange city. Both men are robbed at the beginning of the film: Dr Max of his wallet (he is forced to 'wire', not phone, home for more), Hasari of all he and his family own: this difference should be noted. In the film Hasari saves Max from the monsoon flood (in the book the Westerner only falls into a drain/sewer; in cinema heroes must weather falling trees and twenty-metre depths – Joffe elaborates the sewer to drown the entire city). From this bonding moment Hasari and Max are presented as equal except that one remains a surgeon, the other a rickshaw wallah. Are we supposed to ask, meaningfully: 'Ah, but which one is richer in the spirit?'. Oh joy.

In lieu of analysis (this is fiction, after all), joy works in the film as a romanticist acclamation of the heroism of the poor, and it is not difficult to recognize this also as a curative offering to the Western viewer rather than as a description of the condition of the impoverished in Calcutta. Whose joy is it? Joy which allows Western viewers to feel 'proud' of the heroism of the downtrodden, a heroism activated by the appearance of Swayze. The real 'take' in this film is that it imagines this state of affairs as somehow progressive; sanctified and naturalized by appeal to a universal spirit. When the monsoon breaks in the middle of the film, everyone rushes outside to dance in the downpour. This cleansing rain comes at a time when differences between Max and Hasari have begun to be resolved as Hasari sees that Max does have some answers – although it is through the monsoon floods that he is able to earn extra money with his rickshaw. The establishment of the clinic in spite of the Ghatak opposition is also celebrated with this dance. Joffe says he is not in the business of selling poverty, yet as has been noted, it is very difficult to avoid camera effects which package poverty for the viewers back home. Whatever the 'real', and varied, experience of the poor, there is no reason to think that the material and emotional conditions of Hasari Pal's part of the city are best described with terms – joy – resonant of Christian celebration. Certainly there is a creativity required for a life in Calcutta under conditions of economic hardship, and the success and co-operation of Calcuttan communities should be noted – along with the initiatives of the Marxist parties[3] – but to portray the poor as indomitable, and to accord them a generalized 'courage in adversity' which really leaves them as passive victims, is to idealize their situations for the emotional pleasure of foreign and middle-class audiences.

METAPHORS FOR CINEMA

At a much more abstracted level, it might be possible to agree that the cinema metaphor of the mechanical eye articulates closely with Euro-American hegemony through a specific documentary understanding of the Rest of the World. The actor Hans Zischler, who has appeared in a number of Wim Wenders films, said that 'Film criticism no longer has any meaning', and it is 'reality that we have to analyse in a cinematic way' (in Virilio 1984/1989: 65). Contestations of the nature of 'reality' have become more intense at the same time as cinema becomes popularized – not that a causal relationship can be claimed, but it is interesting to consider the introduction of the techniques of cinema in comparison to an idea of unmediated 'perception of reality' in order to show perception as always mediated, yet not necessarily cinematic. The choice example here could be the effect of editing, which, as Orson Welles said, is 'the only time when you can be in complete control of a film' (Virilio 1984/1989: 65), and which is not as obviously a mechanical process when it comes to unaided human sight (some psychoanalysts might want to disagree). The problem that film presents for critical evaluation is that the interpretative choices, perspectives and moralities of filmmakers and their audiences have remained opaque where the mechanical mode of representation has been understood anthropomorphically as a simple extension of sight. The cinema metaphor for perception must remain 'only' a metaphor, so long as it is recognized that all understandings are metaphorical in some way, all perception is mediated through mechanisms of perception which have various conditioning effects, some more evident to us than others.

In consideration of the effects on perception of various factors, and different theoretical ways to make sense of these factors, the sociologist Manuel Castells came into conflict with Lévi-Strauss at a kind of junction of the screen image and the city. Attempting to explain the variety of processes which structure perception of urban life, Castells, too, hastily rejected the anthropologist's orientation as a wish to find the 'history of a society in the trace of its stones' (Castells 1977: 216), in favour of what seems very much like a late Lévi-Strauss position recommending a 'semiological reading of urban space' which would 'study the expressive mediation through which are realised ideological processes produced by social relations in a given conjuncture' (Castells 1977: 219). Castells's distance from structuralism was not so great when he made use of the cinema metaphor to describe the city:

> In this perspective, urban space is not an already written text, but a screen permanently structured by a symbolic that changes in accordance with the production of ideological content by the social practices that act in and on the urban unit. (Castells 1977: 219)

However clumsy this language may be, the point is valid that social practices − in the case of film, editing, directing, and so on − produce and structure the content − ideas, ideological mode, the symbolic − of our understanding of urban spaces. The complexity of this structuring, of the conditioning effects of productive social practices, or of the dynamics of metaphor, are not easily elucidated, and should be approached with a caution that would avoid simplifications. It is not simply that Joffe's direction − as a filmmaker with access to the huge resources of Western cultural and financial capital − has 'produced' a certain kind of film but, rather, that a range of social practices and conditions, historical relationships, technical effects and particularities of both local experience and the world system have combined to 'produce' a film about another 'culture' that serves a certain set of interests.

The conditioning effects of film, however much Orson Welles may want to assert control, are not all open for easy manipulation at the editing table. The production of film entails what Castells might call productive social processes in ways that are by no means straightforward. While a great degree of choice presents itself under the editor's scissors − to include the last thirty frames or not, to juxtapose close-up with panorama, to edit out a voice or to include some other sound − the choices at the point of exposure of the film are important too − when to press the trigger(?), choice of location, of script, of time of day. Editing also has less than total control over the way a film is received by different viewers; the indeterminacies to be considered here are those of all the perception and choices, selections, interpretations, prejudices and preferences that operate to make any one film mean any number of different things. Yet total indeterminacy is unlikely, too − the very preconceptions and prejudices that influence the choices of director and editor coincide in certain ways with those of the viewers: so much so that some writers have seen film leading towards a dangerous homogenization of the world. This is certainly the case with *City of Joy*, where, so it seems, the narratives of the white man's burden, the Wild Bunch/Magnificent Seven, charity/redemption, and so on, are successfully transplanted to the *strange* location of Calcutta – which becomes *familiar* in the process. Every scene is framed in the same comparative and equalizing rectangle of the screen.

Editing also has its dysfunctions or resistances, as can be seen, curiously enough, in the failure – or irony – of a scene in the James Bond movie *Octopussy*, where the splicing of two shots filmed in separate Indian cities made a tense chase scene into a surreal comedy for Indian viewers, while probably few people in Western audiences noticed the disruption. Having narrowly escaped death, some thugs chase 007, who flees in a specially modified auto-rickshaw past the Taj Mahal in Agra. His auto-scooter has a turbo-charged motor, and faced with a dead end in a market lane alongside the Taj he is able to accelerate up a ramp and leap over the colourful market stall; incredibly, he lands in Udaipur by the Lake Palace some 604 kilometres away. What is for Western observers the same picaresque town full of fabulous 'Eastern' mosques and palaces appears to Indian viewers as two totally different Indian cities in far-separated states. Is it inappropriate to castigate a fiction film for its fictionality? Of course; but the point here is that this conflation of urban India into an amalgam of the sites of its most exotic tourist attractions is exactly the kind of fabrication of the 'Orient' that Said pointed out in 1978, and what is interesting here is the two divergent ways of reading the scene that are also made possible – slapstick or romance? That this is achieved upon the editing table – which has made nothing of the fifteen-hour train trip or three-hour flight that must have separated the two 'takes' for the film crew – underlines the constructed 'reality' of all film, fictional or documentary. The creativity of cinema enables new continuities to emerge across time and distance simply through the removal of sections of film, or turning the camera off and moving it. If the Udaipur scenes had been shot a week before those in Agra, it would make no difference – the comedy of Bond's leap from an already ridiculous Uttar Pradesh market, with too many sword-swallowers and snake-charmers, to a southern Rajasthani one filled with a very different set of people, remains the hidden gift even in this fictional 'Indian' city.

Another curious juxtaposition of cities occurs in a less unreal, but nevertheless disturbing, way in Paul Mazursky's 1990 comedy-drama *Scenes from a Mall*. A middle-class executive couple enter a Los Angeles shopping centre cinema complex and walk into an almost empty auditorium where Mira Nair's *Salaam Bombay* is showing. The husband and wife, Woody Allen and Bette Midler, fall upon each other and fuck in the aisle. Two Sikhs, who are the only other occupants of the theatre, call for silence, but are ignored, while the screen shows scenes of child labour and poverty. Even while a critical point about the shallow lives of middle America is being made, Indian cities are reduced to the generalized image of poverty and distributed unquestioned to (the fornicating residents) of other cities like LA.

Virilio's argument is that the cinema is coming to dominate our understanding and to determine the production of all social relations. In *War and Cinema* he argues for a broad-sweep view of history which moves from urban space to global perception:

> The West, after adjusting from the political illusions of the theatre-city (Athens, Rome, Venice) to those of the cinema-city (Hollywood, Cinecittà, Nuremberg), has now plunged into the transpolitical pan-cinema of the nuclear age, into an entirely cinematic vision of the world. (Virilio 1984/1989: 66)

Rushing too fast into generalization as he does, Virilio perhaps omits recognition that all these cities, and even the present world system, have allowed, or had forced upon them, some space for those who would challenge the hegemony of power that controls the city (or citadel, since here the city has become metaphorical too). The theatre-city allowed a certain space for the public to enter political process through entertainment – as the chorus in the tragedy, as the forum in the Senate. Whatever the great limitations of this participation, the preceding mythological constellation which allowed the gods alone (and their priestly representatives, the authority of the Muse or the deity channelled through the few) to govern life was less inclusive. The cinema-city and capitalist media also includes a somewhat illusory avenue of participation – the game-show, the election-night telecast, the 'real' lives of soap opera – in a way that is less hermetically sealed than the global cinema dominance of MGM and Lucasfilm which would be Virilio's cinematic nuclear world. Within the world market of Sony and Spielberg there are also disruptions and disconnections where people take cameras and – often clumsily in comparison to Lucasfilm techno-effects (and remembering that Joffe's special effects were organized by the same people who brought you *Darth Vadar* and *Alien*) – look at the world somewhat differently. There are sites of resistance to imperialism, sometimes in the very centres of cities like Calcutta, however blind Joffe may be to them – the world market is not sewn up. The films of Mrinal Sen and other Bengalis, although not widely distributed and not accorded equal acclaim, are evidence of 'another' cinema (Roberge 1984).

It may be an error to think that a new regime of urban representation has emerged which demands that we write about or film culture in a wholly different way. The city of Virilio's cinema is Ridley Scott's *Bladerunner*, Jean-Luc Godard's *Alphaville* or Fritz Lang's *Metropolis*, the urban nightmares of Vonnegut's *Slaughterhouse Five* Dresden, or the post-apocalypse genres of Hollywood fantasy or the murky decayed violence of Airstrip One in *1984*. The hyper-real ethnography of Wenders's *Wings of Desire* or the sentimentalized street realism of Mira Nair's *Salaam Bombay* leads now to Joffe's *City of Joy*. Fantastic cities circulate interchangeably. Yet these fantasies, which are crucial to Virilio's conception of cinema cities and a cinematic world, do not technically pose any more difficulty for writing than was present for 'pre-nuclear' (pre-Virilio) commentators. The same critical analysis which must be brought to bear upon Kipling, Maugham, Lévi-Strauss, Grass, and other imperial writers must be brought to the contemporary cinema. At the level of narrative, writing about film presents similar difficulties as does writing about other events, in that the order of one type of narration is interrupted by another in the context of a complicated set of power relations we must continually try to unravel – the peculiar functions of the camera should not divert us too much from this work, while we do take stock of the differences.

Increasingly film approaches the city as a moving entity, even as it is fixed upon a map. Virilio's cities are hardly sedentary, and the speeds of representation provide an illusion of ever more rapid movement. The fast cuts of a frantic cinema coincide with the requirements of a commodity capitalism that now even sells its images in bite-sized fast-food consumable chunks. The spluttering production of this cinema resorts to rapid cutting more often in the Third World or alien city (Joffe's Calcutta), as a representational mode suitable for the expression of difference. Increasingly also in the advertisement and touristic world of our fantasy cities, the myriad images of fragmented lives flash past in quick succession: postcard, news-flash, cartoon, souvenir, snapshot. The curious effects of time-exposure photography or fast-forward film – of traffic at intersections or upon highways, of people seen as ants on footpaths or mounting and dismounting from trains, of crowds entering buildings or crammed onto buses – begin to defy the normal rhythms of life, yet seem more representative on the screen of urban experience than true-to-time scenes. Our imagination allows the city to become a hyperfast flow (yet it doesn't move; again we are flickering on the spot as the still image rushes past the projection bulb), perhaps because the enormity of population numbers no longer allows us to count humans, but instead demands a new kind of statistically calculated species.

The identity effect produced through camera and documentary representation still retains many of the characteristics of the general identity that has dominated European consciousness for a very long time. The optimistic evaluation of the proliferation of video and other electronic media by writer–filmmaker–teacher Gregory Ulmer, who thinks that such media will achieve a major disruption of the 'logos' within which we have thought since the onset of phonetic writing, seems too hasty. Ulmer's experimental exploration of video with reference to the writings of Derrida and Ong (Ulmer 1989) is fascinating, but the disruption he projects onto the camera appears as yet unlikely to be greater than other events (represented by proper names such as Copernicus, Columbus, Kaiser Wilhelm, Gandhi, Oppenheimer, Ho Chi Minh, Fonda, Madonna, etc.) that also threatened to disrupt all the ways we think, yet allowed business as usual.

Views such as those of Ulmer with regard to video, and Virilio's injunction to read the world in a cinematic way, still reside in the geographic and technological space of a visual paradigm not far different from that of other writers considered in this work (such as Clifford, Lévi-Strauss). A vectorial perspective on the city, and a focus on speeds of global transmission, does suggest the beginnings of a rupture of the spatial code, but one so neatly in calibration with new technologies of information flow that the interests of global capital do not seem compromised. It is necessary to continue to watch the circulation of images of Calcutta with an eye to their effects in a representational space that impacts upon a number of levels – for tourists, volunteers, readers, analysts, photographers, cinematographers, and us all.

HAUFF

As an example which begins this critical work, Reinhardt Hauff's 1987 city visit documentary essay *10 Days in Calcutta* can be examined for the ways in which it presents Calcutta as the terrain of the filmmaker Mrinal Sen, as a city that can be filmed in interesting ways, as a city which lends itself, according to Hauff, to the filmic 'discussion' of social issues such as poverty, the political responsibility of the artist, or identity. This version of Calcutta, where intellectuals discuss philosophy while walking amid the cacophony of car horns and crow calls that fills the streets, is importantly different from that which appears in most other European films about the city.

Hauff also begins with the bridge into the city, but in a different way his camera seems to be among the people, focusing upon various workers to make them into 'images' for the film, yet in a way that consciously attempts to tell a story about the city's labour rather than offer some curious gaze upon cultural otherness. Unlike the 'curios' Malle selects, the sequence created by Hauff's camera and editing leads directly into Sen's first comments, which draw Hauff's film more closely into Calcutta:

> We are in the thick of the sprawling city of Calcutta, and I am one of around ten million people living in this city. This is a city which is loved and hated. Kipling called it 'the city of dreadful night'. Lord Clive, the founder of British India, called it 'the most wicked place in the universe'. Nehru called it 'the city of processions, of political manifestations' and Günter Grass called it 'God's excrement'; and you, Reinhardt Hauff, you have probably survived the first shock and have started liking Calcutta. (*10 Days in Calcutta*)

Where Malle first asks 'Why are you here?', in Hauff's film Sen states: 'We are here in Calcutta'. Perhaps this declarative rather than interrogative mode allows a very different kind of documentary. In many ways Hauff's film is a collaborative work with Sen, especially when segments of the latter's films appear as parts of Hauff's film – interestingly enough, this includes a sequence from Sen's 1978 *Parashuram*, a shot of a boy performing a stunt at the top of a pole in the Maidan. This same boy doing the same stunt – spinning high above the audience – also appeared in Malle's *Calcutta*, but where in Malle's film this passes without comment, in Sen's a voice asks the boy, in Hindi, 'Seen him?' and the boy answers: 'Yes, he is lost in the whirl of the city'. In Sen's film, and so repeated a third time in Hauff, the boy spins above his pole, and in both these films the boy speaks of one who is lost in the city. But who is lost? Malle's scene stops with the spinning boy, but Sen's moves on until a woman, confronted with a young man looking for a space on the pavement to sleep, shouts: 'Hey, Young Man! What are you doing there? There's no place for you' (*Parashuram*). In Sen this plays a part in a fictional tale of life on Calcutta streets, but repeated in Hauff's film it resonates with further meanings which question anyone's presence, especially that of a filmmaker, in the life of that street. This question, 'What are you doing?', may be in the same form as that asked by Malle in Mother Teresa's Home for the Dying, but in this context the meaning and the possibilities for exchange of meanings seem very different.

Much of Hauff's film is about the production of politically committed cinema in Calcutta. Rather than presentation of the problem of poverty in a two-dimensional form, Hauff, through Sen/with Sen, is concerned with questions like that of what 'cultural production' might be able to do about poverty on the scale of the city. There are few answers to the many questions which stand like accusations – among the most interesting passages is the one where Hauff discusses the dilemma of filming in slums, and says: 'Can one escape the danger of making suffering photogenic? Can I, with my foreign eyes, perceive anything real at all' (*10 Days in Calcutta*). Is it because, with Mrinal Sen, Hauff is an interlocutor in a way that few visitors to Calcutta can be, and although he does not film so much of Calcutta in his ten days, and much of his Calcutta is put together from bits of Sen spliced on an editing table in Germany, he is able to make more of the city than many other directors could in much longer time.

As an interlocutor, Hauff engages Sen in dialogue which brings out the identity of the Bengali film-maker and his feeling for the city. Towards the end of the film Sen says:

> For the last few days you have been asking me questions about the moral responsibility of a film-maker, of social responsibility, about the role of the cinema itself in social change … the more I think of your film which you are making now, I get this feeling that I discover myself through your film. (*10 Days in Calcutta*)

In a way that identity was always tied up with local concerns for Sen; even the glib clichés of the Indian Tourism Authority slogan 'Discover India, Discover Yourself' find expression in his self-critical evaluation inside Hauff's film. While Sen admits that his love of talking sometimes leads him to talk nonsense, his reflection upon his practice is intense – he presents this to Hauff as the result of a journey:

> I have travelled a long way … and I don't feel tired at all … I am like the city of Calcutta, vibrant, full of vitality. I still continue to serve my own time, do a kind of introspection, self-searching, self-criticism to be more exact, pulling myself by the hair … making myself stand before the mirror. (*10 Days in Calcutta*)

In one example of this reflection, a change is possible in the film, a re-filming or re-evaluation, when Sen realizes that he is not happy with the way he introduced Calcutta the day before. Film does allow such revisions, although Hauff has left the moment as a rupture rather than going back for a repair and a seamless entry to the city. Sen says:

after the shooting, I always feel I have missed something; for instance, yester-day, when I first introduced Calcutta, I very much regretted the fact that I hadn't called Calcutta a city which is full of vitality, a vibrant city. I didn't say that, but even otherwise it is there, but then I would have felt very happy, had I said it. Calcutta is a very vibrant city, it is there in my comment on Calcutta but I would have liked it to be clearer. (*10 Days in Calcutta*)

Often used as a term to defend cities that are disliked, this 'vibrancy' which should be 'clearer' is another sight metaphor in a world of moving shadows – after all, that is what film is: moving shadow. The coexistence of this image and another comment in Sen's film *Calcutta, My Eldorado*, where the city is compared to a kaleidoscope, again confirms the importance of vision, among all senses, in understandings of Calcutta.

This is not to say that Hauff and Sen are concerned only to be publicists for a cosmopolitan city. Many of Sen's films have been very sharp criticisms of Calcutta. For example, John Hood notes that the film *Calcutta 71* is not just about the cruelty and suffering of the city's iniquitous economic system. Instead it 'seeks to identify causes, to lay blame and to point to consequences' (Hood 1993: 36). As such, the film is often dismissed as merely polemical, but it transcends polemic as an intellectual essay. Illustration can be seen, for example, in the 'opening and closing montages [which] sharpen the notion of class conflict and make clear the isolation and abandonment of the poor ... [while] ... the attitude of callous indifference of the establishment stands out as a cause for disquiet' (Hood 1993: 36). Calcutta is not always El Dorado offering gold, but Sen can see that it is a mine for hardworking miners and others in despair. The point of evaluation would be to look at the efficacy of his response – the degree to which his polemic and exploration, even expressed in film, offers more than the charitable 'care' of Modern Lodge, Mother Teresa and her ilk.

In a scene near the end of his film, Hauff follows Sen as he returns to a village in which he had shot a fiction film some years before. Sen again sees the child who had played a part in that film, and discovers that now she wishes to become an actress, and had in fact travelled alone into the city to camp outside Sen's house – although Sen was away from Calcutta at the time. Sen is distressed at this story, and recognizes his complicity in having developed unattainable aspirations in this young villager. The untrained Arati could fit into Sen's film (noting that her name could mean adorable goddess), but once the aspiration to act appears, somehow her authenticity has dissolved. Sen leaves Arati in her village, having her again act out the final scene of the earlier film as a new end for Hauff's. As the car moves off and the camera looks past Hauff and Sen in the back seat, Arati is left framed in the shot by the rear window as she runs waving behind the vehicle.

SELF-REPRESENTATION

In 1990 a group of travellers working at the Preger clinic on Middleton Row decided to make a video about life at the Modern Lodge. This was our reaction to the excess of schmaltz and unreality/alienation we had experienced after watching a particularly bad Channel Four special on the Preger clinic, and after various contacts with television journalists. At about the time when *City of Joy* was becoming a controversial film in the city, various rough scripts for a satire on documentaries about tourist Calcutta were prepared. Scenarios included an invasion of an alien Mother Teresa, and a scene where the Queen Victoria statue from outside the Memorial hitched up her skirts and set up a chai stall outside Modern Lodge. Amateur humour and irony; the final product, put together by Susan Fry, did not follow any such script, but it is a critical, and ironic, piece which does go some way towards representing the viewpoint of Modern Lodge tourists. Jokes about toilets, talks on the rooftop, from the chai stall, along Sudder Street: certain tropes of Calcutta are repeated, sometimes as farce. What is considered curious is collected in cameo appearances, and there is a tendency towards what Hauff calls 'photogenic poverty'. The clinic is shown in a way that does not simply romanticize the charitable 'saintliness' of carers (as some documentaries have) but, rather, focuses on comedy and slip-ups, on the joking banter between volunteers and patients, and the haphazard nature of Western efforts, contrasted to the dedication of the clinic's Bengali doctors. This may not fit the broadcast requirements of conventional documentary, but on the whole the self-critical and roughly cut edges of this video accord it authenticity for those from the *most* Modern. Its status as a document for other audiences will always be more problematic.

In one particular scene, Fiona threatens in a joking way to adopt a woman's child and 'take it back to England'. The mother does not see that this was never a serious intention, and becomes angry. A failure to recognize a sensitive political issue for homeless mothers in a city where Mother Teresa does organize adoptions for wealthy Western visitors became a contentious scene in the video. This was not a case of intentional malice, and an otherwise honest and intelligent person made a mistake which resulted in serious conflict. Negotiations of cultural differences — here in performance and humour — are difficult on a highly politically charged terrain. Is it possible for travellers to become more alert to these difficulties?

In the final sequences of this video I follow the negotiations of an older woman attending the clinic in order to gain a new sari (cotton saris are sometimes given out to those in need). Her repeated requests are refused: she is well known, she is always asking for something. She asks new volunteers and old, she asks each doctor in turn, and finally — with the camera following this as it would an epic adventure — she persuades a clinic administrator to hand over a sari. The last image of the video is a close-up of this woman with her hard-won gift, and its chequered colour pattern.

John Urry points to a shift in the nature of the 'tourist gaze' in the contemporary era. The shift is from a tourism of exemplary 'sites' to one of 'out-of-the-ordinary experiences' (Urry 1990: 102). While the 'new tourism' does not seem that much different, it would include more 'individualistic' pursuits such as sporting or adventure holidays, ironic 'alternative tours' of Calcutta's Marxist monuments, and other off-the-beaten-track variants — perhaps even auto-documentary of the kind described above. Urry's distinction between two 'modes' of tourism might be worth accepting as a heuristic device. Of the first he writes:

> The pleasures of tourism stem from complex processes of both production and consumption. I have emphasised the socially constructed character of the tourist gaze, that both production and consumption are socially organised, and that the gaze must be directed to certain objects or features which are extraordinary, which distinguish that sight/site of the gaze from others. (Urry 1990: 101)

What changes for Urry is perhaps less important than the continuities between the social constructions of production and consumption, and of distinguished 'sights/sites', across his two modes. Nevertheless, he proclaims that 'post-tourism transforms these processes by which the tourist gaze is produced and consumed' (Urry 1990: 101):

> the post-tourist emphasis on playfulness, variety and self-consciousness makes it harder to find simple pleasures ... the post-tourist is above all self-conscious, 'cool' and role-distanced. Pleasure hence comes to be anticipated and experienced in different ways than before ... holidays have become less to do with the reinforcing of collective memories and experiences and more to do with immediate pleasure. (Urry 1990: 101–2)

As if the postmodern self-consciousness of the tourist engaged in white-water rafting down some Himalayan waterway were all that much less 'constructed' and even collective than that of the visitor to some war memorial or other 'historical' site in Europe or Asia! This change has to do, first, with a multiplication of sites for tourism, some of which need no longer be visual but have become experiential; and second, with a fragmentation or segmentation of tourist markets so that ever more diverse numbers of clients can be made to consume the manifold icons of tourism. Calcutta could be a good example here, with *City of Joy* and the reputation of Mother Teresa luring travellers to a form of charity-tourism. Urry (how 'postmodern' this is I don't know) suggests that it 'is an interesting question whether it is in fact possible to construct a postmodern tourist site around absolutely any object' (Urry 1990: 102). Poverty, perhaps? That everything can be consumed is just the correlate of the intellectual point that everything is 'produced', and that market capitalism has colonized every corner of the globe, every corner of our lives – just as Marx promised it would.

But is everything consumed in the same way? Perhaps it is possible to watch *City of Joy* against itself. Just as travellers somewhat mischievously parody postcard tourism with 'found object' mosquito-coil box-tops, as they create alternative anti-tours of the city, and as with the home video of life in the Modern, perhaps also participation in the filming of *City of Joy* can be seen within an ironic frame.

'Joffe is tireless, he invites us all to these long breakfasts at the Oberoi' (Katrina). Here, Joffe's stamina, and the incongruously luxuriant dining-room of the Oberoi Grand Hotel, are gently mocked by hungry backpackers. Much was made of the bit-parts clinic volunteers had in the film – a scene showing them lounging around in the garden of the Fairlawn, and another, which was left on the cutting-room floor, of a group dressed in hippy-trippy pyjamas dancing with Swayze in an ashram (Swayze's dirty dancing failed him on this occasion). The way *City of Joy* can be watched by clinic workers, as well as by Bengali audiences, as incongruity and outrageously miscued farce, does undermine its 'realism' at the very moment where this against-the-grain viewpoint gains in authenticity. At a showing of the film organized by travellers in an open garage opposite Modern Lodge, both travellers and the resident family (Sultana-bibi and children) who watched the film together roared with laughter at many scenes. Hasari Pal's rickshaw style was cause for as much mirth as Swayze's grim dedication. Perhaps this transformation of Joffe's drama into slapstick is the most effective means of critique. As is often apparent, the jokes are always half-true, allowing a nod towards a recognition which shares the critique and then moves past it.

Escape routes are never exempt from reterritorialization. This keeps resistance on the run; so that perhaps only a persistent humour can prevail against the ways in which the 'image' of Calcutta can be marketed to suit the imperatives of charitable world-views. In *City of Joy* poverty is a condition that is to be 'developed' through the intervening benevolence of Doctor Swayze, and by extension by the aid organizations which follow. The space in which Calcutta is produced here is one that does not escape the dominant frame of a capitalist developmental world, of progress, and the world as a manipulable resource. The practice of travellers doing volunteer work slots into this frame and facilitates its global distribution. Joffe picks up hints from the travellers at the Modern; it is quite possible that he was even able to watch the 'home' video. His film occludes real structural disadvantages by presenting the 'solution' in the guise of a virile North American hero, and leaves no space for a rupture in the narrative of underdevelopment plotted in this place.

As a development narrative, the lack of fit with Calcuttan experience for many travellers means that Swayze's proffered 'assistance' as the American-with-the-answers works primarily outside the city. What is 'given' in *City of Joy*? A technology for those who do not 'know' Calcutta to place its aberrant reputation into a well-rehearsed narrative of reassurance – things are bad, but they will/can be improved by our charitable acts. This mental 'gift' is carried into Calcutta by those travellers who now come to work in the organizations 'aiding' the city. Unfortunately, Calcuttan ways of viewing the film are not distributed by the promotions office. While it is also possible to watch against the film in foreign cinema halls, it is the ideological reach of this widely distributed production that has effects which reinforce the 'rumour of Calcutta'. The 'joy' that is attached to this rumour now serves as the reward for charitable souls – come and share the experience is Swayze's call. Many liberal consumers would presumably succumb to this reassuring narrative.

Budget tourism, even in highly ironic and sceptical forms, is little more than a temporary and illusory escape from a privilege based on inequality. The resources of capitalism allocate a little space for alternatives, for a break from more explicit modes of consumption. No wonder Joffe can go to Calcutta and make a film that seems to come from Hollywood. Swayze said at the Melbourne première that while he could normally command a seven-million-dollar fee for a film, he so wanted

to do this one 'for the people of Calcutta' that he accepted just one
million dollars. The film promoters boast that *City of Joy* contributed
$10 million to the Calcuttan economy. Economic justice? No evidence
was presented for this claim. Remember that Joffe and crew were dining
in style at the Oberoi International Hotel chain's Calcutta flagship. Who
gains? It is not unusual to be faced with a seeming paradox of a capitalism which is always the same, yet locally specific. Nikos Papastergiadis
pulls all this together for me in a pertinent formulation:

> The dispersal of signs across the modern world has punctured the borders
> that defined the cultural identity of particular places. Images of distant places
> have crossed many hands. This multiplication of symbolic exchange has done
> little to undermine the basic opposition between the centre and the periphery;
> tourism and migration go in different directions: the decision to visit and the
> decision to leave has a different gravity, let alone price. Furthermore, this
> new global culture has not yet reduced the popular consciousness into a
> homogeneous mulch. Self-definition proceeds through opposition, making
> the asymmetrical relationships to power all too apparent. Increased mobility
> seems to have sharpened the need to know ourselves all the more by defining
> who is and who is not our permissible neighbour, our competitor, our guide.
> (Papastergiadis 1993a: 68)

WHAT IS GIVEN IN CITY OF JOY?
MAX VERSUS MARX

As a coda to this, the scene in *City of Joy* where Max gives a rupee to
the begging children can stand as an emblem for all the themes of Third
World tourism and charity. Max plays this out as a sleight of hand in a
way that recalls Derrida's presentation of Baudelaire's counterfeit-coin
tale. Unlike Lévi-Strauss, who dismisses the begging child's call for one
anna as 'pathetic', Max engages with the children, and amuses them with
coin tricks. Here we can read a routine of savage curiosity over colonial
magic often played out to remind Western audiences of their technological advantages. Max is soon overwhelmed by the numbers of children
his offer of coins attracts and he is forced to flee – the very same scene
appears in John Byrum's 1984 film version of Somerset Maugham's *The
Razor's Edge*, where Bill Murray arrives on the steps of the Ganges in
Varanasi.[4] What does the coin trick signify here? Is it that the Western
visitor has the power to give and yet also to fake the gift, and abandon
the effort when the demand becomes too much?

The coin, as symbol of money, is not, here, the universal marker of
value that it is in the money form for Marx. The burden of money in
Marx is to be a commodity exchangeable both for itself and for all

other commodities. Max's coin cannot be exchanged. The coin, however, is a marker of an exchange in another way – the coin given to a beggar is a marker of power. This is a transaction which shares its structure with the appropriation of photography or film, an abstract directional exchange. Max exchanges his coin for the return that comes to all who give.... The coin he gives has its value 'stripped away' (Marx 1858/1973: 147), and it comes to stand for a social relation, so that the trick of this scene is that the gift of a coin, like any similar scene of 'poverty', is reinvested through the media circuits and wider economy of received images of India. This scene travels. In another context Spivak provides an analysis of this counterfeit, and quotes Marx as saying: 'in the friction with all kinds of hands, pouches, pockets, purses ... the coin rubs off' (in Spivak 1985: 81), recalling that Nietzsche, too, mentions coins which have lost their face through rubbing. This occurs in his famous comment that truths are only metaphors, of which we have forgotten their illusory nature – 'coins no longer of account as coins' (in Spivak intro. to Derrida 1967/1976: xxii). Another formulation; in *Capital*, Marx says: 'During their currency coins wear away' (Marx 1867/ 1967: 125) ['Im Umlauf verschleissen nämlich die Goldmünzen, die eine mehr, die andere weniger' (*Das Kapital* p. 139)]. Some more, some less. Coins are markers of value not by weight, but by sign. Even the coins are a fetish, a rumour of value stored elsewhere. *Was gibt?*

This deceit is played out over and over in the relations of tourism and charity. The exchange of a coin in begging and photographing calls up all manner of other circuits. Marx says that coins are always circulating back towards the mint – they rely upon these double orders:

> Since the producers do not come into social contact with each other until they exchange their products, the specific social character of each producer's labour does not show itself except in the act of exchange. (Marx 1867/1967: 73)

So where is the exchange of tourism and charity if the products of labour are sold and exchanged, and their values set, far away? It would be important not to lose sight of the difference between airline tickets and souvenirs.

That the character Max (and Swayze, and Joffe, travellers, and me) can jet into Calcutta on an overnight plane, and may also instantly leave (allowing for lost passports and Air India delays), is significant too. Many writers point to developments in transportation systems and their contribution to the circumstances of both international travel and international capitalism (the shorthand explanation of change in late capitalism cites development of transport, telecommunications, and technology).

Spivak goes a little further to enable an analysis which impacts upon travel, technology and communications in an urgent way. Noting that the ticker-tape which once marked stock market changes was invented in 1867 and now, because of computers and the development of the market, any attempt to have such a machine keep up with today's market would result in a blur, she reminds us that Marx's *Capital* is also 'a bit of technology from 1867' (Spivak 1985: 188). A contemporary *Capital* (though we do not at present have a Marx) would need to address the contradictions between the possibility of a Swayze or a Joffe jetting into Calcutta to film, build a slum, argue with government leaders and leave in the same time as a local Calcuttan labourer might work in order to earn sufficient to rent the video just to watch Swayze perform. A traveller can take a dozen rolls of film and have them developed in the same day through one of the tourism service facilities along Sudder Street at the same time as the family s/he photographed at one point asks just a few rupees in exchange, and hopes against experience that the traveller will remember to send a copy of the photo to them at an address hastily scrawled on an airline ticket cover. While Western 'Buddhists' jet in to sit at the feet of sharp 'sadhus', ten-year-olds serving tea in guesthouses work from 8 a.m. to 12 p.m. without a break. The ISD stall near the Modern Lodge offers instant phone connections home – it is run by an Oriya man who has not seen his family in four months. These examples are not audacious, and could be multiplied exponentially, some more, some less.

Spivak notes that even as the circulation time (transport, tele-communications) of late-capitalist production attains 'apparent instantaneity', this seeming simultaneity of everything is 'broken up' by capital 'so as to keep the labour reserves in the comprador countries outside' of any 'assimilation of the working class into consumerist-humanism' (Spivak 1985: 84). In the interests of relative exchange value it serves capital (and tourism as part of this) to keep 'the comprador theatre in a state of relatively primitive labour legislation and environmental legislation ... obliged to accept scrapped and out-of-date machinery from the post-industrial economies', and with regard to women workers, with patriarchal super-exploitation of the 'true reserve army of labour' (Spivak 1985: 84). This is the context in which gestures of charity, by Swayze, Mother Teresa and the guests of the Modern Lodge, must be understood. It is patently obvious that consumer boycotts, charity drives and calls for nice 'alternative tourism' are an inadequate intervention on the part of First World activists into the circumstances of global oppression.

As the last scene of *City of Joy* fades into Hollywood schmaltz, words from Hasari Pal appear on the screen: 'All that is not given is lost'. These words offer a fitting point at which I would like to chance my own conclusion. The point has been to show how touristic understandings of the world are arranged according to the needs of a travel-industry 'technic' view of the world. Travellers have views on why they travel – or at least, travellers doing aid work in Calcutta do offer explanations and understandings of what they are doing – and sometimes these are highly self-critical. It is possible to suggest that aid work is not all that different from souvenir-hunting or sightseeing. What is important, however, is that budget travellers, charity workers and other visitors to Calcutta participate in the dissemination of 'versions' of the city that can be described as technology-driven approaches to the world serving objectifying and manipulative ends. It has been one of the main arguments of this work – attending to the metaphorics of travel in words like 'driven' and 'approaches' – that a view of the world, and of Calcutta, as a site to be developed and consumed (collected, manipulated, aided) finds its way through the prevalent representations of Western visitors. That the images of Calcutta which circulate do so according to the basic structure of a capitalist world system, and reinforce – even dysfunctionally – that system, has been the context of this discussion.

It is not to say what Calcutta is really like that is important; it is to question why a film like *City of Joy* needs to ignore the communist parties in the city, how the heroics of Patrick Swayze ignore a commonplace visitor's experience, or how Malle collects trinket-images of the exotic with his camera – all at the same time presenting these myths in a way that reconfirms stereotypes. What is interesting, and revealing, is how Lévi-Strauss responds to beggars asking for rupees, how Günter Grass and Dominique Lapierre can see only garbage, how travellers feel lost in a labyrinthine confusion, discussing their predicament along the banana-pancake trail, looking for familiar images, or organizing 'social projects' within the development mould – Mother T, photogenic poverty – and how the efforts expended in charitable work are squandered in self-interest and folly. These representations *are* Calcutta, but in the service of a wider, tour-ocentric, neocolonial frame which this book has attempted to illustrate, unpacking a city built not with bricks but by rumour. Everything you have heard here is true. 'Built on silt… but gold!'

NOTES

1. There are various works which assess Bengali cinema, though none, to my knowledge, specifically concerned with the representation of the city of Calcutta. John Hood has produced a compact study of Mrinal Sen's films which is excellent (Hood 1993); much of Andrew Robinson's work on the films of Satyajit Ray could be considered here (Robinson 1990); and Roberge (1984) would be helpful. Here I am more interested in the ways Western visitors represent their experience of Calcutta, and cannot attempt any detailed commentary on Bengali film. Biren Das Sharma would be the one who could provide the definitive account.

2. The rest of this discussion was interesting, too – Dutt went on to say that Ray made *Pather Panchali* only to win awards and, absurdly, that he should now make a film about modern India, which, apparently, would be about the greatness of dams. I do not want to be overly critical of Dutt's responses in this interview; it is sufficient to say that her criticisms of Ray are unwarranted, but her point about the reception of such films in the West has *some* import.

3. Consider the efforts of the Left Front, who have been working to improve and eventually to ensure adequate drainage and a reduction of street flooding during the monsoon months – another aspect of communism rendered invisible in the *City of Joy* version of Calcutta.

4. This scene was not in the 1946 version of the film, directed by Edmund Golding and starring Tyrone Power. The 'appearance' of India in this version, replete with Graeco-Roman pillars in the holy Indian city, indicates that there has been a considerable shift in attention to 'authentic' scenery in contemporary films about the country – this, of course, is enabled by international jet travel and the cheaper production costs of Third World location shooting. The documentary realism of *Octopussy* and *City of Joy*'s fabricated slum are, of course, only videographically constructed, and *everyone* knows that trick now.

7

CONCLUSION:

THE GIFTS OF CALCUTTA

'What can we do but try to improve things a little? There's not much hope for this city, but someone has to take responsibility. We have the resources and the knowledge so we have to give it. I don't personally have that many skills, but together, those of us working here, all of us, do. We are lucky to be able to bring this to Calcutta.' (Mitch)

Travellers visiting Calcutta and doing charity work among destitutes are located in a place through which ideological and hegemonic effects are played out in complex yet co-ordinated ways. This book is an attempt to understand the complexities of this situation within the contexts of an international order where specific practices and technologies of tourism, representation and experience combine to reinforce and replicate conditions of contemporary international inequality. It is the Western youth of the budget-travel circuit visiting Calcutta who provide the central illustration, but the ways Calcutta is represented beyond the gossip and traveller-lore of backpackers extends to a variety of forms of representation which reach worldwide. Travel guides, formal literature, maps, postcards, photographic collections, amateur and mainstream cinema, souvenirs, and so on, contribute to the elaboration of a Calcutta which circulates around the world in ways which play a crucial role in the maintenance of the geopolitical hierarchy. Budget travellers can visit the 'Third World' because it is cheap; because there are developed systems of transnational transportation and communication; and because they have the ability – even, perhaps, the need – to leave their usual domestic circumstances in order to travel and 'see the world'. These enabling circumstances are also necessary components of the world system within which all tourism operates: travel, as the largest global industry, is not innocent of capitalism. There is no way that the cultural niceties and 'alternative' tours or celebrations of difference that are a part of budget tourism are not wholly integral to contemporary capitalist relations. Volunteers who thought their activity was significantly different from mainstream tourism would seem to be mistaken. 'Alternative' travel, just as much as the alternative trade promoted by many organized aid groups, works as a reassuring front for continued extension of the logistics of the commodity system, even as it masquerades as a (liberal) project of cultural concern, and despite the best intentions of its advocates. Charity work also operates within a similarly expansionary and uneven development zone. It has been my task to begin to articulate these connections, starting from the very specific experiences of travellers in Calcutta.

Travellers' talk, and their desire to write, about Calcutta displays close affinity to productions which are accorded greater literary status. The metaphorical register, the tropes, the rumour and gossip about Calcutta exchanged on the rooftop of the Modern Lodge and in the travel guides, literature and cinematography of more 'important' Calcutta visitors seems to rehearse so many of the same themes. The anthropological memoirs of Lévi-Strauss are no different, in this respect, from the Hollywood cinematography of Roland Joffe or the throwaway comments of the grungiest backpacker. Indeed, while Günter Grass thinks it is radical to talk about shit and garbage in Calcutta, and Lévi-Strauss laments that 'the first thing we see as we travel round the world is our own filth' (Lévi-Strauss 1955/1973: 38), it is only among budget travellers that I have found any degree of organized Western resistance to these main tropes – although limited, evidence of this is found, despite dysenting stomach disorders, in some travellers' attempts to follow alternative trails through Calcutta and in their interest in and sympathy for the Bengali communist parties. This, however, is the extent of such resistance, and it is easily recouped – I have attempted to extend such moments with a critical reading of the ways conventional Calcutta-for-visitors is produced. What I have taken from the rooftop of the Modern has also informed an attitude to discursive production as a kind of 'gossip', and it is this which has had an influence on the shape of my text. Eclectic. It's not that I don't want to take gossip seriously but, rather, that the multifarious influence of academic and 'serious' texts might be understood better if they are provisionally equated with gossip. That this orientation finds support in the work of Trinh T. Minh-ha, as well as in Malcolm Crick's essay on the similarities between anthropological fieldwork and tourism (Crick 1985), is not accidentally linked to the influence of the rhizomatic thought of Deleuze and

Guattari (1983) imagined as travel. I have intentionally allowed a slip-page between travel, research, writing and rhizome in the metaphors that have guided this project on the rumour of Calcutta, because this 'rumour' is not fixed and immutable, despite its determined effects.

What is produced here is, it must be insisted, only a rumour. The rumour of Calcutta as site of poverty is one whose maintenance suits dominant interests, and the dysfunctional inequities of the global order. If charity were an 'answer' rather than an ideological necessity carefully tended and retained to salve the consciences of the privileged First World and comprador classes, then why haven't greater Western resources been directed towards it? Part of the deceit of this predica-ment is that studies of aid work infrequently ask why so many resources are directed towards government-administered military and industrial projects disguised as aid, while 'helping the poor' is so often left to the haphazard and underorganized efforts of church and community groups. Among travellers working at the Preger Middleton Row clinic, and in Modern Lodge, the community organization was celebrated as a 'people's effort' at the very same time as the usual lament for lack of funding was directed into the air. The tendency to proclaim a local-people-orientated style on the part of Western NGOs is a sham. Instead of concerning themselves so much with their bowels, and projecting this on to what they see in Calcutta, visitors could conceivably strive for something else. Rather than the Calcutta of rumour and charity-squalor, there is a Calcutta that is a part of this world, full of people active in all sorts of projects, works, lives and dreams, alert to prob-lems, as well as successes (a great many) and, whatever the problems of the place, not in need of the patronizing charity of the revolutionary-dancing Patrick Swayze or the caring Christmassy gestures of volunteers and the global NGO apparatus. Photogenic, maybe, but imagine: the Calcutta cinema, the Bengali literary scene, the *adda*, the political to-and-fro, the coffee-houses, the bookshops, the theatre spaces (the rui, the mishti-doi)... Why does so little of this enter the touristic text? No doubt because tourism as charity is self-obsessed; it projects.

It is also clear that the social sciences have sometimes been complicit in maintaining distinctions and privileges among different classes of people, and between First and Third World, by choosing to investigate the conditions of 'the poor' and the 'disempowered' rather than pursuing research into power. This choice – encouraged, no doubt, by funding availability and ease of access – is very much to the benefit of the military–industrial complex, which would like to remain invisible. Interestingly, this occurs in a double movement in work on Calcutta, where transnational industry on one side, and the communist parties on the other, are occluded in favour of a fascination with highly visible photogenic squalor. With protocols like this, academic studies often seem to replicate surveillance: the critique of the gaze, for example, simply institutes another code-word for this project. I have attempted to sidestep these dilemmas by situating this work between those who are disempowered and those who are privileged enough to be travellers in the Third World – those who might even reflexively describe themselves as 'agents of cultural imperialism' (Janet). Several sections of this work attempt a refusal of this agency and the academic social science protocols that go with it – and I have not always indicated where. Suffice it to say that experiments with writing style and convention are also subject to conditioning effects. I do hope some of these are noticed, and open new ways and means for social science, as well as political activism, and tourism. You were warned.

What I want to understand are the ways in which the varied representations of Calcutta produced by these visitors are generated through a series of specific technologies. This is where I have examined traveller talk, writing, mapping and the camera as worked by those who visit Calcutta. There is much to be said about the ways particular characteristics of these technologies allow or confirm specific representational effects. I think it has been useful subsequently to examine these effects within the context of a Heideggerian and Marxist approach to technology. The point of this book has been to make more clear the context in which specific experiences and imagery of Calcutta, as produced by and for visitors, is a part of a wider 'essence of technology' in Heidegger's sense, which is then revealed as a particular orientation to the world as something subjected to technology, something manipulated by apparatus, for profit and gain. With representational technology, this is obviously an orientation destined to produce representations. I have tried to unpack something of what is taken here.

Marx makes it possible to think of this situation in terms of social relations, where technologies of value – symbolized in the money form – are expressive of unequal economic positions. This can be extended to consider the production of meaning in Calcutta as a social illusion. Here, travellers' views, the objects of their photography, that which is given in charity, the guidebooks, the coin and the souvenirs of the tourist economy, are all fetishized and obfuscated relations between really existing peoples. On the one hand, groups of people who are Calcuttans, on the other those who are tourists; on the one side, those who produce local goods and services, on the other those who consume and produce global meanings; those who are visited, those with visas; those who are communists and those who are travellers (some fellow-travellers); those who are written about and those who are writers; the filmed and the filming; and so on. While actual demarcations are never so easily polarized, an attempt to unravel the technologies of commodification and representation which operate in this scene has been the premiss of this work.

In the ways Calcutta is conventionally represented, there is much more at stake than can be explicated by any critique of prejudice or of 'the gaze'. The ways the camera makes poverty photogenic are not only camera effects to be understood within an economy of voyeurism, but more besides. Vision has become supervision. Cultural imperialism, ethnocentrism, ideologies of race, exoticism and romanticism can all be seen in operation within Western experience and evaluation of Calcutta, but any understanding of the interconnections between these things, and of the various examples mentioned throughout this book, is more arduous. Crick's point that 'for all the talk about sacred journeys, cultural understanding, freedom, play and so on, we must not forget the fundamental truth that international tourism feeds off gross political and economic inequalities' (Crick 1991: 9) requires closer attention to the politics of representation in tourism, development and aid, since this 'gross inequality' is too often papered over by brochures and snapshots that forget. What is now demanded is an engagement with the varied and multiple particularities of the contemporary situation in a way that enables the underlying coherence of singular dysfunctional examples to be grasped. Those who preach good works and non-governmental best intentions may also be the worst alternatives. The tenacious grip of the capitalist world-view makes it difficult to keep any critique from the recuperations which attend efforts to reveal and expose its fundamental workings. Heidegger's understanding of the ways certain views of the world come into being through technology (not a simple causal relation) can also open questions about the possibilities and limits of thinking against this frame. Writing about disconnected individual examples (anecdotes) can be co-opted into the same liberal humanitarianism which is found in the 'outrage' of concerned charitable development workers – the self-confessed 'front line of caring colonization' (Janet). We care about this just as we care about the photographs and television images of the shocking conditions of 'the poor' which are recouped into photogenic poverty for sale as postcards and coffee-table books. Allegedly, we care.

In addition to representational apparatuses, experience of Calcutta for travellers is also framed within the context of an attitude which enables a desire or an obligation to intervene in the world at an individual level. There is nothing inherently wrong with this. Indeed, expressive individuality would also be a requisite criterion for a collective social transformatory project that did not reinstate routine. The problem is that the technical apparatus and the conventional possibilities that are currently established for such expression tend easily towards servicing a grossly unequal exploitative system which affects us at every turn. The collection of experiences and souvenirs can be described as an example of this: the traveller goes to Calcutta as a consumer and 'takes', actively. While this should be no surprise within the parameters of what is increasingly becoming a world market where everything is for sale, it is still necessary to attempt to analyse what it means. Why, for example, does the need to intervene manifest as 'charity'? What are its conditions of emergence? Such a complex has implications for all those who feel the need to 'do something' when faced with their experience of Calcutta. Many of those who benefit – in terms of leisure, lifestyle or comforts – from the international divisions of labour also feel compelled to write. I have focused mostly on tourists who are doing charity work. Just as the camera-writing apparatus sets up the world as something to be pictured or written about, the injunctions of charity and responsibility within the context of the development narratives of capitalist (and liberal humanitarian) progress allow Calcutta to be seen as a place in need of (legitimate, legitimized) charitable interventions.

> 'The do-gooders really bug me; they don't realize that the only people who really benefit from charity are the charity workers themselves. Even the people who have worked as volunteers for up to two years sometimes don't know this.' (Ruth)

Charity work allows an investment on the part of the visitor which is both a contribution of value to Calcutta but also an expenditure recouped elsewhere. This is possible because Calcutta is seen as a site amenable to this charitable expenditure, as a site to be worked upon, to be developed, helped. As a place that is seen as one of impoverishment and decay by visitors, its representation as such enables touristic deployment in an economy of improvement, charity and redemption. The 'intention' of charity workers, those who appeal to compassion and care, with concern in the face of a poverty with which they are complicit, is not far removed from the same reform logic that calls for cultural understanding and soft- or low-impact tourism. These 'improvements' are not incompatible with the commodity system, and cultural exchange is not incompatible with ongoing exploitation. Cultural understanding and the 'concern' of charity cannot pose a challenge to the World Bank/IMF/comprador elite/hegemonic order which perpetuates exploitation and oppression. Calcutta as a site for concern only extends this reformist logic and never poses a challenge. Consumption renders passivity bearable – consuming charity redeems the giver. It would not be too far-fetched to imagine charity and redemption as the allegorical accompaniment of travel and the souvenir – I argue that this allegory is discernible in the scene of tourist volunteer work in Calcutta with Calcutta Rescue, and with Mother Teresa, as this circulates from the Modern Lodge and beyond into international cinemas through films like *City of Joy*. The basis for this construction is that the souvenir can be seen as a technology which prepares and allows a certain view of the world to prevail, irrespective of the social relations which, in another view, it might express. Attention to the reification of these relations suggests that the collection of souvenirs serves more than decorative ends.

There is a deceit involved in the souvenir thought as an allegory of giving charity – in that giving charity leaves a trace or memory of charitable work imagined also as experience, just as the souvenir memorializes the encounter or exchange with the 'other'. This scene demands the production of the 'other' – the constitutive power of those who are in a position to give is then also productive of Calcuttan impoverishment, within a demarcated frame, within the developmental narrative, and very much within an international situation of developed world capitalism, where social relations are unequal, but obscured under the soft ideology of tourism of 'other cultures'. Instructively, Andrew Lattas has offered a pithy summary of Marx's investigation of the commodity form as an effort to 'explore the ideological way it conceals and rationalizes the appropriation of surplus value so as to legitimise the power relations between capitalist employers and wage labourers' (Lattas 1993: 108). It would not take too great an adaptation to see this as the basic structure of Third World tourism. Variations, of course, abound. Lattas continues his discussion with a comment on gifts: 'An analysis of gifts has also to ground gifts in those structures of reification, self-mystification and legitimation which gifts make available. It is not a question of denying or dismissing as false the gift's ideology, but of exploring its constitutive power' (Lattas 1993: 108). The gift of charity and the purchase of the souvenir should be understood as constitutive here. In this constitution of Calcutta as a reified site of poverty, exploitative and unequal relations between different classes of people are disguised or routinized as a part of the scenes of travel, aid-work, souvenir-hunting and photography. In the polysemic zone of this book, these tropes are the local particularities of a global rumour.

The charitable tendency has to be understood more closely within the global frame of contemporary capitalist social hegemony. Charity tends towards a permanent institutional form which is manifest in more or less conveniently transportable (or transplantable) ways everywhere. Arjun Appadurai has pointed out in his article on postnationalism that these 'Philanthropies' now 'all constitute one part of a *permanent* frame-work of the emergent postnational order' (Appadurai 1993: 418). While the italicization of 'permanent' and the use of the term 'postnational' perhaps gloss over some specificities, it is clear that a study of these forms of 'organisations, movements and networks' which 'have blurred the boundaries between evangelical, developmental and peace-keeping functions in many parts of the world' (Appadurai 1993: 418) is well overdue. This point has been made explicit by Frank Füredi: 'Global charity initiatives have done more than anything to popularise the view that Third World people need to be looked after and protected, not least from themselves' (Füredi 1994: 113). This is a useful elaboration of Hobson's point that 'Imperialist politicians, soldiers or company directors' utilize the 'protective colours' of disinterested charitable movements and 'instinctively attach themselves to any strong, genuine elevated feeling which is of service' (Hobson 1902/1988: 196–7). In this way they convince themselves and their public, to some extent, that their imperialist activities are for the good. Appadurai identifies a number of new organizational formations which operate both 'within and across national structures, always exploiting their legitimacy' (Appadurai 1993: 420). These are the kinds of groups that present themselves to travellers in Calcutta. Although Appadurai has in mind other examples, what he says does seem to fit well with Mother T and Calcutta Rescue: 'The new organisational forms are more diverse, more fluid, more ad hoc, more provisional, less coherent, less organised' (Appadurai 1993: 420). The examples he offers are Oxfam, Amnesty International and World Vision. It would be easy to extend this list, and many of those travellers and volunteers mentioned in this book could well be found in, or have gone on to begin working in, such organizations. The 'ad hoc', however, is an aspect of international aid enabled by quite formal accountancies, communications networks, media and transport structures, and so on, so that the 'fluidity' of charitable concerns may maintain a certain innocence. Rather than an expression of global and political inequalities, charity masquerades as a 'gift' of concern.

This gift of charity is not given only in the context of Calcutta, or in that particularity which is the exchange between the visitor and the beggar; it is, rather, a gift which has effects in multiple contexts, and which is given its possibility according to already established precepts. Travellers are doing 'what needs to be done' (Natasha), even as what they must do has limited hope of successfully confronting the situation (where success would mean proper care for the sick, preventative practices and medication to combat leprosy, better water facilities, sewerage, and so on: what the Left Front says it is aiming to achieve). A 'solution' would also require a transformation in the ways people are able to think about Calcutta. Is it possible to think otherwise? Perhaps such thinking would be the communism of the Bengali parties, or that reinvented communism of Negri and Guattari (who want to 'rescue communism from its own ill-repute' [1990: 7]). The point is that a change in the world – 'we can only change Calcutta if we change the world' (Peter) – requires a change in thinking and interpretation and the political order on a world scale; the reformist critique of Günter Grass, who can see only piles of garbage and rows of bodies sleeping on the streets, or the critiques of the gaze, or of Eurocentrism, are still insufficient to imagine the possibility of a world where the rumour of Calcutta does not prevail as truth.

But of course, it is not enough just to raise questions about the moral propriety of First World youth taking holidays among the people of the Third World; it is not enough to encourage discussion of such contradictions in cafés along the banana-pancake trail; nor is it sufficient to reflect critically upon the politics of charity, while working – because something must be done – at a 'sound' street clinic. An intervention into the institutional context of such practices would include a critique of cultural consumption in the schools, colleges and universities of the West; in the cinema and media; in the shopping mall and Christmas catalogue – and much else besides. Such interventions would still not suffice to unpack the oppressive structure which belongs to tourism and charity; without interventions into the global balance of power, the commercial realities of the capitalist world system and the cannibalizing machine that is popular culture – in short, without a transformation of everything – tourism and aid remain a running sore. There are reasons to consider a political activism among travellers and 'Third-Worldist' Western youth (those *into* alternative travel, for example) which would seek to extend an awareness of an internationalist responsibility to fight for a redistributive justice that was more than mere charity. This would be informed by recognition of the exploitative structure of capitalist relations; an analysis of how that value which is appropriated from workers in excess of that needed to reproduce life can be redistributed at system-wide advanced and equitable standards; and awareness of the political conditions, organizational forms, and specific tasks needed to achieve this. Ultimately, travel 'alternatives' require transformation of the very conditions in which travel is pursued – a travel activism interested in unlearning its leisured privileges and working for its own demise in a new travel for all. This, however, is generalization beyond speculation at this stage: everything else awaits the next trip.

What is possible at present is to continue to question our representational practices for those truth-effects which maintain the underlying coherence – even in the most dysfunctional inequalities – of a system which produces and circulates the city image of Calcutta as exemplary site of poverty and shit, and also as object of care and development: to insert new and disruptive rumours into the circuits of truth-illusion that maintain complacency. The imagination of a city as a place both inhabited and visited by beings alert to a politics of representation would be the most useful outcome of this book. It is my view that visiting such a Calcutta is already possible – the hostile reception Joffe received when he was trying to make *City of Joy* is evidence that this city exists. Part of what is required now (beyond the absurd utopian call for a moratorium on travel) is a tourists' vigilance, and organizational forms which will attend to a social and political transformatory project adequate to combat the system. This always requires vigilance – of our Eurocentric representations, of the gaze and of our inscriptive zeal – and also of our complicities in the hegemonic production and circulation of this code. Question everything. What this leaves open is the possibility of actively intervening in an imaginary Calcutta that would not simply replicate the market directives of capital. This is the rumour which must be spread; word needs to get around.

BIBLIOGRAPHY

Adorno, Theodor W. (1991) *The Culture Industry: Selected Essays on Mass Culture*, ed. J. M. Bernstein, Routledge, London.

Agamben, Giorgio (1993) *Stanzas: Word and Phantasm in Western Culture*, trans. Ronald L. Martinez, University of Minnesota Press, Minneapolis.

Albers, P. and James, W. (1988) 'Travel Photography: A Methodological Approach', *Annals of Tourism Research* 15: 134–58.

Allen, Charles (ed.) (1975) *Plain Tales from the Raj*, Futura, London.

Appadurai, Arjun (1993) 'Patriotism and its Futures', *Public Culture*, 11: 411–30

Aragon, Louis (1928/1991) *Treatise on Style*, University of Nebraska Press, Lincoln.

Armstrong, Philip, Davis, Kelly and Macdonald, Bradley J. (1990) 'Introduction: Special Issue: In the City', *Strategies: A Journal of Theory, Culture and Politics*, 3: 3–5.

Asad, Talal (1973) *Anthropology and the Colonial Encounter*, Ithaca Press, London.

Bachelard, Gaston (1938/1969) *The Psychoanalysis of Fire*, Quartet, London.

Bachelard, Gaston (1958/1969) *The Poetics of Space*, trans. Maria Jolas, foreword by Etienne Gilson, Beacon Press, Boston, MA.

Bailey, Frederick George (1957) *Caste and the Economic Frontier: A Village in Highland Orissa*, Manchester University Press, Manchester.

Balibar, Étienne (1995) *The Philosophy of Marx*, Verso, London.

Bandyopdhyay, Samik (1987) 'The Discreet Charm of the Small Screen', interview with Mrinal Sen, *Splice*, April: 55–60.

Bandyopadhyay, Saroj (1990) 'In Search of the Meaning of Man: An Introductory Essay', in Mitra, Premendra, *Snake and Other Stories*, Seagull Books, Calcutta.

Banerjee, Alok (1990) 'The City with Two Pasts', in Racine (ed.), *Calcutta 1981: The City, its Crisis and the Debate on Urban Planning and Development*, Concept Publishing Company, New Delhi, pp.89–104.

Banerjee, Amritava (1987) 'Calcutta: Political Culture', in Sinha (ed.), *The Urban Experience: Calcutta*, Riddha-India, Calcutta, pp. 113–121.

Banerjee, Nirmala (1990) 'Making a Living in Calcutta', in Racine (ed.) *Calcutta 1981: The City, its Crisis and the Debate on Urban Planning and Development*, Concept Publishing Company, New Delhi, pp. 209–22.

Banerjee, Sumanta (1980) *In the Wake of Naxalbari*, Subarnarekka, Calcutta.

Banerjee, Sumanta (1984) *India's Simmering Revolution*, Zed Books, London.

Banerjee, Sumanta (1989) *The Parlour and the Streets: Elite and Popular Culture in Nineteenth Century Calcutta*, Seagull Books, Calcutta.

224

Banta, Melissa and Hinsley, Curtis (1986) *From Site to Sight: Anthropology, Photography and the Power of Imagery*, Peabody Museum Press, Cambridge MA.

Basu, Jyoti (1985) *Calcutta*, West Bengal Department of Tourism brochure, 15 February 1985.

Basu, S.C. (1990) 'A Paper not Presented, not Presentable: In Defence of the Calcutta Metropolitan Development Authority', in Racine (ed.) *Calcutta 1981: The City, its Crisis and the Debate on Urban Planning and Development*, Concept Publishing Company, New Delhi, pp. 443–6.

Basu, Sakti and Dasgupta, Shuvendu (1992) *Film Polemics*, Cine Club of Calcutta, Calcutta.

Bataille, Georges (1967/1988) *The Accursed Share: An Essay on General Economy* Volume 1, Zone Books, New York.

Bataille, Georges (1976/1991) *The Accursed Share: An Essay on General Economy*, Volumes 2 and 3, Zone Books, New York.

Bataille, Georges (1989) *Theory of Religion*, Zone Books, New York.

Bate, David (1992) 'The Occidental Tourist: Photography and Colonizing Vision', *After Image*, 20(1): 11–13.

Bateson, Gregory and Mead, Margaret (1942) *Balinese Character: A Photographic Analysis*, New York Academy of Sciences, New York.

Baudrillard, Jean (1975) *The Mirror of Production*, translated with an introduction by Mark Poster, Telos Press, St Louis MO.

Baudrillard, Jean (1981) *For a Critique of the Political Economy of the Sign*, translated and with an introduction by Charles Levin, Telos Press, St. Louis MO.

Baudrillard, Jean (1983) *Simulations*, trans. Paul Foss, Paul Patton and Philip Beitchman, Semiotext(e), New York.

Baudrillard, Jean (1988) *America*, trans. Chris Turner, Verso, London.

Benjamin, Walter (1955/1973) *Illuminations*, edited and with an introduction by Hannah Arendt, trans. Harry Zohn, Schocken, New York.

Benjamin, Walter (1970/1979) *One-way Street, and Other Writings*, trans. Edmund Jephcott and Kingsley Shorter, Verso, London.

Benjamin, Walter (1973) *Charles Baudelaire: A Lyric Poet in the Era of High Capitalism*, trans. H. Zohn, Verso, London.

Benjamin, Walter (1978) *Reflections: Essays, Aphorisms, Autobiographical Writings*, trans. Edmund Jephcott, edited and with an introduction by Peter Demetz, Schocken, New York.

Berger, John (1984) *And Our Faces, My Heart, Brief as Photos*, Pantheon, New York.

Berger, John (1985) *The Sense of Sight*, Pantheon, New York.

Bhabha, Homi (1984) 'Of Mimicry and Man', *October*, 28.

Bharadwaj, Krishna and Kaviraz, Sudipta (eds) (1989) *Perspectives on Capitalism*, Sage, New Delhi.

Bharucha, Rustom (1983) *Rehearsals for Revolution: The Political Theatre of Bengal*, Seagull Books, Calcutta.

Bhatia, A.K. (1986) *Tourism Development: Principles and Practices*, Sterling Publishers, New Delhi.

Birch, David (1989) *Language, Literature and Critical Practice*, Routledge, London.

Blonsky, Marshall (ed.) (1985) *On Signs*, Johns Hopkins University Press, Baltimore MD.

Bohm, Robert (1982) *Notes on India*, South End Press, Boston MA.

Borges, Jorge Luís (1970) *Labyrinths: Selected Stories and Other Writings*, translated and edited by Donald A. Yates and James E. Irby, preface by André Maurois, Penguin, Harmondsworth.

Borges, Jorge Luís (1971) *The Aleph and Other Stories, 1933–1969*, together with commentaries and an autobiographical essay, edited and translated by N.T. di Giovanni in collaboration with the author, E.P. Dutton, New York.

Bose, Netaji and Subhas, Chandra (1935/1948) *The Indian Struggle*, Thackur, Spink & Co., Calcutta.

Bose, Sugata (ed.) (1990) *South Asia and World Capitalism*, Oxford University Press, Delhi.

Boulez, Pierre and Foucault, Michel (1985) 'Contemporary Music and its Public: a conversation', *Melbourne Journal of Politics*, 17: 42–50.

Bourdieu, Pierre (1965/1990) *Photography: A Middle-brow Art*, with Luc Boltanski *et al.*, trans. Shaun Whiteside, Polity, Cambridge.

Bourdieu, Pierre (1977) *Outline of a Theory of Practice*, trans. Richard Nice, Cambridge University Press, Cambridge.

Bourdieu, Pierre (1984) *Distinction: A Social Critique of the Judgement of Taste*, trans. Richard Nice, Routledge & Kegan Paul, London.

Bourdieu, Pierre (1984/1988) *Homo Academicus*, trans. Peter Collier, Polity, Cambridge.

Bourdieu, Pierre (1988/1991) *The Political Ontology of Martin Heidegger*, trans. Peter Collier, Stanford University Press, Stanford CA.

Bowman, Glenn (1989) 'Fucking Tourists: Sexual Relations and Tourism in Jerusalem's Old City', *Critique of Anthropology* 9(2): 77–93.

Bradnock, Robert (1992) *South Asian Handbook*, Trade & Travel Publications, Bath.

Bruner, Edward M. (1989) 'Of Cannibals, Tourists, and Ethnographers', *Cultural Anthropology* 4(4): 438–45.

Buck-Morss, Susan (1989) *The Dialectics of Seeing: Walter Benjamin and the Arcades Project*, MIT Press, Cambridge MA.

Burroughs, William S. (1989) *Interzone*, Picador, London.

Calvino, Italo (1974) *Invisible Cities*, Picador, New York.

Castells, Manuel (1977) *The Urban Question: A Marxist Approach*, Edward Arnold, London.

Castells, Manuel (1988) 'High Technology and Urban Dynamics in the United States', in Dogan, M. and Kasarda, J.D. (eds) *The Metropolitan Era* 1: 85–110.

Castells, Manuel (1989) *The Informational City: Information Technology, Economic Restructuring and the Urban-Regional Process*, Basil Blackwell, Oxford.

CCSG (Chicago Cultural Studies Group) (1992) 'Critical Multiculturalism', *Critical Inquiry* 18(3): 530–54.

Chakrabarty, Dipesh (1991) 'Garbage and Modernity', seminar, Melbourne University.

Chatterjee, Manidip (1990) 'Town Planning in Calcutta: Past, Present and Future', in Chaudhuri (ed.) *Calcutta: The Living City: Vol. II – The Present and Future*, Oxford University Press, Calcutta, pp. 133–7.

Chaube, Shibani Kinkar (1990)'Violence, Crime and Labour Unrest in Calcutta: A comparative analysis in social tension', in Racine (ed.) *Calcutta 1981: The City, its Crisis and the Debate on Urban Planning and Development*, Concept Publishing Company, New Delhi, pp. 237–56.

Chaudhuri, Sukanta (ed.) (1990) *Calcutta: The Living City: Vol. II – The Present and Future*, Oxford University Press, Calcutta.

Chawla, Navin (1992) *Mother Teresa*, Sinclair-Stevenson, London.

Chib, S.N. (1980) 'Tourism and the Third World', *Third World Quarterly* 11(2): 283–94.

Chib, S.N. (1980) 'Tourism Policy – A Political Gimmick', *Eastern Economist*, 5 September, pp. 584–6.

Clastres, Pierre (1974/1987) *Society Against the State*, Zone Books, New York.

Clastres, Pierre (1988) 'On Ethnocide', *Art and Text*, March–May: 50–58.

Clifford, James (1988) *The Predicament of Culture: Twentieth-Century Ethnography, Literature and Art*, Harvard University Press, Cambridge MA.

Clifford, James (1989a) 'The Others: Beyond the Salvage Paradigm', *Third Text* 6.

Clifford, James (1989b) 'Notes on Theory and Travel', *Inscriptions* 5: 177–88.

Clifford, James (1990) 'Response', *Social Analysis* 29: 145–158.

Clifford, James and Marcus, George (1986) *Writing/Culture: The Poetics and Politics of Ethnography*, University of California Press, Berkeley CA.

Cohen, Erik (1972) 'Towards a Sociology of International Tourism', *Social Research* 39: 164–82.

Cohen, Erik (1973) 'Nomads fron Affluence: Notes on the Phenomenon of Drifter-Tourism', *International Journal of Comparative Sociology* XIV(1–2): 89–103.

Cohen, Erik (1984) 'The Sociology of Tourism: Approaches, Issues and Findings', *Annual Review of Sociology* 10: 373–92.

Cohen, Erik (1985) 'Tourism as Play', *Religion* 15: 291–304.

Cohen, Sande (1993) *Academia and the Luster of Capital*, University of Minnesota Press, Minneapolis.

Collier, John Jr and Collier, Malcolm (1986) *Visual Anthropology: Photography as a Research Process*, University of New Mexico Press, Alberquerque.

Conrad, Joseph (1902/1973) *Heart of Darkness*, Penguin Books, Harmondsworth.

Copeland, Douglas (1991) *Generation X: Tales for an Accelerated Culture*, St Martin's Press, New York.

Crapanzano, Vincent (1992) *Hermes' Dilemma and Hamlet's Desire: On the Epistemology of Interpretation*, Harvard University Press, Cambridge MA.

Crary, Jonathan (1990) *Techniques of the Observer: On Vision and Modernity in the Nineteenth Century*, MIT Press, Cambridge MA.

Craven, Paul and Wellmen, Berry (1973) 'The Network City', *Sociological Inquiry* 43: 57–88.

Crick, Malcolm (1976) *Explorations in Language and Meaning: Towards a Semantic Anthropology*, Malaby Press, London.

Crick, Malcolm (1982) 'Anthropological Field Research, Meaning, Creation and Knowledge Construction', in Parkin, D. (ed.), *Semantic Anthropology*, Academic Press, London, pp. 15–37.

Crick, Malcolm (1985) '"Tracing" the Anthropological Self: Quizzical Reflections on Fieldwork, Tourism and the Ludic', *Social Analysis* 17: 71–92.

Crick, Malcolm (1987) 'The Chosen and the Damned: or the Importance of Being Jonathan', *Social Analysis* 21: 84–91.

Crick, Malcolm (1988) 'Sun, Sights, Sex, Savings and Servility', *Criticism, Heresy and Interpretation* 1(1): 37–76.

Crick, Malcolm (1989) 'Shifting identities in the Research Process: an essay in personal anthropology', in John Perry (ed.) *Doing Fieldwork: Eight Personal Accounts of Social Research*, Deaking University Press, Geelong.

Crick, Malcolm (1990) 'Tourists, Locals and Anthropologists: quizzical reflections on "otherness" in tourist encounters and in tourism research' (draft).

Crick, Malcolm (1991) 'Tourists, Locals and Anthropologists', *Australian Cultural History* 10: 6–18.

Crick, Malcolm (1994) *Resplendent Sites, Discordant Voices: Sri Lankans in International Tourism*, Harwood Academic, Chur (read in 1990 draft).

Cronin, Richard (1989) *Imagining India*, Macmillan, Basingstoke.

Crow, Dennis (1990) *Philosophical Streets: New Approaches to Urbanism*, Maisonneuve Press, Washington DC.

Culler, Jonathan (1981) 'Semiotics of Tourism', *American Journal of Semiotics* 1(1–2): 127–40.

Dallery, Arleen B. and Scott, Charles E. (eds) (1989) *The Question of the Other*, State University of New York Press, Albany.

Das, Veena (1992) 'Subaltern as Perspective', *Subaltern Studies VI*, Oxford University Press, Delhi, pp. 310–24.

Dasgupta, S.P. (1990) 'The Structure of Calcutta: Morphology of a Congested City', in Racine, J. (ed.) *Calcutta 1981*, Concept Publishing, New Delhi.

Datta, Partho (1992) 'Review Essay: Celebrating Calcutta', *Urban History* 19(1): 84–98.

Davies, Miranda and Jansz, Nastassia (1990) *Women Travel: Adventures, Advice and Experience*, Harrap Columbus, London.

Davis, Mike (1990) *City of Quartz: Excavating the Future in Los Angeles*, Verso, London.

De Certeau, Michel (1984) *The Practice of Everyday Life*, University of California Press, Berkeley.

De Certeau, Michel (1985) 'Practices of Space', in Marshal Blonsky (ed.) *On Signs*, Johns Hopkins University Press, Baltimore MD, pp. 122–45.

De Souza (1978) *The Indian City: Poverty, Ecology and Urban Development*, South Asia Books, New Delhi.

Dear, M. and Scott, A. (1973) *Urbanization and Urban Planning in Capitalist Society*, Methuen, New York.

Debord, Guy (1970/1983) *Society of the Spectacle*, Black & Red, Detroit MI.

Deleuze, Gilles (1983/1986) *Cinema I: The Movement – Image*, University of Minnesota Press, Minneapolis.

Deleuze, Gilles (1985/1989 *Cinema 2, The Time – Image*, trans. Hugh Tomlinson and Robert Galeta, University of Minnesota Press, Minneapolis.

Deleuze, Gilles (1988) *Foucault*, translated and edited by Sean Hand, Athlone, London.

Deleuze, Gilles and Guattari, Félix (1972/1983) *Anti-Oedipus: Capitalism and Schizophrenia*, trans. Robert Hurley, Mark Seem, and Helen R. Lane, Viking, New York.

Deleuze, Gilles and Guattari, Félix (1983) *On the Line*, Semiotext(e), New York.

Deleuze, Gilles and Guattari, Félix (1987) *A Thousand Plateaus: Capitalism and Schizophrenia*, translated and foreword by Brian Massumi, Athlone, London.

Deleuze, Gilles and Parnet, Claire (1977/1987) *Dialogues*, trans. Hugh Tomlinson and Barbara Habberjam, Athlone, London.

Derrida, Jacques (1967/1976) *Of Grammatology*, translation and introduction by Gayatri Chakravorty Spivak, Johns Hopkins University Press, Baltimore MD.

Derrida, Jacques (1967/1978) *Writing and Difference*, translated, with an introduction and additional notes, by Alan Bass, Routledge & Kegan Paul, London.

Derrida, Jacques (1972/1982) *Margins of Philosophy*, translated, with additional notes, by Alan Bass, University of Chicago Press, Chicago.

Derrida, Jacques (1981) *Positions*, translated and annotated by Alan Bass, University of Chicago Press, Chicago.

Derrida, Jacques (1984/1987) *The Truth in Painting*, trans. Geoff Bennington and Ian McLeod, University of Chicago Press, Chicago.

Derrida, Jacques (1987) *The Post Card: From Socrates to Freud and Beyond*, translated, with an introduction and additional notes, by Alan Bass, University of Chicago Press, Chicago.

Derrida, Jacques (1987/1989) *Of Spirit: Heidegger and the Question*, trans. Geoffrey Bennington and Rachel Bowlby, University of Chicago Press, Chicago.

Derrida, Jacques (1989) 'Interviewed by Christopher Norris', *Deconstruction II*, ed. A.C. Papadakis, Academa Group, London.

Derrida, Jacques (1991/1992) *Given Time: Counterfeit Money*, trans. Peggy Kamuf, University of Chicago Press, Chicago.

Derrida, Jacques (1992) *The Other Heading: Reflections on Today's Europe*, trans. Pascale-

Anne Brault and Michael B. Naas, introduction by Michael B. Naas, Indiana University Press, Bloomington.

Derrida, Jacques (1993a) 'Politics and Friendship: An Interview', in Kaplan, E. Ann and Sprinker, Michael (1993) *The Althusserian Legacy*, Verso, London, pp. 183–232.

Derrida, Jacques (1993b) *Memoirs of the Blind: The Self-portrait and Other Ruins*, University of Chicago Press, Chicago.

Derrida, Jacques (1993c) 'Back from Moscow, in the USSR', in Poster, Mark *Politics, Theory and Contemporary Culture*, Columbia University Press, New York.

Derrida, Jacques (1995a) *Points... Interviews 1974–1994*, Stanford University Press, Stanford CA.

Derrida, Jacques (1995b) *Specters of Marx*, Routledge, London.

Desnoes, Edmundo (1985) 'Cuba Made Me So', in Marshal Blonsky (ed.) *On Signs*, Johns Hopkins University Press, Baltimore MD, pp. 384–403.

Deutsche, Rosalyn (1990) 'Men in Space', *Strategies: A Journal of Theory Culture and Politics* 3: 130–37.

Devi, Mahasweta (1989) *Five Plays*, Seagull Books, Calcutta.

Devi, Mahesweta (1990) *Bashai Tudu*, Thema, Calcutta.

Devi, Mahesweta (1993) *Imaginary Maps*, translation and preface by Gayatri Chakravorty Spivak, Thema, Calcutta.

Diller, Elizabeth and Scofidio, Ricardo (1992) 'Tourism: Suitcase Studies', in *Semiotext(e) Architecture*, pp. 9–16.

Dilley, Robert S. (1986) 'Tourist Brochures and Tourist Images', *The Canadian Geographer*, 30(1): 59–65.

Dogan, M. and Kasarda, J. D. (1988) *The Metropolitan Era, (i) A world of Giant Cities, (ii) Mega-Cities*, Newbury Park, California.

Doniger, Wendy (1992) 'Rationalising the Irrational Other: "Orientalism" and the Laws of Manu', *New Literary History* 23(1): 25–44.

Dumas, Marius (1991) *Approaching Naxalbari*, Radical Impressions, Calcutta.

Dumont, Louis (1970) *Homo Hierarchicus*, Weidenfeld & Nicolson, London.

Duncan, James S. (1978) 'The Social Construction of Unreality: An Interactionist Approach to the Tourist's Cognition of Environment', in Ley and Samuels (eds) *Humanistic Geography: Prospects and Problems*, Croom Helm, London, pp. 269–82.

Duras, Marguerite (1987/1990) *Practicalities*, Collins, London.

Dutta, Krishna and Robinson, Andrew (1992) *Noon in Calcutta*, Viking, New Delhi.

Dwyer, Kevin (1979) 'The Dialogic of Ethnology', *Dialectical Anthropology* 4(3): 205–24.

Dwyer, Kevin (1982) *Moroccan Dialogues: Anthropology in Question*, Johns Hopkins University Press, Baltimore MD.

Eco, Umberto (1983) *The Name of the Rose*, trans. William Weaver. 1st edn, Harcourt Brace Jovanovich, San Diego CA.

Ehrlich, Carol (1986) 'On Commodity Relationships', in *Spectacular Times, The Spectacle* pamphlet.

Eipper, Chris (1991) 'The Predicament of Culture: A Comment', *Social Analysis* 29: 110–15.

Embree, Ainslie (1989) *Imagining India*, Oxford University Press, Delhi.

Erasmus (1511/1971) *Praise of Folly*, Penguin, Harmondsworth.

Evans-Pritchard E.E. (1931) *Social Anthropology*, Cohen & West, London.

Fabian, Johannes (1983) *Time and the Other: How Anthropology Makes its Object*, Cornell University Press, New York.

Fanon, Frantz (1961/1967) *The Wretched of the Earth*, Penguin, Harmondsworth.

Farias, Victor (1987/1989) *Heidegger and Nazism*, Temple University Press, Philadelphia PA.

Feifer, Michelle (1985) *Going Places*, Macmillan, London.
Ferguson, Anna (1993) *Image Place Text: Architecture and its Image in Travel Guides*, BA Hons thesis (draft), Department of Architecture, University of Queensland.
Fishlock, Trevor (1989) *India File*, Rupa & Co., Calcutta.
Foster, David (1987) *Plumbum*, Penguin, Ringwood.
Foucault, Michel (1963/1987) *Death and the Labyrinth: The World of Raymond Roussel*, trans. Charles Ruas, with an introduction by John Ashbery, University of California Press, Berkeley.
Foucault, Michel (1966/1970) *The Order of Things: An Archaeology of the Human Sciences*, Pantheon, New York.
Foucault, Michel (1977) *Discipline and Punish: The Birth of the Prison*, trans. Alan Sheridan, Allen Lane, London.
Foucault, Michel (1979) *Michel Foucault: Power, Truth, Strategy*, edited by Meaghan Morris and Paul Patton, Feral Publications, Sydney.
Foucault, Michel (1980) *Power/Knowledge: Selected interviews and other writings, 1972–1977*, ed. Colin Gordon, trans. Colin Gordon *et al.*, Harvester, Brighton.
Foucault, Michel (1984) *The Foucault Reader*, ed. Paul Rabinow. 1st edn, Pantheon, New York.
Foucault, Michel (1984/1985) *The Uses of Pleasure*, Pantheon, New York.
Foucault, Michel (1985) 'Sexuality and Solitude', in Marshal Blonsky (ed.) *On Signs*, Johns Hopkins University Press, Baltimore MD, pp. 365–72.
Foucault, Michel (1987) *Blanchot: The Thought from Outside*, Zone Books, New York.
Foucault, Michel (1988) *Politics, Philosophy, Culture: Interviews and Other Writings, 1977–1984*, trans. Alan Sheridan and others, edited with an introduction by Lawrence D. Kritzman, Routledge, New York.
Frommers (1984) *Guide to India*, Frommers Guides, London.
Frow, John (1990) 'Tourism and the Semiotics of Nostalgia', *October*, 57: 123–151.
Frow, John (1991) 'New Literary Histories', seminar, Melbourne University
Füredi, Frank (1994) *The New Ideology of Imperialism*, Pluto Press, London.
Fussel, Paul (1980) *Abroad: British Literacy Travelling between the Wars*, Oxford University Press, Oxford.
Gangopadhyay, Sunil (1987) *Arjun*, Penguin, New Delhi.
Garcia, Asun (1988) 'And Why Don't You Go to the Seychelles?', in Rossel (ed.), *Tourism: Manufacturing the Exotic*, IWGIA, Copenhagen.
Geertz, Clifford (1973) *The Interpretation of Cultures*, Basic Books, New York.
Geertz, Clifford (1988) *Works and Lives: The Anthropologist as Author*, Stanford University Press, Stanford CA.
Geertz, Clifford, Geertz, H. and Rosen, L. (1979) *Meaning and Order in the Moroccan Society: Three Essays on Cultural Analysis*, Cambridge University Press, Cambridge.
Gelley, Alexander (1993) 'City Texts; Representations, Semiology and Urbanism' in Poster, Mark, *Politics, Theory and Contemporary Culture*, Columbia University Press, New York.
George, Susan (1976) *How the Other Half Dies: The Real Reasons for World Hunger*, Pelican, Harmondsworth.
Ghosh, Amitav (n.d.) 'Travel Writing'.
Ghosh, Amitav (1986) *The Circle of Reason*, Hamish Hamilton, London.
Ghosh, Amitav (1988) *The Shadow Lines*, Ravi Dayal, Delhi.
Ginsberg, Alan (1990) *Indian Journals*, Penguin, Harmondsworth.
Glass, Ruth (1989) *Clichés of Urban Doom*, Basil Blackwell, Oxford.
Godzich, Wlad (1985) 'The Semiotics of Semiotics', in Marshal Blonsky (ed.) *On Signs*, Johns Hopkins University Press, Baltimore MD, pp.421–47.

Goldmann, Lucien (1977) *Lukács and Heidegger: Towards a New Philosophy*, Routledge & Kegan Paul, London.

Government of West Bengal (1991) *Calcutta's Urban Future: Agonies from the Past and Prospects for the Future*, Government of West Bengal, Calcutta.

Gramsci, Antonio (1977) *Selections from Political Writings 1910–1920*, Lawrence & Wishart, London.

Grass, Günter (n.d.) *The Headbirths are Dying Out*,

Grass, Günter (1977) *The Flounder*, Pan, London.

Grass, Günter (1986/1988) *The Rat*, trans. Ralph Manheim. 1st edn Harcourt Brace Jovanovich, San Diego CA.

Grass, Günter (1989) *Show Your Tongue*, Harcourt Brace Jovanovich, San Diego CA.

Greenblatt, Stephen (1991) *Marvellous Possessions: The Wonder of the New World*, Clarendon Press, Oxford.

Greene, Graham (1980) *Ways of Escape: An Autobiography*, Simon & Schuster, New York.

Greenwood, Darydd J. (1989) 'Culture by the Pound: An Anthropological Perspective on Tourism as Cultural Commoditization', in *Hosts and Guests: the Anthropology of Tourism*, University of Pennysylvania Press, Philadelphia, pp. 171–85.

Gregory, Derek (1990) 'Chinatown, Part Three? Soja and the Missing Spaces of Social Theory', *Strategies: A Journal of Theory, Culture and Politics* 3: 40–104.

Grossberg, Lawrence (1992) *We Gotta Get Out of this Place: Popular Conservatism and Postmodern Culture*, Routledge, New York.

Guattari, Félix (1992) 'Space and Corporeity: Nomads, City, Drawings', *Semiotext(e) Architecture*, pp. 118–25.

Guha, Ranajit (1983) *Elementary Aspects of Peasant Insurgency in Colonial India*, Oxford University Press, Delhi.

Guha, Ranajit (1992) *Subaltern Studies VI*, Oxford University Press. Delhi.

Gupta, R.P. (1990) 'City Life: Calcutta', *Departures*, Jan, 58–65.

Gupta, Sunetra (1993) *The Glassblower's Breath*, Orion, London.

Habermas, Jürgen (1983) *The Theory of Communicative Action*, Vol. 1, Polity, Boston MA.

Halbfass, Wilhelm (1988) *India and Europe: An Essay in Understanding*, State of New York Press, New York.

Hall, Peter (1984) 'Geography – Images of the City', in Rodwin and Hollister (eds), *Cities of the Mind*, Plenum Press, New York, pp. 21–36.

Handlin, Oscar and Burchard, J. (1963) *The Historian and the City*, MIT Press, Cambridge MA.

Hanfi, Zawar (1988) 'On Contradiction', *Criticism, Heresy and Interpretation*, 1: 19–36.

Harvey, David (1989) *The Conditions of Postmodernity*, Basil Blackwell, Oxford.

Hastings, James (ed.) (1951) *Encyclopaedia of Religion and Ethics*, Charles Scribner's Sons, New York.

Hastrup, Kirsten (1990) 'The Ethnographic Present: A Reinvention', *Cultural Anthropology* 5(1): 45–61.

Hauff, Reinhard (1987) *10 Days in Calcutta: A Portrait of Mrinal Sen*, script of film, reconstructed by Anjim Katyal and Samik Bandyopadhyay, Seagull Books, Calcutta.

Healy, Michael (1985) 'Where Does the Music Go When It's Over', *Melbourne Journal of Politics* 17: 51–3.

Hegel, G.W.F. (1899/1959) *The Philosophy of History*, Dover Press, New York.

Heidegger, Martin (1926/1962) *Being and Time*, Basil Blackwell, Oxford.

Heidegger, Martin (1955/1977) *The Question Concerning Technology, and Other Essays*, translated and with an introduction by William Lovitt, 1st edn Harper & Row, New York.

Heidegger, Martin (1966) *Discourse on Thinking: A Translation of Gelassenheit*, trans. John M. Anderson and E. Hans Freund, with an introduction by John M. Anderson, Harper & Row, New York.

Heidegger, Martin (1971) *Poetry, Language, Thought*, translation and introduction by Albert Hofstadter, 1st edn Harper & Row, New York.

Heidegger, Martin (1976) *Gesamtausgabe*, Vol. 9, *Wegmarken*, Klostermann, Frankfurt-am-Main.

Heidegger, Martin (1978) *Basic Writings from 'Being and Time' (1927) to 'The Task of Thinking'* (1964), edited, translated and with general introduction and introductions to each selection by David Farrell Krell, Routledge & Kegan Paul, London.

Heidegger, Martin (1979) *Nietzsche*, 4 vols translated with notes and an analysis by David Farrell Krell, Harper & Row, San Francisco.

Helms, Mary W. (1988) *Ulysses' Sail: An Ethnographic Odyssey of Power, Knowledge and Geographical Distance*, Princeton University Press, Princeton NJ.

Hetherington, Kevin (forthcoming) 'New Age Travellers: Heterotopic Places and Heteroclite Identities', *Theory, Culture and Society*.

Hitchens, Christopher (1992) 'Minority Report', *The Nation*, 13 April: 474.

Hitchens, Christopher (1995) *The Missionary Position*, Verso, London.

Hobson, J.A. (1902/1988) *Imperialism: A Study*, Unwin Hyman, London.

Hodge, Joanna (1995) *Heidegger and Ethics*, Routledge, London.

Hollier, Denis (1974/1989) *Against Architecture: The Writings of Georges Bataille*, MIT Press, Cambridge MA.

Holston, James (1989) *The Modernist City: An Anthropological Critique of Brasìlia*, University of Chicago Press, Chicago.

Holton, R. J. (1986) *Cities, Capitalism and Civilisation*, Allen & Unwin, London.

Home, Stewart (1991) *The Assault on Culture*, A.K. Press, Stirling.

Hood, John (1993) *Chasing the Truth: the Films of Mrinal Sen*, Seagull Books, Calcutta.

Horn, David G. (1989) 'Culture and Power in Urban Anthropology', *Dialectical Anthropology* 13: 189–198.

Horne, Donald (1992) *The Intelligent Tourist*, Margaret Gee Publishing, McMahon's Point.

Hutnyk, John (1987) 'The Authority of Style', *Social Analysis* 21: 59–79.

Hutnyk, John (1988) 'Castaway Anthropology: Malinowski's Tropical Writings', *Antithesis* 2(1): 43–56.

Hutnyk, John (1989) 'Clifford Geertz as a Cultural System', *Social Analysis* 25: 91–107.

Hutnyk, John (1990) 'Comparative Anthropology and Evans Pritchard's Nuer Photography', *Critique of Anthropology* X(1): 81–102.

Hutnyk, John (1993) 'Noir Sociology: Can Academics Map Los Angeles?', *Left Curve* 17: 26–33.

Hymes, Dell (1974) *Reinventing Anthropology*, Vintage Books, New York.

Inden, Ronald (1990) *Imagining India*, Basil Blackwell, Oxford.

Insight Guides (1985) *India*, APA Publications, Hong Kong.

Insight Guides (1991) *Calcutta*, APA Publications, Hong Kong.

Irigaray, Luce (1974) *Speculum de l'autre femme*, Mouton, Paris.

Iyengaer, Vishwapriya (1987) 'Patwardhan's Bombay: Our City, A Blueprint of Irrational Development', *Deep Focus* 1 (1): 62–6.

Iyer, Pico (1989) *Video Night in Kathmandu and Other Reports from the Not-So-Far East*, Black Swan, Ealing.

Jack, Ian (1990) 'Calcutta', *Departures*, Jan./Feb.: 54–7.

Jackson, Peter (1989) *Maps and Meaning*, Unwin Hyman, London.

Jameson Fredric (1991) *Postmodernism, or the Cultural Logic of Late Capitalism*, Verso, London.

Jameson, Fredric (1992) *The Geopolitical Aesthetic: Cinema and Space in the World System*, BFI Publishing, London.

Jha, Makhan (1979) *The Beggars of a Pilgrim's City*, Kishor Vidya Niketan, Varanasi.

Johnston, Barbara R. (ed.) (1990) *Breaking Out of the Tourist Trap: Cultural Survival Quarterly*, special issue, vol 14, pts 1 and 2.

Jones, Emrys (1990) *Metropolis: The World's Great Cities*, Oxford University Press, Oxford.

Josephs, Jeremy (1991) *Dr Jack: Calcutta's Pavement Doctor*, Bloomsbury, London.

Kabbani, Rana (1986) *Europe's Myths of Orient*, Pandora, London.

Kapur, Geeta (1989) 'Francis Newtown Souza: Devil in the Flesh', *Third Text* 8/9: 25–64.

Kapur, Geeta (1990) 'Contemporary Cultural Practice: Some Polemical Categories', *Third Text*, 11, Summer: 109–18.

Keenan, Thomas (1993) 'The Point is to (Ex)change It: Reading *Capital* Rhetorically', in Apter, Emily and Pietz, William (eds), *Fetishism As Cultural Discourse*, Cornell University Press, Ithaca NY.

Keve, Joseph (1990) 'Partnership: 10 Reasons for the Failure of Development Co-operation – an analysis of a development worker from the South', *Debacle* VI(3 & 4): 1–7.

Kirby, Vicki (1989) 'Corporeographies', *Inscriptions* 5: 103–20.

Kirby, Vicki (1991) 'Corpus Delicity: The Body of at the Scene of Writing' in Diprose, R. and Ferrell, R. (eds) (1991) *Cartographies: Poststructuralism and the Mapping of Bodies and Spaces*, Allen & Unwin, London.

Kirby, Vicki (unpub.) 'Feminism, Reading, Postmodernism'.

Koepping, Klaus-Peter (1989) 'Mind, Body, Text: Not Quite Satirical Reflections on the Anthropology of the Trickster', *Criticism Heresy and Interpretation* 2: 37–66.

Kosambi, Meera (1990) 'The Colonial City and its Global Niche', *Economic and Political Weekly*, XXV(51): 2775–2781.

Lafant, Marie-Françoise and Graburn, Nelson H.H. (1992) 'International Tourism Reconsidered: The Principles of the Alternative' in Smith, Valerie and Eadington, William R. (eds), *Tourism Alternatives: Potentials and Problems in the Development of Tourism*, University of Pennsylvania Press, Philadelphia.

Lafleur, William R. (1989)'Hungry Ghosts and Hungry People: Somaticity and Rationality in Medieval Japan', *Zone: Fragments for a History of the Body Part One*, Zone Books, New York

Lambert, Richard D. (1966) 'Some Minor Pathologies in the American Presence in India', *The Annals of the American Academy* 368: 157–70.

Langer, Susan (1953) *Feeling and Form: A Theory of Art*, Charles Scribner's Sons, New York.

Lapierre, Dominique (1985) *The City of Joy*, trans. Kathryn Spink, Doubleday, New York.

Lapierre, Dominique (1986) *Les héros de la cité de la joie*, unsourced.

Lapierre, Dominique and Collins, Larry (1976) *Freedom at Midnight*, Vikas, New Delhi.

Lattas, Andrew (1993) 'Gifts, Commodities and the Problem of Alienation', *Social Analysis*, 34: 102–115.

Lattas, Andrew (unpub.) 'The Aesthetics of Power and the Power of Aesthetics: Nietzsche, Contemporary Intellectuals and Philosophies of Art'.

Lecercle, Jean-Jacques (1985) *Philosophy Through the Looking Glass: Language, Nonsense, Desire*, Hutchinson, London.

Leed, Eric J. (1991) *The Mind of the Traveller: From Gilgamesh to Global Tourism*, Basic Books, New York.

Lefebvre, Henri (1966/1968) *The Sociology of Marx*, Penguin, Hammondsworth.

Lefebvre, Henri (1974/1991) *The Production of Space*, Basil Blackwell, Oxford.

Leiris, Michel (1934) *L'Afrique fantôme*, Gallimard, Paris (1950).

Leiris, Michel (1948/1991) *Scratches: Rules of the Game*, Paragon House, New York.

Leiris, Michel (1960) *Night as Day: Days as Night*, Eridanos Press, Colorado.

Lenaghan, Nick (1992) 'Black Harvest', *Farrago* 10: 30–31.

Lenin, Vladimir Ilyich (1916/1975) *Imperialism, the Highest Stage of Capitalism*, Foreign Language Press, Peking.

Lett, James (1989) 'Epilogue', in *Hosts and Guests: The Anthropology of Tourism*, University of Pennsylvania Press, Philadelphia, pp. 275–9.

Lévi-Strauss, Claude (1955/1973) *Tristes Tropiques*, Jonathan Cape, London.

Lévi-Strauss, Claude (1964/1970) *The Raw and the Cooked*, Harper Torchbooks, New York.

Lévi-Strauss, Claude (1966/1983) *From Honey to Ashes*, University of Chicago Press, Chicago.

Levin, David Michael (ed.) (1993) *Modernity and the Hegemony of Vision*, University of California Press, Berkeley.

Ley, David and Samuels, Marwyn S. (eds) (1978) *Humanistic Geography: Prospects and Problems*, Croom Helm, London.

Llewellyn, Kate (1991) *Angels and Dark Madonnas: Travels in India and Italy*, Hudson Publishing, Hawthorn.

Lowe, Lisa (1991) *Critical Terrain* (unsourced).

Lubell, Harold (1974) *Calcutta: Its Urban Development and Employment Prospects*, International Labor Office, Geneva.

Lubell, Harold (1978) 'Migration and Employment: The Case of Calcutta' in de Souza, *The Indian City: Poverty, Ecology and Urban Development*, South Asia Books, New Delhi: 111–26.

Lukács, Georg (1968/1971) *History and Class Consciousness*, Merlin Press, London.

Lutkehaus, Nancy Christine (1989) 'Excuse Me, Everything is Not Alright: On Ethnography, Film, and Representation', *Cultural Anthropology* 4(4): 422–37.

Lynch, K. (1960) *The Image of the City*, MIT Press, Cambridge MA.

Lyotard, Jean-François (1988/1990) *Heidegger and the Jews*, University of Minneapolis Press, Minnesota.

Lyotard, Jean-François (1986/1992) *The Postmodern Explained to Children, Correspondence 1982–85*, Power Publications, Sydney.

Lyotard, Jean-François (1989) *The Lyotard Reader*, ed. Andrew Benjamin, Basil Blackwell, Oxford.

MacCannell, Dean (1976) *The Tourist: A New Theory of Leisure Class*, Schocken Books, New York; reprinted 1989, with a new introduction, by Random House, New York.

MacCannell, Dean (1992) *Empty Meeting Grounds: The Tourist Papers*, Routledge, London.

MacFarlane, Iris (1975) *The Black Hole or The Makings of a Legend*, George Allen & Unwin, London.

Mallick, Ross (1994) *Indian Communism*, Oxford University Press, New Delhi.

Mani, Lata (1989) 'Multiple Mediations: Feminist Scholarship in the Age of Multinational Reception', *Inscriptions* 5: 1–24.

Manto, Saadat Hasan (1989) *Kingdom's End and Other Stories*, Penguin, New Delhi.

Marcus, G.E. and Cushmen, D. (1982) 'Ethnographies as Texts', *Annual Review of Anthropology* 11: 25–69.

Marcus, George (1991) 'A Broad(er) Side to the Canon: Being a Partial Account of a Year of Travel among Textual Communities in the Realm of Humanities Centers and Including a Collection of Artificial Curiosities', *Cultural Anthropology* 6(3): 385–405.

Marks, Laura U. (1992) 'White People in the Native Camera: Subverting Anthropology', *After Image* 19(10): 18–19.

Marx, Karl (1853/1978) *On Colonialism*, Progress Press, Moscow.

Marx, Karl (1858/1973) *Grundrisse*, Penguin, Harmondsworth.

Marx, Karl (1867/1967) *Capital: A Critique of Political Economy, Vol 1: The Process of Capitalist Production*, edited by Friedrich Engels, trans. S. Moore and E. Aveling, International Publishers, New York.

Marx, Karl (1947) *Notes on Indian History*, Foreign Language Publishing House, Moscow.

Marx, Karl (1973) *The Revolution of 1848*, Penguin/New Left Books, London.

Marx, Karl and Engels, Friedrich (1848/1967) *The Communist Manifesto*, Penguin, Harmondsworth.

Massey, Doreen (1985) 'New Directions in Space', in Gregory, D. and Urry, J. (eds), *Social Directions and Spatial Structures*, Macmillan, London.

Massumi, Brian (1992) *A User's Guide to Capitalism and Schizophrenia: Deviations from Deleuze and Guattari*, MIT Press, Cambridge MA.

Maugham, Somerset (1964) *The Razor's Edge*, Heinemann, London.

McKean, Philip Frick (1989) 'Towards a Theoretical Analysis of Tourism: Economic Dualism and Cultural Involution in Bali', in *Hosts and Guests: The Anthropology of Tourism*, University of Pennsylvannia Press, Philadelphia, pp. 119–38.

McQuire, Scott (1995) *The Migratory Eye: Representation, Memory, Time and Space in the Age of the Camera*, PhD thesis, Dept of Political Science, University of Melbourne.

McQuire, Scott (forthcoming) *Visions of Modernity: Representation, Memory, Time and Space in the Age of the Camera*, Sage, London.

Mehta, Gita (1980) *Karma Cola*, Jonathan Cape, London.

Meigh, Frances (1988) *Destitutes of Calcutta: The Jack Preger Story*, Arnold Publishers, New Dehli.

Menezes, Braz O. (1985) 'Calcutta, India: Conflict or Consistency', *Cities in Conflict*, pp. 61–80, Lee, John and Courtney, John M., A World Bank Symposium.

Michelson, Annette (1989) 'Reading Eisenstein Reading *Ulysses*: Montage and the claims of subjectivity', *Art and Text* 34: 64–78.

Miller, Donald F. (1992) *The Reason of Metaphor: A Study in Politics*, Sage, New Delhi.

Miller, James (1993) *The Passion of Michel Foucault*, Harper Collins, London.

Mitchell, Timothy (1988) *Colonising Egypt*, Cambridge University Press, Cambridge.

Mitchell, W.J.T. (1993) '"In the Wilderness", *Culture and Imperialism* by Edward Said', *London Review of Books*, 8 April.

Mitra, Ashok (1963) *Calcutta: India's City*, New Age Publishers, Calcutta.

Mitra, Ashok (1979) *Calcutta Diary*, Rupa & Co., Calcutta.

Mitra, Ashok (1990) *Calcutta on the Eve of Her Tercentenary*, Abhinav Publications, New Delhi.

Mitra, Premendra (1990) *Snake and Other Stories*, Seagull Books, Calcutta.

Moorhouse, Geoffrey (1971) *Calcutta: The City Revealed*, Penguin, Harmondsworth; reissued with new introduction, 1983.

Muecke, Stephen (1990) 'No Road (Vague Directions for the Study of Tourism)', *Continuum* 3(1): 127–36.

Mukherjee, S.N. (1987) *Calcutta: 'A City of Spendid Palaces and Dingy Streets': Fiction as History*, Faculty of Asian Studies, Canberra.

Mumford, Lewis (1961) *The City in History: Its Tranformation and Its Prospects*, Harcourt, New York.

Murch, Walter (1992) *In the Blink of an Eye*, AFTRS, Sydney.

Murphey, Rhoads (1963) 'The City in the Swamp: Aspects of the Site and Early Growth of Calcutta', *The Geographical Journal*, 130(2): 241–56.

Murphey, Rhoads (1966) 'Urbanisation in Asia', *Ekistics*, 21(122): January.

Murphey, Rhoads (unpubl.), 'Calcutta and the Making of Modern India', paper delivered at Jadavpur University, December 1990.

Nandy, Ashis (1983) *The Intimate Enemy: Loss and Recovery of Self under Colonialism*, Oxford University Press, New Delhi.

Nandy, Ashis (1985) 'An Anti-Secularist Manifesto', *Seminar*, October.

Nandy, Ashis (1992) 'The Other Within: The Strange Case of Radhabinad Pal's Judgement on Culpability', *New Literary History*, 23(1): 45–68.

Nash Denison (1989) 'Tourism as a Form of Imperialism', *Hosts and Guests: The Anthropology of Tourism*, University of Pennsylvania Press, Philadelphia, pp. 37–52.

Negri, Antonio (1988) *Revolution Retrieved: Selected Writings on Marx, Keynes, Capitalist Crisis and New Social Subjects 1967–83*, Red Notes, London.

Negri, Antonio (1991) *Marx Beyond Marx: Lessons on the Grundrisse*, Autonomedia, New York.

Negri, Antonio and Guattari, Félix (1990) *Communist Like Us*, Semiotext(e), New York.

Nietzsche, F.W. 1887/1969) *On the Genealogy of Morals*, Vintage, New York.

Nietzsche, F.W. (1908/1969) *Ecce Homo*, Vintage, New York.

Olalquiaga, Celeste (1992) *Megalopolis: Contemporary Cultural Sensibilities*, University of Minnesota Press, Minneapolis.

Papastergiadis, Nikos (1993a) *Modernity as Exile: The Stranger in John Berger's Writing*, Manchester University Press, Manchester.

Papastergiadis, Nikos (1993b) 'The Ends of Migration', *Agenda* 29: 7–13.

Patnaik, Arun K. (1987) 'Gramsci's Concept of Commonsense: Towards a Theory of Subaltern Consciousness in Hegemony Processes', *Occasional Paper no. 95*, Centre for Studies in Social Sciences, Calcutta.

Pearce, Phillip L. (1977) 'Mental Souvenirs: A Study of Tourists and their City Maps', *Australian Journal of Psychology* 29(3): 203–10.

Peattie, Lisa Redfield and Robbins, Edward (1984) 'Anthropological Approaches to the City', in Rodwin, Lloyd and Hollister, Robert (eds), *Cities of the Mind*, Plenum Press, New York.

Pedretti, Carlo (1980) *Leonardo Da Vinci: Nature Studies from the Royal Library at Windsor Castle*, International Cultural Corporation of Australia.

Phipps, Peter (1990) *The Budget Traveller in India: A Deconstructive Analysis and Cultural Critique*, BA Hons thesis, Department of Anthropology, University of Melbourne.

Pietz, William (1993) 'Fetishism and Materialism: The Limits of Theory in Marx', in Apter and Pretz (eds), *Fetishism as Cultural Discourse*, Cornell University Press, Ithaca NY.

Pocock, D.C. (1972) 'The City of the Mind: A Review of Mental Maps in Urban Areas', *Scottish Geographical Magazine* 88: 116–24.

Poggi, G. (1983) *Calvinism and the Capitalist Spirit*, Macmillan, London.

Pratt, Mary Louise (1992) *Imperial Eyes: Travel Writing and Transculturation*, Routledge, London.

Preziosi, Donald (1990) 'Oublier la Città', *Strategies: A Journal of Theory, Culture and Politics* 3: 260–67.

Raban, Jonathan (1988) *Soft City*, Collins Harvill, London.

Rabinow, Paul (1985) 'Discourse and Power: On the Limits of Ethnographic Texts', *Dialectical Anthropology* 10(1/2): 1–13.

Rabinow, Paul (1989) *French Modern: Norms and Forms of the Social Environment*, MIT Press, Cambridge MA.

Racine, Jean (ed.) (1990) *Calcutta 1981: The City, its Crisis and the Debate on Urban Planning and Development*, Concept Publishing Company, New Delhi.

Radcliffe-Brown, Alfred Reginald (1922) *The Andaman Islanders*, The Free Press of Glencoe, New York (1964).

Ray, Nisith R. (1986) *Calcutta: The Profile of a City*, K.P. Bagchi & Co., Calcutta.

Ray, Satyajit (1976) *Our Films, Their Films*, Orient Longman, Calcutta.

Redfield, Robert (1954) 'The Cultural Role of Cities', *Economic Development and Cultural Change* 4.

Reiner, Thomas A. and Hindery, Michael A. (1984) 'City Planning', in Rodwin and Hollister, *Cities of the Mind*, Plenum Press, New York.

Richter, Linda K. (1989) *The Politics of Tourism in Asia*, University of Hawaii Press, Honolulu.

Roberge, Gaston (1984) *Another Cinema for Another Society*, Seagull Press, Calcutta.

Roberge, Gaston (1989) 'Film Studies in India', manuscript, August.

Roberge, Gaston 1990, 'Images of Calcutta: From Black Hole to Black Box', in Racine (ed.) *Calcutta 1981: The City, its Crisis and the Debate on Urban Planning and Development*, Concept Publishing Company, New Delhi: 15–27.

Roberge, Gaston 1991, 'Tristes Topic: Calcutta and Development', unpublished manuscript.

Robinson, Andrew (1990) *Satyajit Ray: The Inner Eye*, Rupa & Co., Calcutta.

Rodwin, Lloyd and Hollister, Robert (eds) (1984) *Cities of the Mind: Images and Themes of the City in the Social Sciences*, Plenum Press, New York.

Ronell, Avital (1994) *Finitude's Score: Essays for the End of the Millennium*, University of Nebraska Press, Lincoln.

Rossel, Pierre (ed.) (1988) *Tourism: Manufacturing the Exotic*, International Working Group for Indigenous Affairs, Copenhagen.

Roy, Prabudda Nath (1991) 'Calcutta: The Myth of Decay', in *Calcutta's Urban Future*, Government of West Bengal, Calcutta, pp. 84–111.

Rushdie, Salman (1990) *Haroun and the Sea of Stories*, Granta Books, London.

Rushdie, Salman (1991) *Imaginary Homelands*, Granta Books, London.

Ryan, Michael (1982) *Marxism and Deconstruction*, Johns Hopkins University Press, Baltimore.

Said, Edward W. (1978) *Orientalism*, Pantheon, New York.

Said, Edward W. (1981) *Covering Islam: How the Media and the Experts Determine How We See the Rest of the World*, Pantheon, New York.

Said, Edward W. (1986) *After the Last Sky*, Faber & Faber, London.

Said, Edward W. (1989) 'Representing the Colonised: Anthropology's Interlocutor', *Critical Inquiry*, 15(2): 205–25.

Said, Edward W. (1993) *Culture and Imperialism*, Chatto & Windus, London.

Saldana, Muthuvel and Mathray (1988) 'Tourism: the Other Side of the Glamour Story', in *Voices of the Storm*, National Fishermen's Forum, Cochin, pp. 67–70.

Salusinszky, Imre (1987) *Criticism in Society: Interviews with Jacques Derrida, Northrop Frye, Harold Bloom, Geoffrey Hartman, Frank Kermode, Edward Said, Barbara Johnson, Frank Lentricchia, and J. Hillis Miller*, Methuen, New York.

Samaddar, Ranabir (1987) 'The Rebellious and Non-Conformist Youth of Bengal 1966–70', in Sinha, Pradhip (ed.) (1987) *The Urban Experience: Calcutta*, Riddha-India, Calcutta, pp. 94–112.

Samadder, Sivaprasad (1978) *Calcutta Is*, unsourced

Sasnaitis, Jurate (1989) *Sketches*, Nosukumo, Melbourne.

Schor, Naomi (1992) 'Cartes Postales: Representing Paris, 1900', *Critical Inquiry* 18(2): 188–244.

Sealy, I. Allen (1990) *The Trotter-Nama*, Penguin, New Delhi.

Sen, Asok (1989) 'Weber, Gramsci and Capitalism', in Bharadwaj, K. and Kaviraj, S. (eds) *Perspectives on Capitalism*, Sage, New Delhi.

Sen, Mrinal (1983) *In Search of Famine*, Seagull Books, Calcutta

Seth, Vikram (1983) *From Heaven's Lake*, Random House, New York.

Seth, Vikram (1992) *A Suitable Boy*, Phantom Books, London.

Sethuraman, S.V. (1978) 'The Informal Urban Sector in Developing Countries: Some Policy Implications', in de Souza, *The Indian City: Poverty, Ecology and Urban Development*, South Asia Books, New Delhi: pp. 1–16.

Simmel, Georg (1922/1955) *Conflict and the Web of Group Afflictions*, Frans Wolff & Dendix Free Press, New York.

Simmel, Georg (1950) 'The Metropolis and Mental Life', in K. Wolff (ed.), *The Sociology of Georg Simmel*, Free Press, Glencoe.

Sinha, Pradhip (ed.) (1987) *The Urban Experience: Calcutta*, Riddha-India, Calcutta.

Sinha, Surajit (ed.) (1970) *Cultural Profile of Calcutta*, Calcutta.

Sivaramakrishnan K.C. (1978) 'The Slum Improvement Programme in Calcutta: The Role of the CMDA', in de Souza, *The Indian City: Poverty, Ecology and Urban Development*, South Asia Books, New Delhi: 127–144.

Sloterdijk, Peter (1983/1988) *Critique of Cynical Reason*, Verso, London.

Smith, Valerie L. (1989) *Hosts and Guests: The Anthropology of Tourism*, (2nd edn), University of Pennysylvania Press, Philadelphia.

Smith, Valerie L. and Eadington, William R. (eds) (1992) *Tourism Alternatives: Potentials and Problems in the Development of Tourism*, University of Pennsylvania Press, Philadelphia.

Soja, Edward W. (1989) *Postmodern Geographies: The Reassertion of Space in Critical Social Theory*, Verso, London.

Soja, Edward W. (1990) 'Heterotopologies: A Rememberance of Other Spaces in Citadel L.A.', *Strategies: A Journal of Theory, Culture and Politics* 3: 6–39.

Sontag, Susan (1979) *On Photography*, Penguin, Harmondsworth.

Spivak, Gayatri Chakravorty (1976) 'Translator's Preface' to Derrida, J. *Of Grammatology*, Johns Hopkins University Press, Baltimore MD.

Spivak, Gayatri Chakravorty (1985) 'Scattered Speculations on the Question of Value', *Diacritics*, Winter: 73–93.

Spivak, Gayatri Chakravorty (1987) *In Other Worlds: Essays in Cultural Politics*, Methuen, New York.

Spivak, Gayatri Chakravorty (1990a) 'Strategy, Identity, Writing', in *The Post Colonial Critic: Interviews, Strategies, Dialogues*, Routledge, New York (reprinted interview from the *Melbourne Journal of Politics*, 1986).

Spivak, Gayatri Chakravorty (1990b) 'Poststructuralism, Marginality, Postcoloniality and Value', in *Literary Theory Today*, ed. Collier, Peter, and Geyer-Ryan, Helga, Polity, Cambridge, pp. 219–44.

Spivak, Gayatri Chakravorty (1993a) 'Extreme Eurocentrism: Interview with Edward Ball', *Lusitania* 1(4): 55–62.

Spivak, Gayatri Chakravorty (1993b) 'Situations of Value' (interview with Pheng Cheah), *Australian Feminist Studies* 17: 141–62.

Spivak, Gayatri Chakravorty (1993c) *Outside in the Teaching Machine*, Routledge, New York.

Spivak, Gayatri Chakravorty (1996) *The Spivak Reader*, Routledge, London.

Srinivas, M.N. (1962) *Caste in Modern India and Other Essays*, Media Promoters and Publishers, Bombay.

The Statesman, 1989 'Stop This City, I Want to Get Off', 5 February.

Stephens, Julie (1992) *Idioms of Cultural Protest: The 'Sixties' and the Emergence of Postmodernism*, PhD thesis, Faculty of Arts, University of Melbourne.

Strathern, Marilyn (1991) 'Or, Rather, on Not Collecting Clifford', *Social Analysis* 29: 88–95.

Stratton, Jon (1990) *Writing Sites: A Geneaology of the Postmodern World*, Harvester Wheatsheaf, Hemel Hempstead.

Suleri, Sera (1992) *The Rhetoric of English India*, University of Chicago Press, Chicago.

Suraiya, Jug (1985) *Calcutta*, Oxford University Press, New Delhi.

Tagg, John (1990) 'The Discontinuous City: Picturing and the Discursive Field', *Strategies: A Journal of Theory, Culture, and Politics* 3: 138–58.

Tagore, Rabindranath (1913/1988) *Gitangali*, Macmillan, Madras.

Taussig, Michael (1993) *Mimesis and Alterity: A Particular History of the Senses*, Routledge, New York.

Tawadros, Gilane (1989) 'Beyond the Boundary: The Work of Three Black Women Artists in Britain', *Third Text*, 8/9: 121–150.

Tedlock, Denis (1983) *The Spoken Word and the Work of Interpretation*, University of Pennsylvania Press, Philadelphia.

Tempest, Tone (1987) 'Calcutta Tourists Slumming It', from *Los Angeles Times*, reprinted in *The Age*, December.

Thapar, Raj (1980) *The Invincible Traveller*, Vikas House, Ghaziabad.

Tharu, Susie and Lalita, K. (1991) *Women Writing in India*, Vol. I: 600 BC to the Early 20th Century, Feminist Press, New York.

Tharu, Susie and Lalita, K. (1993) *Women Writing in India*, Vol. II: The 20th Century, Harper Collins, London.

Theroux, Paul (1991) 'Subterranean Gothic', *The Best of Granta Travel*, Granta Books, London.

Toynbee, Arnold (1970) *Cities on the Move*, Oxford University Press, Delhi.

Trinh T. Minh-ha (1987) 'She, The Inappropriate/d Other', *Discourse* 8.

Trinh T. Minh-ha (1989) *Women Native Other*, Indiana University Press, Bloomington.

Trinh T. Minh-ha (1992) *Framer Framed*, Routledge, New York.

Tumer, L. and Ash, J. (1975) *The Golden Hordes*, Constable, London.

Turner, Victor (1974) *The Ritual Process: Structure and Anti-Structure*, Pelican, Harmondsworth.

Tylor, Stephen A. (1987) *The Unspeakable: Discourse, Dialogue and Rhetoric in the Postmodern World*, University of Wisconsin Press, Madison.

Ulin, Robert C. (1991) 'Critical Anthropology Twenty Years Later', *Critical Anthropology* vol. II(1): 63–89.

Ulmer, Gregory (1989) *Teletheory: Grammatology in the Age of Video*, Routledge, New York.

Ulmer, Gregory (1993) 'Abject Monumentality: Report on Tourism', *Lusitania* 1(4): 9–16.

Urry, John (1990) *The Tourist Gaze: Leisure and Travel in Contemporary Societies*, Sage, London.

Van den Abbeele, Georges (1992) *Travel as Metaphor: From Montaigne to Rousseau*, University of Minnesota Press, Minneapolis.

Van Gennep, Arnold (1960) *The Rites of Passage*, Routledge & Kegan Paul, London.

Veblen, Thorstein (1925) *The Theory of the Leisure Class*, George Allen & Unwin Ltd, London.

Vir Singh, Tej, Theuns, H.L. and Go, F.M. (eds) (1988) *Towards Appropriate Tourism: The Case of the Developing Countries*, Frankfurt am Main, Bern.

Virilio, Paul and Lotringer, Sylvère (1989) 'Taken by Speed', ABC Radio 24 May 1989, printed in *Agenda: Interview Supplement*, 7/8.

Virilio, Paul (1984/1989) *War and Cinema: The Logistics of Perception*, Verso, London.

Virilio, Paul (1991) *The Lost Dimension*, Semiotext(e), New York.

Vishvanathan, Shiv and Sethi, Harsh (1989) 'Bhopal: A Report from the Future', *Lokayan* 7(3): 47–67.

Viswanathan, Gauri (1989) *Masks of Conquest: Literary Study and British Rule in India*, Columbia University Press, New York.

Wallerstein, Immanuel (1983) *Historical Capitalism*, Verso, London.

Wallerstein, Immanuel (1990) 'Marx, Marxism-Leninism, and Socialist Experiences in the Modern World-System', *Thesis II*, 27: 40–53.

Wallerstein, Immanuel (1990) 'World-Systems Analysis and Historical Particularity: Some Comments', in S. Bose (ed.) *South Asia and World Capitalism*, Oxford University Press, Delhi.

Wallis, Brian (ed.) (1991) *If You Lived Here: The City in Art, Theory and Social Activism*, Dia Art Foundation, Bay Press, Seattle WA.

Washbrook, David (1990) 'South Asia, the World System and World Capitalism', in S. Bose (ed.) *South Asia and World Capitalism*, Oxford University Press, Delhi.

Weber, Max (1958) *The City*, Free Press, Glencoe.

Weber, Max (1961) *General Economic History*, Collier Press, New York.

Weimer, D.R. (1966) *The City as Metaphor*, Random House, New York.

Wheeler, Tony (1982) *India: A Survival Kit*, Lonely Planet, Melbourne; revised 1987.

Wheeler, Valerie (1986) 'Travellers' Tales: Observations on the Travel Book and Ethnography', *Anthropology Quarterly* 59(2): 52–63.

White, Merran (1989) *Going Solo: A Guide for Women Travelling Alone*, Greenhouse Publications, Elwood.

Wigley, Mark (1992) 'Theoretical Slippage', *Fetish: The Princeton Architecture Journal* 4: 88–129.

Williams, Raymond (1989) *The Politics of Modernism*, Verso, London.

Wolin, Richard (1991) *The Heidegger Controversy: A Critical Reader*, Columbia University Press, New York.

Zorbaugh, Harvey (1927) *The Gold Coast and the Slum*, University of Chicago Press, Chicago.

INDEX

Agamben, Giorgio, ix, 14, 153, 162, 167
alternative travellers, ix, x, 11, 19; *see also* Western travellers
anthropologists, 165; as tourists, 157–8
anthropology, 39, 52, 107; of tourism, 138–9
anti-imperialism, 97
Appadurai, Arjun, 221
Aragon, Louis, 138
Artaud, Antonin, 113
Asad, Talal, 98
authenticity, 29
Azmi, Shabana, 177

Bailey, Fred, 184
'banana-pancake trail', 10, 222; lore of the, 42, 64; budget tourists on, 43, 111, 134, 212; conventions of, 70; drugs on the, 79; *see also* Western travellers; Modern Lodge
Basu, Jyoti, 93
Bataille, Georges, 13, 14, 109, 136; *The Accursed Share*, 152–3
Battle of Plassey, 92
Baudrillard, Jean, 145, 167
beggars: commodification of, 68–9
Bengali government, promotional writings of, 87, 93–4
Bengali Women's Trade Union Auxiliary, 155
Bengali writers and artists, 22, 48–9, 102
Benjamin, Walter, 90, 151, 177–8; on Baudelaire, 132
Bhabha, Homi K., ix, 27

Bhatia, A.K., 60–1
Bhopal gas leak, 4
Black Hole, 21, 31, 82–3, 91–2, 110, 140
Borges, Jorge Luís, viii, 124–5, 136
Boulez, Pierre, 129–30
British imperialism, vii, 87, 91
British Raj, 119, 185; histories of, 91–6; *see also* histories of Calcutta
Bruner, Edward, M., 149
budget traveller, *see* Western travellers

Calcutta: alternative maps of, 132–34; cartography of, 117–42; cinematic representations of, 177–8 179–213; codification of, 19; as communist city, 71–7, 115; described, vii; as East or West, 5, 86–8; ethnography of travellers in, 40–9; histories of, 53, 56, 83, 87–8, 92–6, 119, 128; identity of, 6, 71, 83; mythic analysis of, 65–6; mythical construction of, 23, 29, 30, 60, 65, 176; as a pedestrian city, 134–36; photographic identity of, 148–52, 159, 163–67; street names in, 119; *see also* poverty in Calcutta; representations of Calcutta; Western travellers, views of
Calcutta Rescue group, ix, 220, 221
Calcutta Social Project, 100
camera, the, 19, 158; democratization and, 147, 164, 172; as technology, 20, 143, 163; tourism, and, 143–7
capitalism, 33, 56, 163, 208; as 'global',

23; production of space by, 120–4, 140
cartography: national identity formed by, 125–6; of perception, 165; *see also* maps; Calcutta, cartography of; Western travellers, orientation in Calcutta
Castells, Manuel, 14, 196–7
charity, viii–x, 18, 59, 160–1, 180, 204, 214; capitalism and, 24–6, 50, 53, 76–7, 207–10, 219; communism and, 74–7; as gift, 221–2; morality of, 67; protocols of, 33; recipients of, 12; tourism and, 35, 207, 210, 214; *see also* volunteers; Western travellers, as volunteers
Charnock, Job, 2, 92, 106
Chaudhuri, Sukanta, *Calcutta, The Living City*, 65
cinema: critical evaluation of, 196–201; modes of framing, 185–7; as a mode of perception, 177–9 urban representation in, 199–201
classes, 172; maintaining divisions between, 34, 216; *see also* middle class; Western travellers as middle class
Clifford, James, 14, 27, 28, 34, 49, 114, 201; *The Predicament of Culture*, 26, 51–2
Clive, Robert (Clive of India), 91–2
Cold War, end of, 72–3
Collins, Larry, *Freedom at Midnight*, 94–5
commodification, 14, 169; of identity, 167
commodity system, 19, 24, 31
communism, 72–7, 78, 84, 180
Communist Party of India – Marxist (CPI(M)), 72, 76–7, 84, 189
Communist Party of India Marxist-Leninist (CPI(M-L)), 76–7, 84
Community Aid Abroad (CAA), 155
consumption of cultural goods, 3, 151; of the exotic, 21, 134; of India, 69, 150; purpose of, 25, 220; tourism and, 9–11, 172, 208
contra-tourism, 33
counterfeit economy, vii, 21
Crapanzano, Vincent, 130
Crary, Jonathan, 86, 143–4, 164
Crick, Malcolm, 10, 61, 139, 149–50, 157, 215, 218
cultural identity, 147

cultural imperialism, viii; and mapping, 120
culture: notion of, 26; production of, 203

De Certeau, Michel, 135
Dear, M. (with A. Scott), 141
Debord, Guy, *The Society of the Spectacle*, 121
Deleuze, Gilles, ix, 14, 34, 215; on cinema, 194; on enframing, 172, 186; on ideology, 111–14; on maps, 118, 125, 130, 134; on world market, 10–11; *see also* Félix Guattari
Derrida, Jacques, ix, 14, 26, 34, 107, 201; on Artaud, 54; on Baudelaire, 160–1, 209–10; on gifts, 156–7; on Lévi-Strauss, 28; on postcards, 79; on process of communication, 30–1; on status of technology, 171; on travelogues, 90
Devi, Mahasweta, viii, 97
drugs, 79–80
Dumont, Louis, 182
Duras, Marguerite: *The Vice-Consul*, 4; *India Song*, 4
Dutt, Nargis, 184

Eadington, William, R., 10
East India Company, vii, 55, 87, 88, 91
Eco, Umberto, *The Name of the Rose*, 136
enframing, 47, 208; apparatus of, 42; concept of, 17–18, 21–2; maps as, 141; recognition of ways of, 33; technologies of, viii, 17, 146, 166, 184; *see also* Martin Heidegger
ethnographic text, 32
ethnographers: authenticity of, 27–8
ethnography, 165; as polytextual, 51–2
Expositions, European, 162–3

Fanon, Frantz, 7
film-making, process of, 197–8
Foster, David, *Plumbum*, 81
Foucault, Michel, ix, 14, 46, 99, 143; power/knowledge and, 31
Frommers guide, 1–2
Fry, Susan, 205
Füredi, Frank, 221
Fussel, Paul, 158

Gandhi, Rajiv, 111
'gaze', the, 144, 172, 186; voyeurism of, 151; tourists and, 206
Geertz, Clifford, *Works and Lives*, 122
gender, 191
geography, 141
George, Susan, 12
Ghatak, Ritwik, 177
Ghosh, Amitav, 145; *The Shadow Lines*, 43, 55
Ginsberg, Allen, *Indian Journals*, 81, 112
Gordon, Leonard, 110
gossip, 29–31, 35; as a tool, 34, 42
Graburn, Nelson H.H., *Tourism Alternatives* (with Marie-François Lafant), 138
Gramsci, Antonio, 97
Grass, Günter, viii, 21, 35, 56, 78, 83, 87, 105–17 *passim* 153, 200, 212, 215, 222; *Flounder*, 99, 100; *The Headbirths Are Dying Out*, 99; reception of, in Calcutta, 110; *Show Your Tongue*, 82, 99, 100–4, 111
Greenblatt, Stephen, 124
Greene, Graham, 52
Greenwood, Darydd J., 137, 138, 170
Guattari, Félix, ix, 172, 215, 222 on commodification, 170; on deterritorialization, 127–128; on ideology, 111–14; on maps, 118; *see also* Gilles Deleuze
Gupta, Sunetra, *The Glassblower's Breath*, 193–4

Habermas, Jürgen, 170–1
Hanfi, Zawar, 58
Hauff, Reinhardt, *10 Days in Calcutta*, 176, 201–5
Healy, Michael, 129
Hetherington, Kevin, 46–7
Heidegger, Martin, viii, 13–15, 34, 37–8 121, 123, 141, 173; *Being and Time*, 18, 31; on deception, 24; on enframing, 17–18, 21, 31, 124, 143; on 'idle talk', 31; 'Letter on Humanism', 16; on technology, 16–19, 144, 171–2, 217, 218; 'What are Poets for?', 15–16
heterotopia: concept of, 46–7
Hetleb, Dieter, *Calcutta, One Day*, 186
Hollier, Denis, 136
Hood, John, 204

Horne, Donald, 5
hybrid texts, 3
hybridity: concept of, 127

ideological production, 164; through charity work, viii; from Western travel guides, viii
imperialism, 7, 19, 23, 56, 155, 163; of meaning, 32; and charity, 67
Inden, Ronald, *Imagining India*, 116, 122
Independence, 87
India, 64; economy of, 76–7
Indian English, 7, 48
Indian independence struggle, vii, 101
Indian nationalist movement, 87
Indian Tourism Development Corporation, 118
Indiana Jones and the Temple of Doom, 140
Information Unit on Militarization and Demilitarization in Asia (IUMDA), 4
International Monetary Fund (IMF), 10, 11, 68, 76–7, 220
Iyengar, Vishwapriya, 54
Iyer, Pico, 139

Jameson, Fredric, ix, 28, 34, 127
Joffe, Roland, *City of Joy*, viii, 35, 38, 44, 79, 174, 179–81, 182, 185, 187–95, 198, 205, 207, 209–212 *passim*, 215, 220; censorship of film in India, 163, 223; making the film, 62, 189, 193–4; role of the West in, 68; treatment of charity in, 24, 59, 176, 177, 208; urban representation, 200

Kabbani, Rana, 8, 139–40, 159
Kafka, Franz, *The Trial*, 136
Kali, 92, 99, 110, 183
Keenan, Thomas, 123, 169
Kerouac, Jack, *On the Road*, 61, 112
Kipling, Rudyard, 55, 56, 87, 93, 140, 176, 200

Lafant, Marie-François, *Tourism Alternatives* (with Nelson H.H. Graburn), 138
Lafleur, William R., 153
Lambert, Richard, 8
language: use of local languages, 47, 65; as technology, 47

Lapierre, Dominique: *The City of Joy*, 35, 55, 82, 87, 95–6, 97, 99, 100, 111, 114, 212; *Freedom at Midnight*, 94–5
Lattas, Andrew, 220
Lefebvre, Henri, *The Production of Space*, 120–21
Leiris, Michel, viii, 13, 49, 51; *L'Afrique fantôme*, 114, 115; *Rules of the Game*, 114
Lenaghan, Nick, 23
leprosy, 53–4, 104, 105–6, 184, 222
Lett, James, 137–8
Lévi-Strauss, Claude, viii, 13, 24, 65–6, 87, 102, 114, 115, 121, 124, 132, 153, 196–7, 200, 201, 209, 212, 215; on the culture industry, 27–8; *Tristes Tropiques*, 88–90
linguistic diversity, 47–8
Llewellyn, Kate, 101
local culture, 6–7
Lonely Planet, *India: A Travel Survival Kit*, 8, 41, 43, 53, 55, 59, 62, 72, 73, 87; anecdotal character of, 50, 64; maps in the, 118, 125, 133, 134; other guidebooks and, 90; popularity of, 63
Lubell, Harold, 168
Lukács Georg, 14, 163
Lyotard, Jean-François, 173

MacCannell, Dean, 10, 123
MacFarlane, Iris, *The Black Hole, or The Makings of a Legend*, 91–2
Malle, Louis, viii, 56, 176, 212; *Phantom India*, 181; *Calcutta*, 181–5, 202
Mallick, Ross, 3
maps, 117–142; *see also* cartography
Marcus, George, 49
Marx, Karl, viii, 13–16, *passim*, 22, 34, 124, 144, 155, 160, 173, 217, 220; on the 'Black Hole of Calcutta', 91–2; *Capital*, 15, 162, 169, 211; on commodity fetishism, 31, 143–4, 161–2; on exchange analysis, 24–5, 123, 209–10; on social production, 171; on surplus value, 153
Massumi, Brian, 167
materialism, 16
Maugham, Somerset, *The Razor's Edge*, 81, 176, 200, 209
Mazursky, Paul, *Scenes from a Mall*, 198
McKean, Philip F., 61, 138

McQuire, Scott, 164, 178
Mehta, Gita, *Karma Cola*, 79, 81
Missionaries of Charity, vii, 75, 144, 183
Mitchell, Timothy, 118
Mitra, Ashok, 94
Mitra, Premendra, 104
Mitra, Radharaman, n35
Modern Lodge Guest House, viii, ix, 2, 4, 9, 11, 12, 13, 35, 40–3, 45, 54, 59, 60, 62, 64, 66, 72, 78, 79, 81, 133, 134, 216; ethnographic details of, 43–5; as a refuge for travellers, 46; as heterotopic site, 46–9; staff at, 83, 168; video made by guests of, 205–6
Moorhouse, Geoffrey, 8, 25, 31; *Calcutta: The City Revealed*, 90–1, 92, 93, 97, 98, 99, 166
Mother Teresa, vii, ix, 42, 44, 50, 53, 56, 59–60, 71, 75, 84, 105, 144, 153, 183, 202, 205, 212, 220
Mountbatten, Lord Louis, 95
movie camera, the, 192–3; as travelling eye, 178
Muecke, Stephen, 52
Mukherjee, S.N., 97
Murch, Walter, 178

Nair, Mira, *Salaam Bombay*, 199, 200
Nandy, Ashis, ix, 5, 6; *The Intimate Enemy*, 66, 86–7
Nash, Denison, 62, 138
nationalism: cartography and, 125–6
Naxalites, 92, 98, 116, 181
Negri, Antonio, 222
neo-imperialist, 48
Newby, Eric, *Slowly Down the Ganges*, 81
Nietzsche, Friedrich W., 13
non-governmental organizations (NGOs), 41, 42, 48, 76, 100, 152, 172, 216
nostalgia, 144–6

Octopussy, viii, 140, 198
Olalquiaga, Celeste, 152
otherness, 138; ethical problems of, 9; notion of, 26
Oxfam, 155, 221

Papastergiadis, Nikos, 13, 36, 123, 209
Parnet, Claire, 125, 134
passivity, theme of, 189–90

Patwardhan, Anand, *Bombay, Our City*, 54
Phipps, Peter, 23
photography, 144–75
Picasso, Pablo, 147–8
Pietz, William, 169
post-structuralism, 29
postcards, 79–81
poverty in Calcutta: as common trope, 56–8, 150, 164; politics of, 86, 192, 204; as photogenic, 203, 204; representations of, 8, 11, 35, 66–7, 74–7, 149, 164, 180, 183–5, 195–6; tourist consumption of, 20–1, 96; voyeurism and, 11; *see also* representations of Calcutta
Pratt, Mary Louise, 49, 98, 120
Preger clinic, 59, 66, 75, 111, 176, 190, 205, 216; *34 Middleton Row*, 41
Preger, Jack, x, 40–2, 96
Puri, Om, 177, 187

Racine, Jean, 1–2, 65, 66; *Calcutta 1981*, 194
racism, 45, 63, 126
Radcliffe-Brown, A.R., 49
Ray, Satyajit, vii, 106, 177, 182, 189; *Pather Panchali*, 185
reading, morality of, 104
representation: discrepancies of, 56; ethnocentrism of, 146, 150, 177, 191; issues of, 27, 29, 48, 58; politics of, 43, 218, 223
representational fictions, 12
representational technologies, 2
representations of Calcutta, 8, 20, 34, 64, 69–70, 108, 110–11, 133, 148, 212; as appropriated by West, 6; politics of, 8, 18; modes of, 19
representations: authenticity of, 159–61
revealing, 19; concept of, 17–18
rickshaws, 188, 194
Roberge, Gaston, 65, 66, 96, 184, 200
Roussel, Raymond, 115
rumour, 29, 34
'rumour of Calcutta', 2–3, 21, 148, 208, 216; production of the, 35, 69, 163, 176
'rumour of poverty', 20
Rushdie, Salman, 127; *Midnight's Children*, 5, 97, 109

Said, Edward, ix, 14, 27, 35, 198;

Orientalism, 7–8, 10, 126; *Culture and Imperialism*, 126
Salon Indien, 179
Schor, Naomi, 79
Scott, A. (with M. Dear) 141
Sen, Mrinal, 6, 156, 177, 184, 199, 201–5; *Parashuram*, 202; *Calcutta, My Eldorado*, 204; *Calcutta 71*, 204
Seth, Vikram, *From Heaven's Lake*, 81
Sethi, Harsh, 4
Sharma, Biren Das, 68
'sick tours', 21
Situationist International, 121
Smith, Valerie, L., 10
social sciences, 29–34, 82, 122, 157–9, 216–7
Soja, Edward W., 14
Sontag, Susan, 147, 164
souvenirs, 144, 154–7, 158, 159–61
Spivak, Gayatri Chakravorty, ix, 12, 14, 26, 31, 34, 54, 97, 98, 125, 153, 210–11
Stephens, Julie, 31
Stratton, Jon, 12
street clinics, 40
street-dwellers, 41
Subaltern Studies collective, 97–8
Suleri, Sera, 8
Suraj-ud-daula, 91, 119
surplus value, defined, 153
Swayze, Patrick, 44, 62, 111, 176, 208–9

Taussig, Michael, 99, 165–6
technologies, viii, x, 3, 9, 14, 16; of film, 176; as homogenizers, 24; of identity formation, 82; as instruments in enframing, 17–19, 34, 143; of perception, 21; of representation, viii, 2, 15, 20, 35, 86, 108, 115, 163, 214; of reproduction, 146–7; *see also* camera; Heidegger; maps; photography; travel literature
Third World, ix, 11, 19, 102, 147, 158; cultural attraction of, 21; economic relations between First World and, 15, 25, 77–8, 151, 214; tourism in, 11, 154, 217, 220
tourism, ix, 8, 9, 15, 18, 32; as 'alternative', 206–7, 211; economics of, 24, 68–9, 120, 153; ideology of, 10, 123, 157–8; as industry, x, 2, 10, 14, 61–2, 122, 154–5, 170, 172,

211, 214–15; photography and, 143–6; postmodernist forms of, 207; studies of, 138–39, 144

travel guidebooks, x, 3, 21, 26, 56, 63, 82, 98–9, 117, 131, 133, 214; academic texts and, 51–2; history of India in, 92; language of, 6; writers of, 51

travel literature, 81–2, 87–116, 125, 128, 138, 148; canon of, 111; links with colonialism and, 139–40

Trinh T. Minh-ha, ix, 34, 215; on anthropology as gossip, 29–31

Turner, Victor, 61;

Ulmer, Gregory, *Lusitania*, 153, 164, 201

United Nations, 100

Urry, John, *The Tourist Gaze*, 10 147, 164, 168, 206–7

Van Der Abbeele, Georges 123

Van Gennep, Arnold, 61

Vir Singh, Tej, 45

Virilio, Paul, ix, 5, 14, 148, 165, 196; *War and Cinema*, 18–19, 199–201

Vishvanathan, Shiv, 4, 8

voluntary services, x, 40–42

volunteers: dominant identity taken by travellers, 44; motivation of, 58–9; *see also* Western travellers; charity

Wallerstein, Immanuel, 169

Welles, Orson, 196, 197

West Bengal Government Publications, 92–3

West Bengal Tourism Authority, 125

West, 5–6, 23, 30, 129; 'development' discourse of, 48; India as not non-West, 86–7; *see also* Western

Western: charity workers, viii, 59; views of Calcutta, viii, documents

of the 'Third World', 19–20

Western aid agencies, 41; intervention of, 56–8, 68

Western scholarship, 27

Western thought, 129–30, 145

Western travellers, ix, 2, 4, 6, 9, 11, 16, 22, 23, 29; as agents of global exploitation, 12–13, 26, 139, 170, 172; as 'alternative', ix, 156, 206; attitudes to beggars, 67–9; behaviour directives to, 70–1; books and, 81, 96; budgets of, 153–4; communities of, 61–3, 70; connections with 'home', 78–80; economic advantages of, 9, 21, 68–9, 154–7; expectations of, 19, 64; health problems of, 40; identities of, 7, 44, 61–3, 81, 81, 111, 149–50, 167; loneliness of, 80; as middle class, ix, 9, 48, 74, 80, 157; orientation in Calcutta, 117–20, 123–25, 128, 130–142; perception of communism, 72–7; photographs and souvenirs of, 144, 153–7; politicization of, 53, 74–7; stereotypes of, 61; views of Calcutta by, 55–8, 66; as volunteers for charity work, 40–77; as voyeurs, 5, 149, 166; 'world-view' of, 35, 44, 212; *see also* volunteers; charity; Modern Lodge

Wheeler, Tony, 6, 63–4

women, 45

World Bank, 10, 11, 68, 76–7, 172, 220

World Development Movement, 77

World Vision, 75, 221

writing: process of, 104–105, 107–9, 112–14

Zischler, Hans, 196